BROKEN IMAGE

Foreign Critiques of America

America, you have it better.

GOETHE

BROKEN IMAGE

Foreign Critiques of America

———————◆———————

*Selected & Edited
with Notes & Introduction by*

Gerald Emanuel Stearn

RANDOM HOUSE

New York

IN MEMORY OF
P. H. Noyes

CONTENTS

INTRODUCTION : page xi

Corneille De Pauw : 3
We have depicted Americans as being a race of men who have all the faults of children, as a degenerate species, cowardly, impotent, without physical strength, without vitality, without elevation of mind.

Felix de Beaujour : 14
There is scarcely a civilized country in the world in which there is less generosity of sentiment, less elevation of soul and less of those soft and brilliant illusions which constitute the charm of life.

Sydney Smith : 20
In the four quarters of the globe, who reads an American book? or goes to an American play?

Thomas Hamilton : 29
Misery, discontent, and turbulence will spread through the land. A change of fashion, a war, the glut of a foreign market are liable to produce this. . . . At all events, let no man appeal to the stability of the American government.

Frances Anne Kemble : 38
If I make you sick with these disgusting stories, I cannot help it; they are the life itself here.

Charles Dickens : 48
I believe the heaviest blow ever dealt at liberty's head will be dealt by this nation in the ultimate failure of its example to the earth.

José Martí : 68

Osceola lay down and died in his war paint because he "did not have the heart to kill the white man like a bear or a wolf, although he comes upon us with friendship in one hand and a serpent in the other."

Eleanor & Edward Aveling Marx : 81

The cowboys are as much at the mercy of the capitalist as a New England cotton-worker.

Knut Hamsun : 89

If a man emerges in that democratic mob who believes in anarchism as the eventual, most ideal form of society, this man is too free—the Americans hang him!

Paul Bourget : 107

If two horsemen saw one another at five miles' distance on the prairie, each would turn in the opposite direction. Strange desert, which man sought to make still more deserted, and where he dreaded nothing but his own kind!

M. I. Ostrogorski : 117

You collect your impressions and you realize what a colossal travesty of popular institutions you have just been witnessing.

W. T. Stead : 130

I discussed with policemen, saloon keepers, gamblers and keepers of houses of ill fame what Christ would think of the poisonous, fiery and venomous city of Chicago!

Lepel Henry Griffin : 146

America is the country of disillusion and disappointment. I can think of none except Russia in which I would not prefer to reside.

Hugo Munsterberg : 160

The foreigner cannot see these charming American girls without a constant feeling that there is something unhealthy in their nervous make-up, an over-irritation, a pathological tension.

Maxim Gorky : 172

Everywhere is toil, everything is caught up in its whirlwind, everybody obeys the will of some mysterious power hostile to man and to nature. A machine, a cold, unseen, unreasoning machine, in which man is but an insignificant screw!

H. G. Wells : 189

Three unfortunate Negroes were burned to death, apparently because they were Negroes. It was a sort of racial sacrament. The edified Sunday-school children hurried from their gospel-teaching to search for souvenirs among the ashes, and competed with great spirit for a fragment of charred skull.

V. I. Lenin : 202

American imperialism—the freshest, strongest and latest in joining in the world-wide slaughter of nations for the division of capitalist profits—at this very moment has turned an exceptionally tragic page in the bloody history of bloody imperialism.

Sigmund Freud : 214

Hate America? I don't hate America, I regret it! I regret that Columbus ever discovered it!

Georges Duhamel : 225

By what frightful miracle does this land, which stretches from the tropics to the icebergs, find itself so degraded and made ugly?

Emilio Cecchi : 237
Branching out in the most tangled way, ultimate political power often passes finally into the hands of the last gangster.

Adolph Hitler : 246
When one reads a book like this about them, one sees that they have the brains of a hen!

Kingsley Martin : 254
The effect of the [McCarthyite] witch hunt is to produce a general level of conformity, a new orthodoxy from which a man dissents at his economic peril.

David Holbrook : 262
Few Americans know what it is like to be bombed, blown up, invaded or to have one's country wasted. Mentally they are back in the "Spirit of '76": a fatal anachronism. No wonder they are so preoccupied with the dinosaur: Tyrannosaurus rex *could be their symbol.*

Michel Legris : 268
American pornographers, by pushing specialization to an extreme degree, have succeeded in catering to the infinite variety of tastes and desires, if not perversions, of their clients.

Edward Thorpe : 283
"When you see one of those sonsa-bitches make the peace sign you're gonna be drilled so's you can place your baton right between his goddammed fingers."

SOURCES : 289

INTRODUCTION

In 1909, Dr. Sigmund Freud came to America to deliver a series of lectures on the new subject of psychoanalysis. After returning to Europe, he remarked to a group of curious friends, "America is a mistake; a gigantic mistake, it is true, but a mistake none the less." Freud's view of America was a common one: most visitors found the republic fascinating, novel, often exciting, but inevitably unattractive. "The experiment has been made," a nineteenth-century English traveler said, "and it has failed."

Broken Image is a biased, distorted, unfair, arbitrary and slanted collection (in rough chronological order, from 1770 to 1970) of foreign critical views of the American experience. Anthologies of the American image usually begin with the heroic writings of Hector St. John Crevecouer ("We are the most perfect society now existing in the world!"), lead on to the brilliant insights of Alexis de Tocqueville, pause for the delightful praise of Lord Bryce and continue with the admiring prose of Winston Churchill and D. W. Brogan. Until recently, American historians exercised an almost conditioned hostility to foreign criticisms. Listen, for example, to the formidable Henry Steele Commager, writing in his introduction to *America in Perspective: The United States Through Foreign Eyes**:

> The wanton attacks, the envy, the misunderstanding, the patronage, are all to be found readily enough—but jaundiced criticism came from the second-rate commentators rather than from the magisterial ones. The most judicious, the most learned, the most perspicacious, the most profound interpreters of America returned a verdict that ranged from sympathy to enthusiasm . . .

* New York, Random House, 1947.

But there has been another view of America, more provocative, certainly harsher and, until recently, out of fashion. The "other America" has been described as a land of contradiction and hypocrisy, where whites enslaved blacks under a supposedly democratic constitution; where violence and instability reigned in place of kings; where feudal degradation gave way to capitalist oppression; where corruption became synonymous with universal (white) male suffrage; where feminine idiosyncrasies counterpointed male vulgarity; where culture was frail and mediocrity dominant. And, finally, a country where the future appeared bleak, since America, though born in revolution, had become opposed to radical, though urgent, change.

My concern here is with the unattractive, the dismal, the dark sides of America. Selections have been made with a desire for thematic relevance, using the 1960's as a watershed in American history, so that earlier foreign quibbles often become prescient, incisive and revealing observations today. Consequently, many of these essays are brutal, even gory. Some lack delicacy and restraint and appear to have been written simply to offend Americans. Several contributors are openly bigoted, sharing the distorted values of a people they observed in order to condemn. Rumor, myth and fantasy often mingle in these essays with embarrassing fact. This, then, is a very harsh book, composed of a series of briefs submitted by foreign prosecutors and directed against one obviously vulnerable defendent. It is at best only an indictment, not a verdict. My role, as I see it, is that of a historical court reporter. The evidence, such as it is, and for what it is worth, follows.

When Christopher Columbus sailed home to Europe after making his epic discovery, he wrote reassuringly to his Spanish patrons, King Ferdinand and Queen Isabella, that the New World appeared a choice and inviting land. "I have so far found no human monstrosities, as many expected," Columbus remarked. But America and the Western Hemisphere were frequently seen as environments hostile to civilization. In the eighteenth century the Dutch Abbé CORNEILLE DE PAUW (1770) described America as a horrible place filled with strange animals and weird plants, attacked by a climate which steadily undermined human capabilities. Columbus' discovery, De Pauw concluded, was a tragic and dangerous mistake. "The truth is," W. H. Auden wrote of America in the 1960's, "nature never intended human beings to live here."

After the successful American revolution, questions of people and government became more important than those of climate. The French official FELIX DE BEAUJOUR (1810) saw the young republic as an unstable, materialistic experiment, run by crass lawyers, and doomed to failure. A weak central authority endangered private property, the true basis of freedom. Sectional differences between the money-grubbing Yankee and the genteel cavalier implied dissolution of the fragile Union. Even the continental ambitions of Americans were futile. Fierce nomadic Indians, using effective techniques of guerrilla warfare, were unconquerable. America may have been a mistake, Beaujour said, but it was certainly no threat to the world.

The English writer SYDNEY SMITH (1820) demanded spectacular achievements from the democratic republic. He complained of the absence of "great men" in North America, echoing De Pauw's earlier theme of cultural degeneracy. Smith mixes a smug condescension with a sharp moral fervor to chastise Americans for their lack of culture, their foolish and hollow pride and their slaveholding hypocrisy.

The chapter by the English traveler THOMAS HAMILTON (1833) on working-class discontent in New York during the Age of Jackson is important for its appraisal of early industrialism and its profound influence on the theories of Karl Marx. Hamilton's is the first modern essay in the book, one that speaks to the present despite its Tory hauteur and melancholy patronization. The self-sustaining myth of enraged workers seizing power begins with Hamilton, is embraced by Marxists throughout the nineteenth century and repeated in our time by the disciples of Lenin and Mao.

The sensitive English actress FRANCES ANNE KEMBLE (1839) and the brilliant novelist CHARLES DICKENS (1842) provide two extraordinary essays on the agonizing contradictions between white democrats and black slaves. Miss Kemble's description of plantation life details the formerly unspoken consequences of the sexual bondage masters held over female slaves. Dickens is concerned with slavery as a moral abomination, but he perceived as well the wretched brutalization of all Americans as a consequence of the "peculiar institution." The America Dickens visited was a violent republic, apparently doomed to self-destruction.

On the eve of the Civil War, foreign critics had already sketched a land of natural turbulence, political instability, cultural emptiness, threatening industrialism, and inhuman slavery. The war ended slavery. By the end of the century industrialism transformed the economy. The last frontiers of the West were crossed and the Indians crushed. Somewhat different foreign travelers and observers now wrote about America. Tory aristocrats and middle-class journalists competed with left- and right-wing ideologues. The polite tones of scoffing reprimands were replaced by specific and biting exposés.

The Cuban poet JOSÉ MARTÍ (1889) saw the raucous Oklahoma Land Rush as a symbolic event which underlined several of the more outrageous features of American life. First the land was stolen from some Indians, promised to newly freed Negroes —and other Indians—and then given to an avaricious band of white entrepreneurs who staked out bogus claims which were fantically defended by brute force. Like De Pauw and Beaujour, Martí equated the Wild West of stark deserts and bleak plains with the wild Americans who came to resemble their surroundings and behave like instinctive animals battling against nature and themselves for survival.

Today, along the road leading from Moscow's airport to its inner city, are a series of billboards filled, not surprisingly, with

pro-Soviet, anti-American propaganda. One large poster carica-
tures the Statue of Liberty, her "crown" filled with drawings
of KKK hooded figures, nooses ready for lynchings, and gun-
toting cowboys, their heads covered with outlandish ten-gallon
hats, ready for shoot-outs. Late in the nineteenth century,
American Wild West shows toured the world. Cowboys and
Indians re-created battles, craven red savages bit the dust, shot
down by noble white horsemen. When Karl Marx's daughter,
ELEANOR AVELING MARX, and her husband visited America in
1887, they extended her father's theories of repressive capitalism to the romantic cowboy, whom they transformed into an
exploited member of the proletariat.

The young Marxs visited Chicago in hopes of aiding the
anarchist victims of judicial lynching, the condemned men of
the infamous Haymarket Square bomb episode. Haymarket was
the first prominent case of radical suppression by government
which drew world-wide sympathy to the victim's cause and,
with equal fervor, violent indictments of the American legal
system. In the twentieth century, the names of Sacco-Vanzetti,
Scottsboro, Rosenberg, and more recently, the Black Panthers,
the Chicago Seven, and Attica, among others, have evoked similar foreign protests. The Norwegian writer KNUT HAMSUN
(1889) dismissed all American claims to freedom of speech and
the press by illustrating the repressive consequences of Haymarket and the pervasive judicial corruption of the Gilded Age.
No doubt a brave exponent of freedom, Hamsun concluded that
America was a legal and cultural swamp, lacking excellence
and still further corrupted by ever-present, uppity, animal-like
Negroes.

PAUL BOURGET (1895), a French visitor near the end of the
century, illuminates the sheer terror of the West by relating the
failure of two Europeans who had hoped to establish ranches in
America but were frustrated by repeated threats and violence.

A frequent complaint against young America of the late
eighteenth and early nineteenth centuries had been the political
turmoil produced by excessive democracy. Universal suffrage

created puffed-up bosses floating on a sea of petty corruption and steering the ship of state into a whirlpool of degradation. The Russian liberal scholar M. I. OSTROGORSKI (1896) writes movingly of the subversion of the democratic process caused by the emergence of mass political parties. He provides a detailed account of the bedlam and sham called national presidential conventions. A case study of urban political corruption at work and the plight of young women forced into prostitution is described by the English Victorian crusader W. T. STEAD (1894), who entitled his exposé *If Christ Came To Chicago*.

Columbus had told the King and Queen of Spain that the New World contained "numerous rivers, good and large . . . trees as green and beautiful as they are in Spain in May, some of them flowering." Nightingales and other birds sang sweetly. "And there is honey," Columbus said, "and a great variety of fruits." Less than four hundred years after Columbus, a retired Anglo-Indian official, SIR LEPEL HENRY GRIFFIN (1885), wrote an early, biting attack on polluted landscapes and environmental desecration. Griffin blamed the commercial numbness of Americans, their lust for dollars being so great that aesthetic considerations were dismissed, beauty sacrificed and nature tortured.

America, by 1900, was a land of severe contrast. Great new cities sheltered depressing slums which were filled with millions of immigrants seeking a better life in what had been described to them as the Promised Land. Another promise, that of black equality following the Reconstruction, dissolved into betrayal. Segregation and lynching in the South and discrimination in the North faced the children of slaves. Violence between business and labor was uncommonly intense. Yet the industrial richness of the country and the rising standard of living for the broad middle sections of the population were undeniable. "The ship of [European] Socialism," a German sociologist wrote in the 1900's, "founders in America on the shoals of roast beef and apple pie."

The frenetic pace of life caused what a number of primitive

psychologists referred to as "American nervousness." The German psychologist HUGO MUNSTERBERG (1901) characterized American women as pathologically tense, and he found grave dangers in their predominant educational role which, he discovered, was leading to the "effeminization of culture."

The lower depths of city life were brilliantly sketched by the great Russian radical writer MAXIM GORKY (1906). H. G. WELLS (1906) employed his prophetic sense to describe black life at its nadir. Unlike most of his white foreign contemporaries, Wells interviewed two black leaders, the conservative Booker T. Washington and the militant W. E. B. Du Bois, whose more radical approach he favored. Wells broke with the traditional foreign attitude that the "Negro Question" was an essentially Southern problem.

The Russian Marxist V. I. LENIN (1914, 1918) viewed the Negro as a victim of bourgeois politics and capitalist reformers. But his main argument was directed against American "imperialism" during and after the First World War. America, for a time, considered massive intervention into Soviet affairs; American troops fought on Russian soil to help overthrow the Bolshevik revolution led by Lenin; and American diplomacy excluded Russia from the councils of the League of Nations. Lenin is unique in this collection in that he makes a rigid distinction about his animosities. His criticisms are directed against an American class—the bourgeoisie—not the entire nation or its culture.

The ideology of Marx had little attraction for SIGMUND FREUD (1925). The founder of psychoanalysis was almost irrational in his distaste for everything American. Much the same was true of the French writer GEORGES DUHAMEL (1931), who repeats some of the themes of degeneracy publicized by De Pauw and Beaujour nearly one hundred years before his visit to America. Duhamel also is livid in his attacks on pollution, the horrors of industrialism and the empty civilization of America as it appeared during the Great Depression.

EMILIO CECCHI's intemperate judgments (1938) stimulated wide interest in Italy a few years before the Second World War. Like Griffin, Hamsun and other foreign critics, Cecchi is a racist with little affection for blacks who yet becomes outraged by bloody accounts of lynchings, details of which he reprints at length.

That ADOLPH HITLER (1942) would be critical of the United States is, of course, not surprising. The chapter included is a cartoon pamphlet issued by the Nazi government during the Second World War. Essentially propaganda, it summarizes the themes of vulnerability exploited by American enemies in the twentieth century, from fascism to communism.

The revolution in communications has modified the need for the travel reports or secondhand accounts of American life which filled thousands of articles and books for over two hundred years. Since 1945 a few major crises have evoked criticisms which transcend mere policy differences. KINGSLEY MARTIN (1952) writes on the domestic life of America during the McCarthyite period of the 1950's. DAVID HOLBROOKE (1967) sees the Vietnam war as a true reflection of American defects. The French journalist MICHEL LEGRIS (1970) reports on a tour of pornography from New York to California. One traditional objection to American life had been its lingering Puritan ethic, criticized, for example, by Hamsun and Gorky. Legris finds distasteful the new open society which foreigners demanded for so long. The concluding essay is by a young English novelist, EDWARD THORPE (1970). His report on campus riot control training sessions at the New Mexico State Police Academy is a chilling study in the perennial theme of institutional American violence.

Foreign criticisms from England, France, Germany, Russia, Austria, Cuba, Italy, Holland and Norway have been collected. I confess to having been unable to find substantive remarks on America from Africa or Asia, remarks that might fit into my admittedly arbitrary scheme. No doubt foreign criticisms will continue to appear and, in future, more intrepid researchers may find a wider range of material.

Some of our bitterest foreign commentators denied the greatness of America because its achievements had come too easily. The land was already there waiting for the disciplined industry and imagination of Western man. All our wars were of "happy consequence." We were indeed the richest nation in the history of mankind. And if we chased after the almighty dollar, the world, thank God, merely chased after pennies. We could be forgiven our greed once they shared it. What we lacked in order to be a great nation, they said, was a great sadness, a humbling defeat, some catastrophic event which would turn our energy and imagination inward, which would create, after the great "conflagration" Gorky wanted, a spiritual revival of values, not things.

Quite possibly, America, in the last third of the twentieth century, has finally caught up with history. Internal battles which other nations fought against rival tribesmen hundreds, even thousands of years ago, are now concluded. Waves of immigrants no longer respond to Emma Lazarus' heroic invitation. Now we have what might almost be termed an indigenous population. There is a sense of completeness about us too, a recognition of most if not all our faults, a sense of finality in the limits of our achievements. In the last decade, American technology has blazed a path to the moon and made the Cuyahoga river combustible. In the more than four hundred and fifty years of our existence we have borrowed a language from the English, accepted a culture from the West; applied, with a vengeance, the materialist ethic of Puritanism; fashioned a government from classical Greek and Roman idealism; grabbed a land from the Indians; lured most of our people from Europe, Asia and Latin America, and stolen the rest from Africa; drained oil and other natural resources from most of the world; and if it were at all possible we would, no doubt, steal the moon and the stars from the universe. Now we have a general sadness about us, too.

In 1842 Charles Dickens wrote *American Notes* and, frightened by the future of America, he described himself as a "Lover of Freedom, disappointed." But the next year, when he published *Martin Chuzzlewit*, a comic novel which contained some nasty chapters on America, he had added hope to understanding:

> "Why, I was a-thinking, sir," returned Mark, "that if I was a painter and was called upon to paint the American Eagle, how should I do it?" "Paint it as like an Eagle as you could, I suppose." "No," said Mark. "That wouldn't do for me, sir. I should want to draw it like a Bat, for its shortsightedness; like a Bantam, for its bragging; like a Magpie, for its honesty; like a Peacock, for its vanity; like an Ostrich, for putting its head in the mud, and thinking nobody sees it——"
> "And like a Phoenix, for its power of springing from the ashes of its faults and vices, and soaring up anew into the sky!" said Martin.
> "Well, Mark. Let us hope so."

Gerald Emanuel Stearn

Croton-on-Hudson, New York

March–September, 1971

BROKEN IMAGE

Foreign Critiques of America

Corneille De Pauw

We have depicted Americans as being a race of men who have all the faults of children, as a degenerate species, cowardly, impotent, without physical strength, without vitality, without elevation of mind.

On the eve of the American revolution, a French philosopher offered a prize for the best essay in response to the following questions:

> Was the discovery of America a blessing or a curse to mankind? ... If it was a curse by what means are we to repair the damage?

The questions were asked rhetorically. Many of the learned men of the day considered the discovery at once the greatest event in history and one filled with the most evil consequences.

Corneille De Pauw, *Recherches philosophiques sur les Americains* (Berlin, 1770), from Vol. I, pp. 1–12, 31–34, 38–40; Vol. II, pp. 107–122. Translated by Daniel Webb as *Philosophical Investigations on the Americans* (London, R. Cruttwell, 1775), pp. 1–21, 23–37.

Serious debate on the validity of Columbus' work began with the publication a Dutch monk's diatribe on the Western Hemisphere, the Abbé Corneille De Pauw's *Philosophical Investigations of the Americans*. De Pauw (1739–1801) argued against colonization out of fear that Europe would be drained of talent by the new lands opening to settlement. He denied that genius could thrive in America; that creativity could flourish in such a climate. Others had suggested that the new world permanently damaged its inhabitants, the Indians. But De Pauw went beyond this speculative judgement and included the European and his children as victims of the environment. No further proof was needed than the demonstrable absence of great men of learning from either the North or South American continents. Even Harvard confirmed the enduring "degeneracy": "It has not been observed that the professors of the University of Cambridge in New England have educated any young Americans to the point of being able to display them in the literary world."

In the essay below when De Pauw speaks of "Americans" he means the original inhabitants, the Indians.

———————◆———————

NO EVENT is more memorable for the human race than the discovery of America. Looking back from the present to the most remote ages, we see no event that can be compared with it; and indeed it is an impressive and terrible spectacle to see one-half of this globe so ill-favored by nature that all it contains is either degenerate or monstrous.

Would any physicist of Antiquity ever have suspected that this same planet had two hemispheres so different one from the other, one of which would be conquered, subjugated and devoured by the other just as soon as it was discovered, after having been lost for centuries in the dark abyss of time?

This astonishing revolution that has altered the face of the earth and the fortunes of nations was an absolutely instantaneous phenomenon, for by an almost unbelievable fatality, there was no balance between attack and defense. All strength and all injustice were on the side of the Europeans. Americans had only weaknesses; they were therefore bound to be exterminated, and exterminated in an instant's time.

Whether this was due to a fatal combination of our destinies, or whether it was instead the necessary consequence of so many crimes and errors, it is nevertheless certain that the conquest of the New World, so celebrated and so unjust, has been the greatest of all misfortunes to befall mankind.

After the rapid massacre of some millions of savages, the heinous conqueror found himself attacked in turn by an epidemic disease which, attacking both the origins of life and the source of propagation, quickly became the most horrible scourge of the civilized world. Already crushed under the burdens of existence, man encountered, as his crowning misfortune, the germs of death in the arms of pleasure and in the very bosom of enjoyment. Easily could he believe that an irate Nature had vowed his ruin.

The annals of the universe reveal no other similar period, nor perhaps will there ever be another. If such disasters could occur more than once, the earth would be a dangerous abode where our species, succumbing under all these evils or exhausted from resisting its destiny, would become extinct, abandoning this planet to happier or less afflicted beings.

If we have depicted Americans as being a race of men who have all the faults of children, as a degenerate species of the human race, cowardly, impotent, without physical strength, without vitality, without elevation of mind, we offer nothing in such a portrait that would surprise the imagination by its novelty, for the history of man in his natural state has been more neglected than one might think.

At the time of the discovery of America, its climate was unfavorable to most quadruped animals, which in fact are one-sixth smaller in the New World than their counterparts on the old continent. In particular, the climate was injurious to the natives who, to an astonishing degree, were stupefied, enervated, and vitiated in all the parts of their organism.

The land itself, either bristling with mountain peaks or covered with forests and marshlands, presented the aspect of an immense and sterile desert. The first adventurers to settle there all underwent the horrors of famine or the great sufferings of thirst.

The Spaniards, from time to time, were forced to eat Americans and even other Spaniards for lack of nourishment. The Floridians, observing these horrible repasts, understood immediately the ferocity of such a conqueror for whom hunger held no fears.

The first French colonists sent into this hapless world also ended by eating each other. The English who conquered Virginia returned home famished on the ships of Commodore Drake; in London, they were taken for ghosts and for many years thereafter no one was found in all of England who would embark for such a land. But when it was learned that the earth there held inexhaustible treasures in its depths, the thirst for gold affronted all dangers, overcame all obstacles, and conquered nature itself.

The surface of the earth, full of putrefaction, was flooded with lizards, snakes, serpents, reptiles, and insects that were monstrous by their size and the power of their poison extracted from the juice of this earth, so barren, so vitiated, so abandoned, where the nutritive sap became sour like milk in the breasts of animals that do not propagate.

There, caterpillars, butterflies, centipedes, scarabs, spiders, frogs, and toads were found in gigantic size for their species, and multiplied beyond imagining. Glancing at the excellent drawings made in Surinam by Mademoiselle Merian, we are struck by the prodigious growth of butterflies that equal our birds in size.

Iguana lizards and fighting cocks, eaten by so many Americans, hastened, unbeknown to them, the progress of the disease to which all men and many animals are subject from the Straits of Magellan to Labrador, where venereal disease stops to make way for the muriatic scurvy which appears to be only a variation of the same disease.

Americans, though light and agile in racing, were deprived of the lively physical force that comes from the tension and resistance of muscles and nerves. The weakest European overcame them easily in any combat. What a difference between them and the ancient savages of Gaul and Germany who became so famous for the strength of their limbs and their massive and indefatigable bodies!

The constitution of Americans, so little defective in appearance, is fundamentally weak. They collapse under the slightest burden. In transporting the belongings of the Spaniards, more than two hundred thousand of them died in less than one year under the weight of these loads, even though ten times more men were used for these transports than would have been required in Europe.

At first Americans were not thought to be men, but rather orang-outangs, or large monkeys, that could be destroyed without remorse and without reproach. Finally, to add the ridiculous to the calamities of that era, a certain pope issued a bull in which he decreed that, as he wished to establish dioceses in the richest regions of America, it pleased him and the Holy Spirit to recognize Americans as true men. Thus, without this decision made by an Italian, the inhabitants of the New World would still today be, in the eyes of the faithful, a race of dubious animals. There has never been another example of such a decision since the world was first inhabited by both monkeys and men.

Americans were particularly distinguished by the fact that most of them had no eyebrows and none had beards. We cannot infer from this defect alone that they were debilitated in their reproductive organs, since the Tartars and the Chinese have more or less the same characteristics. Nevertheless, these peoples are far from fecund, and are not inclined to love. And yet it is not true that the Chinese and the Tartars are absolutely beardless. When they are about thirty years old, a thin mustache grows on their upper lip and a few tufts grow on their chin.

In addition to being beardless, Americans also completely lacked hair on any part of their bodies and on their genitals, and this distinguished them from all other peoples of the earth. It is from this fact that we can draw some conclusions about the weakness and the deterioration of these very members, although nothing unusual or irregular was noted about them save the smallness of the organ and the length of the scrotum, which in some was excessive.

The little inclination, the little warmth of Americans toward women, unquestionably demonstrated their lack of virility and the deterioration of their reproductive organs. Love exerted over them hardly half its usual power. They experienced neither the torments nor the delights of this passion, because the most ardent and the most precious spark of nature died out in their tepid and phlegmatic souls.

The blood was certainly poorly constituted, for in certain places, fully grown men had milk in their breasts. This gave rise, in some old travel accounts, to the legend that in South American provinces only the men breast fed the children. This exaggeration was entirely gratuitous for a phenomenon that needs no elaboration and which in fact deserves to be discussed in a special treatise wherein the author, at his ease, could consider all the details and develop all the causes of such a surprising effect. But to forestall boredom and cut short this physiological study, I will say in a few words what I believe to be sufficient to explain this difficulty.

I am persuaded that humidity of temperament in the inhabitants of the New World caused this defect which, as one can easily understand, necessarily influenced their physical and moral faculties. We can therefore say that in the New World, men were more like women, more cowardly, more timid, and more afraid of the dark, than we can possibly conceive.

It is a great problem to know whether Europe would not have been truly happier if two Italians had not, in the fifteenth century, shown it the way to the New World. Without speaking here of that cruel malady that poisoned the reproductive organs of mankind, a malady that could not be compensated by all the treasures of Potosi and Brazil, it is certain that we have not gained from America all the benefits we think.

A brutish insensibility forms the basis of the character of all Americans; their indolence prevents them from being attentive to any instruction; they know no passion strong enough to move their souls, to transcend their nature. Superior to animals in the use they make of their hands and their tongue, they are nevertheless truly inferior to the lowest Europeans. Deprived of both intelligence and perfectability, they can only obey the impulse of their instincts. No incentive for fame can enter their heart; their unpardonable weakness forces them either into a state of servitude where it keeps them, or into a savage existence they are too cowardly to quit. America was discovered nearly three centuries ago; since that time, Americans have constantly been brought to Europe. Attempts have been made to give them all sorts of education and culture, and never has one of them succeeded in making a name for himself in the sciences, in the arts, or in the trades.

As it was thought that transporting Americans to Europe was harmful to their temperament, attempts were made to educate some in their own country. These attempts were no more successful than the others, but the results of observations made on this occasion are very curious: it is admitted that the children of this race show some glimmer of intelligence until the age of sixteen or seventeen. During this period, they learn to read and write a little and give some promise to their teachers that their labors will not be lost if they continue to study. But towards the twentieth year, a stupor suddenly overcomes them. At that point, the harm is done. They regress instead of developing, and so completely forget what they have learned that one is obliged to give up all attempts at educating them, and to abandon them to their fate.

I have not attempted to discover with all possible exactitude the secret causes of such an astonishing effect. I only note the stupidity that overcomes them around the age of puberty. To be sure, it is true that even in Europe we see many young people whose intelligence declines at that age. That period of life is a terrible and critical moment that destroys or consumes all one had hoped for from the child's alertness. It is possible that in some cases the first effusions of the prolific fluid obstructs some passages and dulls their vital spirits. And yet it has been proved by experience that even immoderate enjoyment of women is not harmful to the development of the mind, whereas castration performed in early childhood is manifestly harmful and produces only men who are pusillanimous, indolent, without vivacity, and whose souls are as degraded as their bodies, for the violence of this operation turns back the seminal matter and diverts the fibers.

I am far from supposing that the zeal of our missionaries has not always been as fervent as they tell us it is, but I flatter myself to think that most of them, if they are sincere, will not contradict me if I state as a fact that no American native has ever understood a word of the Christian religion. Women and children go regularly to church and enjoy themselves singing hymns; as for the men, their only pleasure comes in ringing the church bell, without paying the slightest attention to the words of the catechist. One cannot attach himself sincerely to a religion without knowing its dogmas and its mysteries. The Christian mysteries are too metaphysical to be able to satisfy Americans, who do not understand them.

No one realized the missions' lack of success among the savages better than when the English took Canada. Several were questioned on the articles of faith, which turned out to be entirely unknown to them, although these dogmas had been preached in their lands for already two centuries. Others had a very confused notion of the story of Christ, and when asked who Christ was, they answered that he was a *jongleur*, of French nationality, whom the English hanged in London, that his mother was French, and Pontius Pilate was a lieutenant in the service of Great Britain. M. Douglas, who cites these details, infers from this that Catholic preachers, in order to incite the Iroquois against the English, had intentionally taught them these false things. But I cannot believe that anyone would abuse religion in such a criminal way, and I prefer to impute these childish replies to the Americans' lack of understanding rather than to the sacrilegious intrigues of missionaries.

If there had been found, in the New World, men inspired by generous sentiments, capable of feeling the incentive of fame, and eager to become learned in the arts and sciences, all the advantage of the discovery of America would have been theirs. By exchanging their gold, their pearls, their emeralds, and their cochineal for our understanding and our secrets; by profiting from our knowledge, our discoveries, our inventions and our instruments, they would have blessed fate for having brought to their shores such clever masters, whom they could repay with some insects, some shining stones, and some yellow dirt. Many nations of ancient Europe recognized that coming under the yoke of the Roman Empire, they ceased being barbarians, for their conquerors had taught them the arts and letters they lacked, and in this they were not mistaken. But the stupidity and laziness of Americans caused them to lose the only advantage they could draw from the arrival of the Europeans.

If they had defended themselves even a little against the invaders, these would not have made bold to slaughter them like animals; if they had shown the slightest inclination for learning, we would not have come to think of them as the lowest form of the human species. To say that a Spaniard born in America is an "American" is to insult him so cruelly that he can never forgive the offender. Portuguese and English Creoles also consider themselves sorely insulted when they are called "Americans," so superior do they consider themselves to the men of that race; and indeed they are superior in many respects, though not quite so much as they think.

Since it is principally to the climate of the New World that that we have attributed the causes vitiating the essential qualities of men and the degeneration of human nature, we are doubtless justified in asking if any derangement has been observed in the faculties of Creoles, that is, of Europeans born in America of parents native to our continent. This interesting question, very important in itself, merits our attention. All animals taken from the Old World to the New have undergone, without any exception, a noticeable deterioration, either in their form or in their instinct. This would lead us immediately to presume that men also have experienced some effects caused by the air, the land, the water, and the food; but since men were better able than animals to preserve themselves against these first influences of the climate, the change in their constitution and the weakening of their mind was not immediately recognized. Yet, in later comparing them with freshly arrived Europeans, some differences seemed to begin to appear; and after repeated observations, it was evident that the degeneracy earlier believed possible was indeed a reality. Finally, we can now affirm with assurance that Creoles of the fourth and fifth generation have less genius, less capacity for knowledge, than Europeans.

The Jesuits have published some impressive accounts of their college at Santa Fe, where they say they have often counted as many as ten thousand students. It is particularly surprising that of this vast number of students there has come no great teacher, no philosopher, no doctor, no physician, no scientist whose name has crossed the seas and become known in Europe.

It is useless to protest that this total lack of famous men is due to the ignorance and barbarity of the professors, and to the deplorable state to which the sciences are reduced in the West Indies. Those who have received from nature the priceless gift of intellect easily surmount the obstacles of a poor education, and rise by means of their own efforts, just as all great men have risen above their age and above their own masters to whom they never owe the least part of their talents and their fame. Thus, the lack of success of Creoles sent by their parents to the different colleges of the New World must be ascribed to a real defect and physical deterioration of constitution, in an unhealthy climate harmful to the human race.

Felix de Beaujour

There is scarcely a civilized country in the world in which there is less generosity of sentiment, less elevation of soul and less of those soft and brilliant illusions which constitute the charm of life.

Napoleon's Counsel General, Felix de Beaujour, wrote this *Sketch* in 1810, but it remained largely unknown until the English writer William Walton translated the book in 1814 as part of a larger propaganda campaign against his country's enemy, the United States, in the continuing War of 1812. Walton quite frankly admitted that the translation was made to show the faults and dangerous future of the former colony. "North America," Walton wrote in his introduction to the *Sketch*, "amidst the horrors of European warfare" used her neutrality to add to her riches and population, becoming an "asylum of the oppressed as well as the lawless." But, as his

Le Chevalier Felix de Beaujour, *Sketch of the United States of North America, at the Commencement of the Nineteenth Century, from 1800 to 1810*, trans. by William Walton (London, J. Booth, 1814), pp. 64–69, 133–34, 145–47, 157–65.

sometime French enemy Beaujour makes clear, America is no true friend of Europe but a detached, "haughty" and selfish merchant possessing, thank God, all the elements of her own dissolution.

In his "Author's Preface" Beaujour claimed that he was a detached observer: "I have neither wished to praise them in order to pass censure on some nations or disparage them to flatter the pride of others. . . . One ought to repeat to nations more frequently: such a one is your friend [who] presents to you the mirror of your vices, rather than he who hides . . . deformity under the cover of flattery."

Beaujour's *Sketch* was enormously popular in Europe. It established America's reputation as an unstable, money-loving, corrupt land with a bleak future.

THE GOVERNMENT of the United States, since its institution, has scarcely evinced any thing else but proofs of weakness; and, in future, greater vigour cannot be expected from it, as long as it is conducted by lawyers, a species of men the least proper to govern others, because they have nearly all a false judgment and dull character; and because, with their confined ideas and mean passions, they think they can govern empires, in the same manner as they would govern a club.

Nevertheless, it must be confessed in praise of this government, that it presents a species of phenomenon in the political world; and that, like this hand of Providence, it governs without being felt, and almost without being perceived; for to know that it exists, it is necessary to seek it in the bosom of the woods, and, like certain birds of passage, it disappears in the fine season.

This government, which, in Europe, has the reputation of being the most liberal in the world, is, in reality, no more so than the British government; and in the United States, there is not more real liberty than in England, notwithstanding there is more apparent freedom. Consequently, it is this appearance of liberty which most flatters the pride of man, as well as his taste for independence; and if the great art of governing a people is to hide the chains which they every where drag after them, it must be acknowledged that the American government is the most clever of all others. But, is it not rather to be presumed, that what has been attributed to the cleverness of this government, is no other than the work of its own weakness?

An essential defect in the American government is, that, in itself, it has no sufficient guarantee against the people. If an attempt was made to perfect this government, it would be necessary to strengthen it, and balance its powers in a better manner, in order to maintain them in a more perfect equilibrium. An executive power with more force; a senate composed of permanent members, to protect the people against the executive power, and the executive power against the people; a representative body composed of great freeholders; and finally, a legislative code, clear and precise, in order to get rid of the vermin of lawyers;—such are the improvements which the Americans ought to introduce into their government and administration. They ought never to forget, that governments have been essentially established to protect property, and that the best of all is that which protects it most.

The Americans have no more stability in their character than in their opinions. Each state, nay, almost each district, has different manners; and in these there are none of those general and striking resemblances, which give to a whole people a particular colour and a distinct physiognomy. The people of the United States possess the habits of every other people; but they have hitherto none of their own. The climate alone has modified these habits; but their institutions have not yet blended them. In the northern states the inhabitants are bold and enterprising, inconstant and light in the middle states, and heedless and lazy in those of the south. A Bostonian would go in search of his fortune to the bottom of Hell; a Virginian would not go across the road to seek it. An inhabitant of New York, Philadelphia, or Baltimore can never die content, if, during his life time, he has not changed his profession three or four times.

The American never loses an opportunity of enriching himself. Gain is the subject of all his discourse, and the lever of all his actions; so that there is scarcely a civilized country in the world, in which there is less generosity of sentiment, less elevation of soul, and less of those soft and brilliant illusions which constitute the charm or the consolation of life. There a man weighs every thing, calculates all, and sacrifices all to his own interest. He lives only in himself, and for himself, and regards all disinterested acts as so many follies, condemns all talents that are purely agreeable, appears estranged to every idea of heroism and of glory, and in history beholds nothing but the romance of nations.

Virtue has always been considered as the principle, or the chief spring of all republics; but that of the American republic seems to be an unbounded love of money. This is the effect of the political equality that reigns there, and which leaves to the citizens no other distinction than that of riches, and invites them to fill their coffers by every means in their power. Every thing among them favours this vile cupidity; their disdain for the agreeable arts, their taste for the comforts of life, their coarse intemperance, which deprive them of all love and activity for every thing that is not personal; and in short, even their laws, which by their ambiguity, seem to be the secret accomplices of fraud and bad faith. With them, justice is the result of calculation, but never of sentiment. She is deaf to the cries of the wretched, and particularly of the foreigner; and in the greatest part of their commercial towns, bankruptcy, who would believe it, is the shortest as well as the surest road to arrive at a fortune.

But although honesty is not the favourite virtue of the American merchants, it is not, as is usually believed in Europe, entirely banished from among them; and we still find, even amidst the corruption of their maritime cities, some persons of great uprightness and rigid probity. In the country, and among the villagers embosomed in the woods, considerable candor and good faith is to be met with, and, in general, good and upright characters are hardly less frequent in the United States, than in other countries; but high spirited and lofty souls, generous and magnanimous hearts, in a word, great and noble characters are there infinitely rarer than in other parts, and particularly than in the South of Europe, where they shine amidst the universal depravity that surrounds them, like stars in the obscurity of night.

Writers who have never gone out of their own country have sought to regulate the lot of the United States, have traced out for that extended country the most brilliant destinies; some have promised it, in the course of a few years, a population equal to that of China; and others have predicted easy conquests, and the entire possession of all North America.

But men do not people the land as fish increase and multiply in a breeding-pond; and unless Europe becomes depopulated and its inhabitants go over to settle there, men, abandoned to the impulse of nature alone, will never populate so large an extent, more than they have peopled so many other countries, still more favoured by Heaven. It may even be conjectured, that the United States will become less peopled than South America, because the land is there less fertile, and man more voracious. If we except the Delta and valley of the Mississippi, which in goodness equal those of the Nile, there is not in the whole of North America, but one country destined to maintain a large population. This is the beautiful table-land of Mexico, which gently declines towards the two seas, and presents on these two slopes, all the productions of the tropics, and on the centre, all those of temperate climates; but Mexico was not created to become a prey to the North Americans.

Nature has arrested, by barriers more or less strong, the enterprises of one nation against another; and if the people of the United States ever cross the mountains which separate the waters of the Mississippi from those of the river Del Norte, they will find in these vast solitudes, a race of men, like the Tartars, hardened to the chase, indefatigable horsemen who would continually harass them, would cut off their convoys and provisions and end by destroying them in detail. They would have to carry on against such a people as these, the same species of warfare the Romans waged against the Parthians, and this war would be eternal, because there is no means of stopping a wandering people.

The inhabitants of the United States, undoubtedly, by the extent of their territory and particularly by that of their coasts, are called upon to act a great part in the affairs of the world; but if they seek to make their appearance too soon, they will become fatal victims of their own dissentions, and will dissolve before they have been formed into a great body of a nation. The principles of this dissolution already exist; and so extended an empire as theirs, can never be kept together by so feeble a bond as a federative government.

Sydney Smith

In the four quarters of the globe, who reads an American book? or goes to an American play?

The Reverend Sydney Smith (1771–1845), churchman, wit, doctor, justice and architect, wrote about America with a tone of arrogance and shrewdness mixed with a certain affection. In his role as Whig publicist, he wished well for "Brother Jonathan" (a common sobriquet for the U.S.A. before "Uncle Sam" became fashionable) and used selected attributes of the former colonies to criticize the British Tories of his day. "Americans," he wrote in the *Edinburgh Review*, which he helped revive in 1802, "have been treated with ridicule and contempt. But they are becoming a little too powerful . . . for this cavalier sort of management." Government, for one thing,

---

The Works of the Reverend Sydney Smith (London, Longman, Brown, 1859), Volume I, pp. 243–44, 247–49, 292.

was far cheaper than that of Britain; American "Kings" and "Vice-Kings" were paid little. Unlike Britain, the military establishment in the United States was modest and taxes, therefore, were limited.

Smith was known as a great wit. "He sometimes verged upon buffoonery," said a contemporary biographer. "You have been laughing at me for seven years," his friend Lord Dudley is reported to have told him, "and you have not said a word that I wished unsaid." But Smith's charge about American intellectual inconsequence, if meant as a joke, was resented for years.

After a varied and nomadic career Smith inherited a fortune of five hundred thousand pounds. Some money was spent to improve his status in the Church of England. (In time he became Canon of St. Paul.) Some was invested in the lucrative but risky bonds of American states. In one of his last published writings, Smith in vain petitioned the government of Pennsylvania to resume interest and principle payments on securities defaulted by the state. The object of his poetic contempt ended by taking his money.

In the following selection I've combined several essays by Smith and "framed" a long review of two important travel journals: Francis Hall's *Travels in Canada and America in 1816–1817* (London, 1818); and Henry Bradshaw Fearon's *A Narrative of a Journey . . . [to America]* (London, 1818). References in the text are to the original editions.

———◆———

LITERATURE the Americans have none—no native literature, we mean. It is all imported. They had a Franklin, indeed; and may afford to live for half a century on his fame. There is, or was, a Mr. Dwight, who wrote some poems; and his baptismal name was Timothy. There is also a small account of Virginia by Jefferson, and an epic by Joel Barlow; and some pieces of pleasantry by Mr. Irving. But why should the Americans write books, when a six weeks' passage brings them, in their own tongue, our sense, science, and genius, in bales and hogsheads? Prairies, steam-boats, grist-mills, are their natural objects for centuries to come. Then, when they have got to the Pacific Ocean—epic poems, plays, pleasures of memory, and all the elegant gratifications of an ancient people who have tamed the wild earth, and set down to amuse themselves.—This is the natural march of human affairs.

In his honest endeavours to better his situation, and in his manly purpose of resisting injury and insult, we must cordially sympathise. We hope he will always continue to watch and suspect his Government as he now does— remembering, that it is the constant tendency of those entrusted with power, to conceive that they enjoy it by their own merits, and for their own use, and not by delega- tion, and for the benefit of others. Thus far we are the friends and admirers of Jonathan. But he must not grow vain and ambitious; or allow himself to be dazzled by that galaxy of epithets by which his orators and newspaper scribblers endeavour to persuade their supporters that they are the greatest, the most refined, the most enlightened, and the most moral people upon earth. The effect of this is unspeakably ludicrous on this side of the Atlantic—and, even on the other, we should imagine, must be rather humiliating to to the reasonable part of the population. The Americans are a brave, industrious, and acute people; but they have hitherto given no indications of genius, and made no approaches to the heroic, either in their morality or character. They are but a recent offset indeed from England; and should make it their chief boast, for many generations to come, that they are sprung from the same race with Bacon and Shakespeare and Newton. Consider- ing their numbers, indeed, and the favourable circumstances in which they have been placed, they have yet done marvelously little to assert the honour of such a descent, or to show that their English blood has been exalted or refined by their republican training and institutions. Their Franklins and Washingtons, and all the other sages and heroes of their revolution were born and bred subjects of the King of England—and not among the freest or most valued of his subjects. And, since the period of their separation, a far greater proportion of their statesmen and artists and political writers have been foreigners, than ever occurred before in the history of any civilised and educated people. During the thirty or forty years of their independence, they have done absolutely nothing for the Sciences, for the Arts, for Literature, or even for the statesman-like studies of Political Economy. Confining ourselves to our own country, and to the period that has elapsed since they had an independent existence, we should ask, Where are their Foxes, their Burkes, their Sheridans, their Windhams, their Horners, their Wilberforces?— where their Arkwrights, their Watts, their Davys?—their Robertsons, Blairs, Smiths, Stewarts, Paleys, and Malthuses? —their Porsons, Parrs, Burneys, or Bloomfields?—their Scotts, Rogers's Campbells, Byrons, Moores, or Crabbes?— their Siddons, Kembles, Keans, or O'Neils?—their Wilkies, Lawrences, Chantrys?—or their parallels to the hundred other names that have spread themselves over the world from our little island in the course of the last thirty years, and blest or delighted mankind by their works, inventions, or examples? In so far as we know, there is no such parallel to be produced from the whole annals of this self-adulating race. In the four quarters of the globe, who reads an American book? or goes to an American play? or looks at an American picture or statue? What does the world yet owe to American physicians or surgeons? What new substances have their chemists discovered? or what old ones have they analysed? What new constellations have been discovered by the telescopes of Americans? What have they done in the mathematics? Who drinks out of American glasses? or eats from American plates? or wears American coats or gowns? or sleeps in American blankets? Finally, under which of the old tyrannical governments of Europe is every sixth man a slave, whom his fellow-creatures may buy and sell and torture?

When these questions are fairly and favourably answered, their laudatory epithets may be allowed: but till that can be done, we would seriously advise them to keep clear of superlatives.

The great curse of America is the institution of Slavery —of itself far more than the foulest blot upon their national character, and an evil which counterbalances all the excise-men, licensers, and tax-gatherers, of England. No virtuous man ought to trust his own character, or the character of his children, to the demoralising effects produced by command-ing slaves. Justice, gentleness, pity, and humility, soon give way before them. Conscience suspends its functions. The love of command—the impatience of restraint, get the better of every other feeling; and cruelty has no other limit than fear.

" 'There must doubtless,' says Mr. Jefferson, 'be an un-happy influence on the manners of the people produced by the existence of slavery among us. The whole commerce between master and slave is a perpetual exercise of the most boisterous passions; the most unremitting despotism on the one part, and degrading submissions on the other. Our children see this and learn to imitate it; for man is an imita-tive animal. The parent storms, the child looks on, catches the lineaments of wrath, puts on the same airs in the circle of smaller slaves, gives loose to the worst of passions; and thus nursed, educated, and daily exercised in tyranny, can-not but be stamped by it with odious pecularities. The man must be a prodigy who can retain his morals and manners undepraved by such circumstances.' " (Hall, p. 459)

The following picture of a slave song is quoted by Mr. Hall from the "Letters on Virginia."

"I took the boat this morning, and crossed the ferry over to Portsmouth, the small town which I told you is opposite to this place. It was court day, and a large crowd of people was gathered about the door of the court house. I had hardly got upon the steps to look in, when my ears were assailed by the voice of singing; and turning round to discover from what quarter it came, I saw a group of about thirty negroes, of different sizes and ages, following a rough-looking white man, who sat carelessly lolling in his sulky. They had just turned round the corner, and were coming up the main street to pass by the spot where I stood, on their way out of town. As they came nearer, I saw some of them loaded with chains to prevent their escape; while others had hold of each other's hands, strongly grasped, as if to support themselves in their affliction. I particularly noticed a poor mother, with an infant sucking at her breast as she walked along, while two small children had hold of her apron on either side, almost running to keep up with the rest. They came along singing a little wild hymn, of sweet and mournful melody, flying, by a divine instinct of the heart, to the consolation of religion, the last refuge of the unhappy, to support them in their distress. The sulky now stopped before the tavern, at a little distance beyond the court house, and the driver got out. 'My dear Sir,' said I to a person who stood near me, 'can you tell me what these poor people have been doing? What is their crime? And what is to be their punishment?' 'O,' said he, 'it's nothing at all, but a parcel of negroes sold to Carolina; and that man is their driver, who has bought them.' 'But what have they done, that they should be sold into banishment?' 'Done,' said he, 'nothing at all, that I know of; their masters wanted money, I suppose, and these drivers give good prices.' Here the driver, having supplied himself with brandy, and his horse with water (the poor negroes of course wanted nothing), stepped into his chair again, cracked his whip, and drove on, while the miserable exiles followed in funeral procession behind him."—(Hall, pp. 358–60)

The law by which slaves are governed in the Carolinas is a provincial law as old as 1740, but made perpetual in 1783. By this law it is enacted, that every negro shall be presumed a slave, unless the contrary appear. The 9th clause allows two justices of the peace, and three free-holders, power to put them to any manner of death; the evidence against them may be without oath.—No slave is to traffic on his own account.—Any person murdering a slave is to pay 100 shillings—or 14 shillings if he cuts out the tongue of a slave.—Any white man meeting seven slaves together on a high road may give them twenty lashes each. —No man must teach a slave to write, under penalty of 100 shillings currency. We have Mr. Hall's authority for the existence and enforcement of this law at the present day. Mr. Fearen has recorded some facts still more instructive.

"Observing a great many coloured people, particularly females, in these boats, I concluded that they were emigrants, who had proceeded thus far on their route towards a settlement. The fact proved to be, that fourteen of the flats were freighted with human beings for sale. They had been collected in the several States by slave dealers, and shipped from Kentucky for a market. They were dressed up to the best advantage, on the same principle that jockeys do horses upon sale. The following is a specimen of advertisement on this subject:—

TWENTY DOLLARS REWARD

Will be paid for apprehending and lodging in gaol, or delivering to the subscribers, the following slaves, belonging to JOSEPH IRVIN of Iberville.—TOM, a very light Mulatto, blue eyes, 5 feet 10 inches high, appears to be about 35 years of age; an artful fellow—can read and write, and preaches occasionally.—CHARLOTTE, a black wench, round, and full faced, tall, straight, and likely—about 25 years of age, and wife of the above named Tom.—These slaves decamped from their owner's plantation on the night of the 14th September inst."—(Fearon, p. 270)

"The three 'African churches,' as they are called, are for all those native Americans who are black, or have any shades of colour darker than white. These persons, though many of them are possessed of the rights of citizenship, are not admitted into the churches which are visited by whites. There exists a penal law, deeply written in the mind of the whole white population, which subjects their coloured fellow-citizens to unconditional contumely and never-ceasing insult. No respectability, however unquestionable— no property, however large—no character, however unblemished, will gain a man, whose body is (in American estimation) cursed with even a twentieth portion of the blood of his African ancestry, admission into society! ! ! They are considered as mere Pariahs—as outcasts and vagrants upon the face of the earth! I make no reflection upon these things, but leave the facts for your consideration."—(Fearon, pp. 168, 169)

That such feelings and such practices should exist among men who know the value of liberty, and profess to understand its principles, is the consummation of wickedness. Every American who loves his country should dedicate his whole life, and every faculty of his soul, to efface this foul stain from its character. If nations rank according to their wisdom and their virtue, what right has the American, a scourger and murderer of slaves, to compare himself with the least and lowest of the European nations?—much more with this great and humane country, where the greatest lord dare not lay a finger upon the meanest peasant? What is freedom where all are not free? where the greatest of God's blessings is limited, with impious caprice, to the colour of the body? And these are the men who taunt the English with their corrupt Parliament, with their buying and selling votes. Let the world judge which is the most liable to censure—we who, in the midst of our rottenness, have torn off the manacles of slaves all over the world; —or they who, with their idle purity, and useless perfection, have remained mute and careless, while groans echoed and ships clanked around the very walls of their spotless Congress. We wish well to America—we rejoice in her prosperity—and are delighted to resist the absurd impertinence with which the character of her people is often treated in this country: but the existence of slavery in America is an atrocious crime, with which no measures can be kept—for which her situation affords no sort of apology —which makes liberty itself distrusted, and the boast of it disgusting.

Thomas Hamilton

*Misery, discontent, and turbulence will
spread through the land. A change of
fashion, a war, the glut of a foreign market
are liable to produce this. . . . At all events,
let no man appeal to the stability of the
American government.*

The professional Scottish soldier Captain Thomas Hamilton
(1789–1842) traveled to America in 1830 to ease the sadness
caused by the death of his young wife the previous year. A
friend of Sir Walter Scott and William Wordsworth, Hamilton retired from the army and turned to writing after being
severely wounded in the Peninsular Campaign. In 1827 he wrote
a popular novel, *Cyril Thornton*. His book on America was intended as a warning to Britain on the revolutionary possibilities
of an industrialized society.

Hamilton noticed the paradox of American men willing to
do unbelievably strenuous work in pursuit of money but who
considered personal service demeaning: "Mammon is his god,
he prays to him, not merely with his lips, but with all the force
of his body and mind . . . A young English nobleman is sent

Thomas Hamilton, *Men and Manners in America* (Philadelphia,
Carey, Lea and Blanchard, 1833), pp. 299–310.

to the [private schools of] Westminster or Winchester to brush
coats and wash tea cups, while the meanest American store-
keeper would redden with virtuous indignation at the very
thought of the issue of his loins contaminating his plebian blood
by the discharge of such functions." The reasons for this,
Hamilton concluded, had to do with race, rather than with
class, consciousness. "In England, the menial offices in question
form the duties of *freemen*; in America, even in those States
where slavery has been abolished, domestic service being discharged by Negroes, is connected with a thousand degrading
associations." Hamilton believed that the New York Workingman's party, the "Workies," would eventually overthrow the
rich: "The event may be distant, but it is not the less certain on
that account." A modern French scholar, Maximilien Rubel,
who has studied Marx's manuscripts and the notes used in
writing *Das Kapital,* found that the father of "scientific socialism" copied large extracts from Hamilton on the "Workies." In
America, Marx wrote at the time, "pauperism is making the
most delightful progress." Rubel concludes: "In Thomas Hamilton [Marx] found what Tocqueville failed to notice: the revolutionary implications of American democracy." Tocqueville
and his colleague Gustave de Beaumont argued with Hamilton
(and, by indirection, Marx) about the levels of inequality in
America as well as the idea of a distant, though certain, working-class revolution, a prophecy which Marx and Engels embraced so willingly. Tocqueville said that the "wretchedness"
of some parts of the working class was "a monstrous exception
in the general aspect of society" and that "a slow and gradual
rise of wages is one of the general laws of democratic communities."

———◆———

IN NEW YORK CITY a separation is rapidly taking place between the different orders of society. The operative class
have already formed themselves into a society, under the

name of "*The Workies*," in direct opposition to those who, more favoured by nature or fortune, enjoy the luxuries of life without the necessity of manual labour. These people make no secret of their demands, which to do them justice are few and emphatic. They are published in the newspapers, and may be read on half the walls of New York. Their first postulate is "EQUAL AND UNIVERSAL EDUCATION." It is false, they say, to maintain that there is at present no privileged order, no practical aristocracy, in a country where distinctions of education are permitted. That portion of the population whom the necessity of manual labour cuts off from the opportunity of enlarged acquirement, is in fact excluded from all the valuable offices of the State. As matters are now ordered in the United States, these are distributed exclusively among one small class of the community, while those who constitute the real strength of the country, have barely a voice in the distribution of those loaves and fishes, which they are not permitted to enjoy. There does exist then—they argue—an aristocracy of the most odious kind —an aristocracy of knowledge, education, and refinement, which is inconsistent with the true democratic principle of absolute equality. They pledge themselves, therefore, to exert every effort, mental and physical, for the abolition of this flagrant injustice. They proclaim it to the world as a nuisance which must be abated, before the freedom of an American be something more than a mere empty boast. They solemnly declare that they will not rest satisfied, till every citizen in the United States shall receive the same degree of education, and start fair in the competition for the honours and the offices of the state. As it is of course impossible—and these men know it to be so—to educate the labouring class to the standard of the richer, it is their condition with the former; to prohibit all supererogatory knowledge; to have a maximum of acquirement beyond which it shall be punishable to go.

But those who limit their views to the mental degradation of their country, are in fact the MODERATES of the party. There are others who go still further, and boldly advocate the introduction of an AGRARIAN LAW, and a periodical division of property. These unquestionably constitute the *extrême gauche* of the Worky Parliament, but still they only follow out the principles of their less violent neighbours, and eloquently dilate on the justice and propriety of every individual being equally supplied with food and clothing; on the monstrous iniquity of one man riding in his carriage while another walks on foot, and after his drive discussing a bottle of Champagne, while many of his neighbours are shamefully compelled to be content with the pure element. Only equalize property, they say, and neither would drink Champagne or water, but both would have brandy, a consummation worthy of centuries of struggle to attain.

All this is nonsense undoubtedly, nor do I say that this party, though strong in New York, is yet so numerous or so widely diffused as to create immediate alarm. In the elections, however, for the civic offices of the city, their influence is strongly felt; and there can be no doubt that as population becomes more dense, and the supply of labour shall equal, or exceed the demand for it, the strength of this party must be enormously augmented. Their ranks will always be recruited by the needy, the idle and the profligate, and like a rolling snowball it will gather strength and volume as it proceeds, until at length it comes down thundering with the force and desolation of an avalanche.

This event may be distant, but it is not the less certain on that account. It is nothing to say, that the immense extent of fertile territory yet to be occupied by an unborn population will delay the day of ruin. It will delay, but it cannot prevent it. The traveller, at the source of the Mississippi, in the very heart of the American Continent, may predict with perfect certainty, that however protracted the wanderings of the rivulet at his foot, it much reach the ocean at last. In proportion as the nearer lands are occupied, it is very evident that the region to which emigration will be directed must of necessity be more distant. The pressure of population therefore will continue to augment in the Atlantic States, and the motives to removal become gradually weaker. Indeed, at the present rate of extension, the circle of occupied territory must before many generations be so enormously enlarged, that emigration will be confined wholly to the Western States. Then, and not till then, will come the trial of the American constitution; and until that trial has been passed, it is mere nonsense to appeal to its stability.

Nor is this period of trial apparently very distant. At the present ratio of increase, the population of the United States doubles itself in about twenty–four years, so that in half a century it will amount to about fifty millions, of which ten millions will be slaves, or at all events a degraded caste, cut off from all the rights and privileges of citizenship. Before this period it is very certain that the pressure of the population, on the means of subsistence, especially in the Atlantic States, will be very great. The price of labour will have fallen, while that of the necessaries of life must be prodigiously enhanced. The poorer and more suffering class, will want the means of emigrating to a distant region of unoccupied territory. Poverty and misery will be abroad; the great majority of the people will be without property of any kind, except the thews and sinews with which God has endowed them; they will choose legislators under the immediate pressure of privation; and if in such circumstances, any man can anticipate security of property, his conclusion must be founded, I suspect, rather on the wishes of a sanguine temperament, than on any rational calculation of probabilities.

It is the present policy of the government to encourage and stimulate the premature growth of a manufacturing population. In this it will not be successful, but no man can contemplate the vast internal resources of the United States—the varied productions of their soil,—the unparalleled extent of river communication,—the inexhaustible stores of coal and iron which are spread even on the surface,—and doubt that the Americans are destined to become a great manufacturing nation. Whenever increase of population shall have reduced the price of labour to a par with that in other countries, these advantages will come into full play; the United States will then meet England on fair terms in every market of the world, and in many branches of industry at least, will very probably attain an unquestioned superiority. Huge manufacturing cities will spring up in various quarters of the Union, the population will congregate in masses, and all the vices incident to such a condition of society will attain speedy maturity. Millions of men will depend for subsistence on the demand for a particular manufacture, and yet this demand will of necessity be liable to perpetual fluctuation. When the pendulum vibrates in one direction, there will be an influx of wealth and prosperity; when it vibrates in the other, misery, discontent, and turbulence will spread through the land. A change of fashion, a war, the glut of a foreign market, a thousand unforeseen and inevitable accidents are liable to produce this, and deprive multitudes of bread, who but a month before were enjoying all the comforts of life. Let it be remembered that in this suffering class will be practically deposited the whole political power of the state; that there can be no military force to maintain civil order, and protect property; and to what quarter, I should be glad to know, is the rich man to look for security, either of person or fortune?

There will be no occasion however for convulsion or

violence. The *Worky* convention will only have to choose representatives of their own principles, in order to accomplish a general system of spoliation, in the most legal and constitutional manner. It is not even necessary that a majority of the federal legislature should concur in this. It is competent to the government of each state to dispose of the property within their own limits as they think proper, and whenever a *numerical* majority of the people shall be in favour of an Agrarian law, there exists no counteracting influence to prevent, or even to retard its adoption.

I have had the advantage of conversing with many of the most eminent Americans of the Union on the future prospects of their country, and I certainly remember none who did not admit that a period of trial, such as that I have ventured to describe, is according to all human calculation inevitable. Many of them reckoned much on education as a means of safety, and unquestionably in a country where the mere power of breathing carries with it the right of suffrage, the diffusion of sound knowledge is always essential to the public security. It unfortunately happens, however, that in proportion as poverty increases, not only the means but the desire of instruction are necessarily diminished. The man whose whole energies are required for the supply of his bodily wants, has neither time nor inclination to concern himself about his mental deficiencies, and the result of human experience does not warrant us in reckoning on the restraint of individual cupidity, where no obstacle exists to its gratification, by any deliberate calculation of its consequences on society. There can be no doubt, that if men could be made wise enough to act on an enlarged and enlightened view of their own interest, government might be dispensed with altogether; but what statesman would legislate on the probability of such a condition of society, or rely on it as a means of future safety?

The general answer, however, is, that the state of things

which I have ventured to describe, is very distant. "It is enough," they say, "for each generation to look to itself, and we leave it to our descendants some centuries hence to take care of their interests as we do of ours. We enjoy all manner of freedom and security under our present constitution, and really feel very little concern about the evils which may afflict our posterity." I cannot help believing, however, that the period of trial is somewhat less distant than such reasoners comfort themselves by imagining; but if the question be conceded that democracy necessarily leads to anarchy and spoliation, it does not seem that the mere length of road to be travelled is a point of much importance. This, of course, would vary according to the peculiar circumstances of every country in which the experiment might be tried. In England the journey would be performed with railway velocity. In the United States, with the great advantages they possess, it may continue a generation or two longer, but the termination is the same. The doubt regards time, not destination.

At present the United States are perhaps more safe from revolutionary contention than any other country in the world. But this safety consists in one circumstance alone. *The great majority of the people are possessed of property;* have what is called a stake in the hedge; and are therefore, by interest, opposed to all measures which may tend to its insecurity. It is for such a condition of society that the present constitution was framed; and could this great bulwark of prudent government, be rendered as permanent as it is effective, there could be no assignable limit to the prosperity of a people so favoured. But the truth is undeniable, that as population increases, another state of things must necessarily arise, and one unfortunately never dreamt of in the philosophy of American legislators. The majority of the people will then consist of men without property of any kind, subject to the immediate pressure of want, and then will be decided the great struggle between property and numbers; on the one side hunger, rapacity, and physical power; reason, justice, and helplessness on the other. The weapons of this fearful contest are already forged; the hands will soon be born that are to wield them. At all events, let no man appeal to the stability of the American government as being established by experience, till this trial has been overpast. Forty years are no time to test the permanence, or, if I may so speak, the vitality of a constitution, the immediate advantages of which are strongly felt, and the evils latent and comparatively remote.

Frances *Anne* Kemble

If I make you sick with these disgusting stories, I cannot help it; they are the life itself here.

During the Civil War, on September 22, 1862, Abraham Lincoln issued a preliminary Proclamation of Emancipation freeing all slaves in areas still controlled by the Confederacy after January 1, 1863. A few weeks later, the London *Times* called the Proclamation "more contemptible than it is wicked. The most consummate folly ever perpetuated by a ruler." The Chancellor of the Exchequer, William Gladstone, reassured the country: "We may anticipate with certainty the success of the Southern states . . . Jefferson Davis and other leaders of the Confederacy have made an army; they are making, it appears, a navy; and they have made, what is more important than

Frances Anne Kemble, *Journal of a Residence on a Georgian Plantation, 1838–1839* (New York, Harper and Brothers, 1863), pp. 214–16, 229–31, 255–57, 269–70.

either, they have made a nation." The partial abolition of
slavery and still powerful pro-Confederate British sympathies
finally persuaded an English actress, Frances Anne ("Fanny")
Kemble (1809–1893), to publish an extraordinary though long-
suppressed memoir of her life on a Georgia plantation in 1839.

The diary shocked and appalled mid-Victorians on both
sides of the Atlantic. Mrs. Kemble revealed the full degree of
brutality and degradation of slavery: she listed in clinical detail the extent of suffering, both physical and psychic; and she
pointed out the dark world of forced sexuality which turned
bondage into rape.

Fanny Kemble was born into a famous English theatrical
family. Her aunt Sarah Siddons had world-wide fame. Her
father was a prominent actor. On tour in America in 1832
she met and married Pierce Butler, a wealthy Philadelphian
whose family drew its riches from vast slave-run plantations.
Her husband reluctantly took her with him to visit one of his
holdings in Georgia. "I am going prejudiced against slavery,"
she wrote friends, "for I am an Englishwoman, in whom the absence of such a prejudice would be disgraceful." She stayed in
Georgia for two months; but the *Journal* remained unpublished
for nearly twenty-five years. For a time the *Journal* rivaled
Uncle Tom's Cabin as a description of the "peculiar institution"
of slavery. Recently, historians have turned to it again as a
major source for accounts of the ante-bellum South. Mrs.
Kemble's special insights and great passion reveal the corrupting effects of the system on both slave and master. Arguments
have been made that the publication of the *Journal* in 1863
changed public opinion in Britain and turned it away from the
Confederacy, thus saving the Union by preventing armed British intervention on behalf of the South. But the book did not
appear in London until May, 1863. Two months later, in July,
it was published in America. That month, however, Grant took
Vicksburg and Lee fled back to Virginia after his defeat at
Gettysburg. Whatever its immediate consequence, the *Journal*

still impresses as it impressed a reviewer in 1863: "A sadder book the human hand never wrote."

Soon after her plantation experience Fanny Kemble's marriage broke up. She lost custody of her children and returned to London and the stage, existing amidst the common triteness of Victorian scandal until her death in 1893. But she knew and won the affection of the young Henry James, who said that "She could invite the spirit of mirth, flinging herself, in the joy of high places, on the pianos of mountain inns, joking, punning, botanizing, encouraging the lowly and abasing the proud (that was almost her mission in life) and startling infallibly all primness of propriety. . . . From the first she had abundantly lived."

Her *Journal* consisted of a series of "letters" never sent though addressed to "Elizabeth," probably her cousin who lived in Philadelphia.

———————◆———————

THIS MORNING [FEBRUARY 28] I had a visit from two of the women, Charlotte and Judy, who came to me for help and advice for a complaint, which it really seems to me every other woman on the estate is cursed with, and which is a direct result of the conditions of their existence; the practice of sending women to labor in the fields in the third week after their confinement is a specific for causing this infirmity, and I know no specific for curing it under these circumstances. As soon as these poor things had departed with such comfort as I could give them, and the bandages they especially begged for, three other sable graces introduced themselves, Edie, Louisa, and Diana; the former told me she had had a family of seven children, but had lost them all through "ill luck," as she denominated the ignorance and ill-treatment which were answerable for the loss of these, as of so many other poor little creatures their fellows. Having dismissed her and Diana with the sugar and rice they came to beg, I detained Louisa, whom I had never seen but in the presence of her old grandmother, whose version of the poor child's escape to, and hiding in the woods, I had a desire to compare with the heroine's own story.

She told it very simply, and it was most pathetic. She had not finished her task one day, when she said she felt ill, and unable to do so, and had been severely flogged by driver Bran, in whose "gang" she then was. The next day, in spite of this encouragement to labor, she had again been unable to complete her appointed work; and Bran having told her that he'd tie her up and flog her if she did not get it done, she had left the field and run into the swamp.

"Tie you up, Louisa!" said I; "What is that?"

She then described to me that they were fastened up by their wrists to a beam or a branch of a tree, their feet barely touching the ground, so as to allow them no purchase for resistance or evasion of the lash, their clothes turned over their heads, and their backs scored with a leather thong, either by the driver himself, or, if he pleases to inflict their punishment by deputy, any of the men he may choose to summon to the office; it might be father, brother, husband, or lover, if the overseer so ordered it. I turned sick, and my blood curdled listening to these details from the slender young slip of a lassie, with her poor piteous face and murmuring, pleading voice.

"Oh," said I, "Louisa; but the rattlesnakes—the dreadful rattlesnakes in the swamps; were you not afraid of those horrible creatures?"

"Oh, missis," said the poor child, "me no tink of dem; me forget all 'bout dem for de fretting."

"Why did you come home at last?"

"Oh, missis, me starve with hunger, me most dead with hunger before me come back."

"And were you flogged, Louisa?" said I, with a shudder at what the answer might be.

"No, missis, me go to hospital; me almost dead and sick so long, 'spec driver Bran him forgot 'bout de flogging."

I am getting perfectly savage over all these doings, E[lizabeth], and really think I should consider my own throat and those of my children well cut if some night the people were to take it into their heads to clear off scores in that fashion.

You will see how miserable the physical condition of many of these poor creatures is; and their physical condition, it is insisted by those who uphold this evil system, is the only part of it which is prosperous, happy, and compares well with that of Northern laborers. Judge from the details I now send you, and never forget, while reading them, that the people on this plantation are well off, and consider themselves well off, in comparison with the slaves on some of the neighboring estates.

Fanny has had six children; all dead but one. She came to beg to have her work in the field lightened.

Nanny has had three children; two of them are dead. She came to implore that the rule of sending them into the field three weeks after their confinement might be altered.

Leah, Caesar's wife, has had six children; three are dead.

Sophy, Lewis's wife, came to beg for some old linen. She is suffering fearfully; has had ten children; five of them are dead. The principal favor she asked was a piece of meat, which I gave her.

Sally, Scipio's wife, has had two miscarriages and three children born, one of whom is dead. She came complaining of incessant pain and weakness in her back. This woman was a mulatto daughter of a slave called Sophy, by a white man of the name of Walker, who visited the plantation.

Charlotte, Renty's wife, had had two miscarriages, and

was with child again. She was almost crippled with rheumatism, and showed me a pair of poor swollen knees that made my heart ache. I have promised her a pair of flannel trousers, which I must forthwith set about making.

Sarah, Stephen's wife; this woman's case and history were alike deplorable. She had had four miscarriages, had brought seven children into the world, five of whom were dead, and was again with child. She complained of dreadful pains in the back, and an internal tumor which swells with the exertion of working in the fields; probably, I think, she is ruptured. She told me she had once been mad and had run into the woods, where she contrived to elude discovery for some time, but was at last tracked and brought back, when she was tied up by the arms, and heavy logs fastened to her feet, and was severely flogged. After this she contrived to escape again, and lived for some time skulking in the woods, and she supposes mad, for when she was taken again she was entirely naked. She subsequently recovered from this derangement, and seems now just like all the other poor creatures who come to me for help and pity. I suppose her constant childbearing and hard labor in the fields at the same time may have produced the temporary insanity.

Sukey, Bush's wife, only came to pay her respects. She had had four miscarriages; had brought eleven children into the world, five of whom are dead.

Molly, Quambo's wife, also only came to see me. Hers was the best account I have yet received; she had had nine children, and six of them were still alive.

This is only the entry for today, in my diary, of the people's complaints and visits. Can you conceive a more wretched picture than that which it exhibits of the conditions under which these women live? Their cases are in no respect singular, and though they come with pitiful entreaty that I will help them with some alleviation of their pressing physical distresses, it seems to me marvelous with what desperate patience (I write it advisedly, patience of utter despair) they endure their sorrow-laden existence. Even the poor wretch who told that miserable story of insanity, and lonely hiding in the swamps, and scourging when she was found, and of her renewed madness and flight, did so in a sort of low, plaintive, monotonous murmur of misery, as if such sufferings were "all in the day's work."

I asked these questions about their children because I think the number they bear as compared with the number they rear a fair gauge of the effect of the system on their own health and that of their offspring. There was hardly one of these women, as you will see by the details I have noted of their ailments, who might not have been a candidate for a bed in a hospital, and they had come to me after working all day in the fields.

In the afternoon I made my first visit to the hospital of the estate, and found it, as indeed I find everything else here, in a far worse state even than the wretched establishments on the rice island, dignified by that name; so miserable a place for the purpose to which it was dedicated I could not have imagined on a property belonging to Christian owners. The floor (which was not boarded, but merely the damp hard earth itself) was strewn with wretched women, who, but for their moans of pain, and uneasy, restless motions, might very well each have been taken for a mere heap of filthy rags; the chimney refusing passage to the smoke from the pine-wood fire, it puffed out in clouds through the room, where it circled and hung, only gradually oozing away through the windows, which were so far well-adapted to the purpose that there was not a single whole pane of glass in them. My eyes, unaccustomed to the turbid atmosphere, smarted and watered, and refused to distinguish at first the different dismal forms, from which cries and wails assailed me in every corner of the place. By degrees I was able to endure for a few minutes what they were condemned to live their hours and days of suffering and sickness through; and, having given what comfort kind words and promises of help in more substantial forms could convey, I went on to what seemed a yet more wretched abode of wretchedness.

This was a room where there was no fire because there was no chimney, and where the holes made for windows had no panes or glasses in them. The shutters being closed, the place was so dark that, on first entering it, I was afraid to stir lest I should fall over some of the deplorable creatures extended upon the floor. As soon as they perceived me, one cry of "Oh missis!" rang through the darkness; and it really seemed to me as if I was never to exhaust the pity, and amazement, and disgust which this receptacle of suffering humanity was to excite in me. The poor dingy supplicating sleepers upraised themselves as I cautiously advanced among them; those who could not rear their bodies from the earth held up piteous beseeching hands, and as I passed from one to the other I felt more than one imploring clasp laid upon my dress, to solicit my attention to some new form of misery. One poor woman, called Tressa, who was unable to speak above a whisper from utter weakness and exhaustion, told me she had had nine children, was suffering from incessant flooding, and felt "as if her back would split open." There she lay, a mass of filthy tatters, without so much as a blanket under her or over her, on the bare earth in this chilly darkness. I promised them help and comfort, beds and blankets, and light and fire—that is, I promised to ask Mr. [Butler] for all this for them; and, in the very act of doing so, I remembered with a sudden pang of anguish that I was to urge no more petitions from his slaves to their master. I groped my way out, and, emerging on the piazza, all the choking tears and sobs I had controlled broke forth, and I leaned there crying over the lot of these unfortunates till

I heard a feeble voice of "Missis, you no cry; missis, what for you cry?" and, looking up, saw that I had not yet done with this intolerable infliction. A poor crippled old man, lying in the corner of the piazza, unable even to crawl toward me, had uttered this word of consolation, and by his side (apparently too idiotic, as he was too impotent, to move) sat a young woman, the expression of whose face was the most suffering, and, at the same time, the most horribly repulsive I ever saw. I found she was, as I supposed, halfwitted; and, on coming nearer to inquire into her ailments and what I could do for her, found her suffering from that horrible disease—I believe some form of scrofula—to which the Negroes are subject, which attacks and eats away the joints of their hands and fingers—a more hideous and loathsome object I never beheld; her name was Patty, and she was granddaughter to the old crippled creature by whose side she was squatting.

After my return home I had my usual evening reception, and, among other pleasant incidents of plantation life, heard the following agreeable anecdote from a woman named Sophy, who came to beg for some rice. In asking her about her husband and children, she said she had never had any husband; that she had had two children by a white man of the name of Walker, who was employed at the mill on the rice island; she was in the hospital after the birth of the second child she bore this man, and at the same time two women, Judy and Scylla, of whose children Mr. K[ing] was the father, were recovering from their confinements. It was not a month since any of them had been delivered, when Mrs. K[ing] came to the hospital, had them all three severely flogged, a process which *she* personally superintended, and then sent them to Five Pound—the swamp Botany Bay of the plantation, of which I have told you— with further orders to the drivers to flog them every day for a week. Now, E[lizabeth], if I make you sick with these disgusting stories, I cannot help it; they are the life itself here; hitherto I have thought these details intolerable enough, but this apparition of a female fiend in the middle of this hell I confess adds an element of cruelty which seems to me to surpass all the rest. Jealousy is not an uncommon quality in the feminine temperament; and just conceive the fate of these unfortunate women between the passions of their masters and mistresses, each alike armed with power to oppress and torture them.

Sophy went on to say that Isaac was her son by driver Morris, who had forced her while she was in her miserable exile at Five Pound. Almost beyond my patience with this string of detestable details, I exclaimed—foolishly enough, heaven knows: "Ah! but don't you know—did nobody ever tell or teach any of you that it is a sin to live with men who are not your husbands?"

Alas! E[lizabeth], what could the poor creature answer but what she did, seizing me at the same time vehemently by the wrist: "Oh yes, missis, we know—we know all about dat well enough; but we do anything to get our poor flesh some rest from de whip; when he made me follow him into de bush, what use me tell him no? he have strength to make me."

I have written down the woman's words; I wish I could write down the voice and look of abject misery with which they were spoken. Now you will observe that the story was not told to me as a complaint; it was a thing long past and over, of which she only spoke in the natural course of accounting for her children to me. I make no comment; what need, or can I add, to such stories? But how is such a state of things to endure? And again, how is it to end?

Charles Dickens

I believe the heaviest blow ever dealt at liberty's head will be dealt by this nation in the ultimate failure of its example to the earth.

When Charles Dickens arrived in America in 1842 he was greeted like a lion: "There never was a king or emperor upon the earth," he wrote home, "so cheered and followed by crowds, and entertained in public at splendid dinners. . . . It is all heart. There never was, and never will be such a triumph." When his critical report *American Notes* appeared in 1842 he was called a mere "penny-a-liner," "the most flimsy—the most childish—the most trashy—the most contemptible" visitor the young country ever suffered.

Dickens' popularity here, as the author of *Boz, Pickwick Papers, Oliver Twist* and *The Old Curiosity Shop*, was enormous. But if America read his books with intense interest, they

Charles Dickens, *American Notes* (New York, Harper and Brothers, 1842), pp. 266–84.

refused to pay him (or other European writers) royalties. The United States did not recognize the International Copyright Agreement and Dickens reminded his audiences throughout his visit that this was criminal neglect. Americans were outraged to be lectured to by a "self-serving Englishman." Newspapers called him a mercenary scoundrel who returned the lavish hospitality with a beggar's request for payment. Dickens knew the American sensitivity to criticism: "The wonder is that a breathing man can be found with temerity enough to suggest . . . the possibility of their having done wrong." He attacked slavery and dueling; prison conditions and poor sanitation (he was livid on the profuse habit of spitting). He found the press a haven of degradation and vulgarity; the government bad enough to shame the Founding Fathers in their graves. "I love and honor very many people here," he told a friend, "but the 'mass' (to use our monarchial terms) are miserably dependent in great things, and miserably independent in small ones. . . . The nation is a body without a head; the arms and legs are occupied in quarreling with the trunk and each other, and exchanging bruises at random." America, he concluded, "is not the Republic of my imagination."

Slavery especially disturbed him, as well as other foreign visitors at the time. His friend Harriet Martineau wrote: "A walk through a lunatic asylum is far less painful than a visit to the slave quarter of an estate. . . . It is well known that the most savage violences that are now heard of in the world take place in the Southern and Western States of America. Burning alive, cutting the heart out and sticking it on the point of a knife . . . are heard of only there." Another traveler, who came on the charred ashes of a slave executed for killing an overseer, was told by American friends that this "mode of punishment [burning alive] is sometimes inflicted on Negroes when the crime is very flagrant, to deprive them of the mental consolation arising from the hope that they will after death return to their own country."

Before he left England for the New World, Dickens said that foreigners had been too hostile to America. He would tell the truth, in candor and affection. Thinking men must "utterly forget, and put out of sight the Old [World] and bring none of its customs or observations into comparison." After his tour, Dickens wrote a friend that "I cannot change my secret opinion of this country—its follies, vices, grievous disappointments. . . . I believe the heaviest blow ever dealt at Liberty's head will be dealt by this nation in the ultimate failure of its example to the Earth."

THE UPHOLDERS OF SLAVERY IN AMERICA—of the atrocities of which system I shall not write one word for which I have not ample proof and warrant—may be divided into three great classes.

The first are those more moderate and rational owners of human cattle who have come into the possession of them as so many coins in their trading capital, but who admit the frightful nature of the Institution in the abstract, and perceive the dangers to society with which it is fraught: dangers which, however distant they may be, or howsoever tardy in their coming on, are as certain to fall upon its guilty head as is the Day of Judgment.

The second consists of all those owners, breeders, users, buyers, and sellers of slaves, who will, until the bloody chapter has a bloody end, own, breed, use, buy, and sell them at all hazards; who doggedly deny the horrors of the system, in the teeth of such a mass of evidence as never was brought to bear on any other subject, and to which the experience of every day contributes its immense amount; who would, at this or any other moment, gladly involve

America in a war, civil or foreign, provided that it had for its sole end and object the assertion of their right to perpetuate slavery, and to whip and work and torture slaves, unquestioned by any human authority, and unassailed by any human power; who, when they speak of Freedom, mean the Freedom to oppress their kind, and to be savage, merciless, and cruel; and of whom every man on his own ground, in Republican America, is a more exacting, and a sterner, and a less responsible despot than the Caliph Haroun Alraschid in his angry robe of scarlet.

The third, and not the least numerous or influential, is composed of all that delicate gentility which cannot bear a superior, and cannot brook an equal; of that class whose Republicanism means, "I will not tolerate a man above me: and, of those below, none must approach too near"; whose pride, in a land where voluntary servitude is shunned as a disgrace, must be ministered to by slaves; and whose inalienable right can only have their growth in negro wrongs.

It has been sometimes urged that, in the unavailing efforts which have been made to advance the cause of Human Freedom in the republic of America (strange cause for history to treat of!), sufficient regard has not been had to the existence of the first class of persons; and it has been contended that they are hardly used, in being confounded with the second. This is, no doubt, the case; noble instances of pecuniary and personal sacrifice have already had their growth among them; and it is much to be regretted that the gulf between them and the advocates of emancipation should have been widened and deepened by any means: the rather as there are, beyond dispute, among these slave-owners, many kind masters who are tender in the exercise of their unnatural power. Still it is to be feared that this injustice is inseparable from the state of things with which humanity and truth are called upon to deal. Slavery is not a whit the more endurable because some hearts are to be found which can partially resist its hardening influences; nor can the indignant tide of honest wrath stand still, because in its onward course it overwhelms a few who are comparatively innocent among a host of guilty.

The ground most commonly taken by these better men among the advocates of slavery is this: "It is a bad system; and for myself I would willingly get rid of it, if I could, most willingly. But it is not so bad as you in England take it to be. You are deceived by the representations of the emancipationists. The greater part of my slaves are much attached to me. You will say that I do not allow them to be severely treated; but I will put it to you whether you believe that it can be a general practice to treat them inhumanly, when it would impair their value, and would be obviously against the interests of their masters."

Is it the interest of any man to steal, to game, to waste his health and mental faculties by drunkenness, to lie, forswear himself, indulge hatred, seek desperate revenge, or do murder? No. All these are roads to ruin. And why, then, do men tread them? Because such inclinations are among the vicious qualities of mankind. Blot out, ye friends of slavery, from the catalogue of human passions, brutal lust, cruelty, and the abuse of irresponsible power (of all earthly temptations the most difficult to be resisted), and when ye have done so, and not before, we will inquire whether it be the interest of a master to lash and maim the slaves, over whose lives and limbs he has an absolute control!

But again: this class, together with that last one I have named, the miserable aristocracy spawned of a false republic, lift up their voices and exclaim, "Public opinion is all-sufficient to prevent such cruelty as you denounce." Public opinion! Why, public opinion in the slave States *is* slavery, is it not? Public opinion in the slave States has delivered the slaves over to the gentle mercies of their masters. Public opinion has made the laws, and denied the slaves legislative protection. Public opinion has knotted the lash, heated the branding-iron, loaded the rifle, and shielded the murderer. Public opinion threatens the abolitionist with death, if he venture to the South; and drags him with a rope about his middle, in broad unblushing noon, through the first city in the East. Public opinion has, within a few years, burned a slave alive at a slow fire in the city of St. Louis; and public opinion has to this day maintained upon the bench that estimable Judge who charged the Jury, impanelled there to try his murderers, that their most horrid deed was an act of public opinion, and, being so, must not be punished by the laws the public sentiment had made. Public opinion hailed this doctrine with a howl of wild applause, and set the prisoners free, to walk the city, men of mark, and influence, and station, as they had been before.

Public opinion! what class of men have an immense preponderance over the rest of the community in their power of representing public opinion in the legislature? The slave-owners. They send from their twelve States one hundred members, while the fourteen free States, with a free population nearly double, return but a hundred and forty-two. Before whom do the presidential candidates bow down the most humbly, on whom do they fawn the most fondly, and for whose tastes do they cater the most assiduously in their servile protestations? The slave-owners always.

Public opinion! hear the public opinion of the free South as expressed by its own members in the House of Representatives at Washington. "I have a great respect for the chair," quoth North Carolina, "I have a great respect for the chair as an officer of the House, and a great respect for him personally; nothing but that respect prevents me from rushing to the table, and tearing that petition which has just been presented for the abolition of slavery in the district of Columbia to pieces."—"I warn the abolitionists," says South Carolina, "ignorant, infuriated barbarians as they are, that if chance shall throw any of them into our hands, he may expect a felon's death."—"Let an abolitionist come within the borders of South Carolina," cries a third, mild Carolina's colleague, "and if we can catch him, we will try him, and, notwithstanding the interference of all the governments on earth, including the Federal Government, we will HANG him."

Public opinion has made this law.—It has declared that in Washington, in that city which takes its name from the father of American liberty, any justice of the peace may bind with fetters any negro passing down the street, and thrust him into gaol: no offence on the black man's part is necessary. The justice says, "I choose to think this man a runaway," and locks him up. Public opinion empowers the man of law, when this is done, to advertise the negro in the newspapers, warning his owner to come and claim him, or he will be sold to pay the gaol fees. But supposing he is a free black, and has no owner, it may naturally be presumed that he is set at liberty. NO: HE IS SOLD TO RECOMPENSE HIS GAOLER. This has been done again, and again, and again. He has no means of proving his freedom; has no adviser, messenger, or assistance of any sort or kind; no investigation into his case is made, or inquiry instituted. He, a free man, who may have served for years, and bought his liberty, is thrown into gaol on no process, for no crime, and on no pretence of crime: and is sold to pay the gaol fees. This seems incredible, even of America, but it is the law.

Public opinion is deferred to in such cases as the following; which is headed in the newspapers—

INTERESTING LAW-CASE

"An interesting case is now on trial in the Supreme Court, arising out of the following facts. A gentleman residing in Maryland had allowed an aged pair of his slaves substantial though not legal freedom for several years. While thus living, a daughter was born to them, who grew up in the same liberty, until she married a free negro, and went with him to reside in Pennsylvania. They had several children, and lived unmolested until the original owner died, when his heir attempted to regain them; but the magistrate before whom they were brought decided that he had no jurisdiction in the case. *The owner seized the woman and her children in the night, and carried them to Maryland.*"

"Cash for negroes," "cash for negroes," "cash for negroes," is the heading of advertisements in great capitals down the long columns of the crowded journals. Woodcuts of a runaway negro with manacled hands, crouching beneath a bluff pursuer in top-boots, who, having caught him, grasps him by the throat, agreeably diversify the pleasant text. The leading article protests against "that abominable and hellish doctrine of abolition, which is repugnant alike to every law of God and nature." The delicate mamma, who smiles her acquiescence in this sprightly writing as she reads the paper in her cool piazza, quiets her youngest child who clings about her skirts by promising the boy "a whip to beat the little niggers with."—But the negroes, little and big, are protected by public opinion.

Let us try this public opinion by another test, which is important in three points of view: first, as showing how desperately timid of the public opinion slave-owners are in their delicate descriptions of fugitive slaves in widely-circulated newspapers; secondly, as showing how perfectly contented the slaves are, and how very seldom they run away; thirdly, as exhibiting their entire freedom from scar, or blemish, or any mark of cruel infliction, as their pictures are drawn, not by lying abolitionists, but by their own truthful masters.

The following are a few specimens of the advertisements in the public papers. It is only four years since the oldest among them appeared; and others of the same nature continue to be published every day in shoals.

"Ran away, Negress Caroline. Had on a collar with one prong turned down."

"Ran away, a black woman, Betsy. Had an iron bar on her right leg."

"Ran away, the negro Manuel. Much marked with irons."

"Ran away, the negress Fanny. Had on an iron band about her neck."

"Ran away, a negro boy about twelve years old. Had round his neck a chain dog-collar with 'De Lampert' engraved on it."

"Ran away, the negro Hown. Has a ring of iron on his left foot. Also, Grise, *his wife*, having a ring and chain on the left leg."

"Ran away, a negro boy named James. Said boy was ironed when he left me."

"Committed to jail, a man who calls his name John. He has a clog of iron on his right foot which will weigh four or five pounds."

"Detained at the police jail, the negro wench, Myra. Has several marks of LASHING, and has irons on her feet."

"Ran away, a negro woman and two children. A few days before she went off, I burnt her with a hot iron, on the left side of her face. I tried to make the letter M."

"Ran away, a negro man named Henry; his left eye out, some scars from a dirk on and under his left arm, and much scarred with the whip."

"One hundred dollars reward, for a negro fellow, Pompey, 40 years old. He is branded on the left jaw."

"Committed to jail, a negro man. Has no toes on the left foot."

"Ran away, a negro woman named Rachel. Has lost all her toes except the large one."

"Ran away, Sam. He was shot a short time since through the hand, and has several shots in his left arm and side."

"Ran away, my negro man Dennis. Said negro has been shot in the left arm between the shoulders and elbow, which has paralysed the left hand."

"Ran away, my negro man named Simon. He has been shot badly, in his back and right arm."

"Ran away, a negro named Arthur. Has a considerable scar across his breast and each arm, made by knife; loves to talk much of the goodness of God."

"Twenty-five dollars reward for my man Isaac. He has a scar on his forehead, caused by a blow; and one on his back, made by a shot from a pistol."

"Ran away, a negro girl called Mary. Has a small scar over her eye, a good many teeth missing, the letter A is branded on her cheek and forehead."

"Ran away, negro Ben. Has a scar on his right hand; his thumb and forefinger being injured by being shot last fall. A part of the bone came out. He has also one or two large scars on his back and hips."

"Detained at the jail, a mulatto, named Tom. Has a scar on the right cheek, and appears to have been burned with powder on the face."

"Ran away, a negro man named Ned. Three of his fingers are drawn into the palm of his hand by a cut. Has a scar on the back of his neck, nearly half round, done by a knife."

"Was committed to jail, a negro man. Says his name is Josiah. His back very much scarred by the whip, and branded on the thigh and hips in three or four places, thus (J M). The rim of his right ear has been bit or cut off."

"Fifty dollars reward, for my fellow Edward. He has a scar on the corner of his mouth, two cuts on and under his arm, and the letter E on his arm."

"Ran away, negro boy Ellie. Has a scar on one of his arms from the bite of a dog."

"Ran away, from the plantation of James Surgette, the

following negroes: Randal, has one ear cropped; Bob, has lost one eye; Kentucky Tom, has one jaw broken."

"Ran away, Anthony. One of his ears cut off, and his left hand cut with an axe."

"Fifty dollars reward for the negro Jim Blake. Has a piece cut out of each ear, and the middle finger of the left hand cut off to the second joint."

"Ran away, a negro woman named Maria. Has a scar on one side of her cheek, by a cut. Some scars on her back."

"Ran away, the Mulatto wench Mary. Has a cut on the left arm, a scar on the left shoulder, and two upper teeth missing."

I should say, perhaps, in explanation of this latter piece of description, that, among the other blessings which public opinion secures to the negroes, is the common practice of violently punching out their teeth. To make them wear iron collars by day and night, and to worry them with dogs, are practices almost too ordinary to deserve mention.

"Ran away, my man Fountain. Has holes in his ears, a scar on the right side of his forehead, has been shot in the hind parts of his legs, and is marked on the back with the whip."

"Two hundred and fifty dollars reward for my negro man Jim. He is much marked with shot in his right thigh. The shot entered on the outside, halfway between the hip and knee joints."

"Brought to jail, John. Left ear cropt."

"Taken up, a negro man. Is very much scarred about the face and body, and has the left ear bit off."

"Ran away, a black girl named Mary. Has a scar on her cheek, and the end of one of her toes cut off."

"Ran away, my mulatto woman, Judy. She has had her right arm broke."

"Ran away, my negro man, Levi. His left hand has been burnt, and I think the end of his forefinger is off."

"Ran away, a negro man, NAMED WASHINGTON. Has lost a part of his middle finger, and the end of his little finger."

"Twenty-five dollars reward for my man John. The tip of his nose is bit off."

"Twenty-five dollars reward for the negro slave Sally. Walks *as though* crippled in the back."

"Ran away, Joe Dennis. Has a small notch in one of his ears."

"Ran away, negro boy, Jack. Has a small crop out of his left ear."

"Ran away, a negro man, named Ivory. Has a small piece cut out of the top of each ear."

While upon the subject of ears, I may observe that a distinguished abolitionist in New York once received a negro's ear, which had been cut off close to the head, in a general post letter. It was forwarded by the free and independent gentleman who had caused it to be amputated, with a polite request that he would place the specimen in his "collection."

I could enlarge this catalogue with broken arms, and broken legs, and gashed flesh, and missing teeth, and lacerated backs, and bites of dogs, and brands of red-hot irons innumerable: but, as my readers will be sufficiently sickened and repelled already, I will turn to another branch of the subject.

These advertisements, of which a similar collection might be made for every year, and month, and week, and day; and which are coolly read in families as things of course, and as a part of the current news and small-talk; will serve to show how very much the slaves profit by public opinion, and how tender it is in their behalf. But it may be worth while to inquire how the slave-owners, and the class of society to which great numbers of them belong, defer to public opinion in their conduct, not to their slaves, but to each other; how they are accustomed to restrain their passions; what their bearing is among themselves; whether they are fierce or gentle, whether their social customs be brutal, sanguinary, and violent, or bear the impress of civilisation and refinement.

That we may have no partial evidence from abolitionists in this inquiry either, I will once more turn to their own newspapers, and I will confine myself, this time, to a selection from paragraphs which appeared from day to day during my visit to America, and which refer to occurrences happening while I was there. The italics in these extracts, as in the foregoing, are my own.

These cases did not ALL occur, it will be seen, in territory actually belonging to legalised Slave States, though most, and those the very worst among them, did, as their counterparts constantly do; but the position of the scenes of action in reference to places immediately at hand, where slavery is the law; and the strong resemblance between that class of outrages and the rest; lead to the just presumption that the character of the parties concerned was formed in slave districts, and brutalised by slave customs.

HORRIBLE TRAGEDY

"By a slip from *The Southport Telegraph*, Wisconsin, we learn that the Hon. Charles C. P. Arndt, Member of the Council for Brown county, was shot dead *on the floor of the Council chamber*, by James R. Vinyard, Member from Grant county. *The affair* grew out of a nomination for Sheriff of Grant county. Mr. E. S. Baker was nominated and supported by Mr. Arndt. This nomination was opposed by Vinyard, who wanted the appointment to vest in his own brother. In the course of debate, the deceased made some statements which Vinyard pronounced false, and made use of violent and insulting language, dealing largely in personalities, to which Mr. A. made no reply. After the adjournment, Mr. A. stepped up to Vinyard, and requested him to retract, which he refused to do, repeating the offensive words. Mr. Arndt then made a blow at Vinyard, who drew back a pace, drew a pistol, and shot him dead.

"The issue appears to have been provoked on the part of Vinyard, who was determined at all hazards to defeat the appointment of Baker, and who, himself defeated, turned his ire and revenge upon the unfortunate Arndt."

THE WISCONSIN TRAGEDY

"Public indignation runs high in the territory of Wisconsin, in relation to the murder of C. C. P. Arndt, in the Legislative Hall of the Territory. Meetings have been held in different counties of Wisconsin, denouncing *the practice of secretly bearing arms in the Legislative chambers of the country*. We have seen the account of the expulsion of James R. Vinyard, the perpetrator of the bloody deed, and are amazed to hear, that, after this expulsion by those who saw Vinyard kill Mr. Arndt in the presence of his aged father, who was on a visit to see his son, little dreaming that he was to witness his murder, *Judge Dunn has discharged Vinyard on bail*. The Miners' Free Press speaks *in terms of merited rebuke* at the outrage upon the feelings of the people of Wisconsin. Vinyard was within arm's length of Mr. Arndt, when he took such deadly aim at him, that he never spoke. Vinyard might at pleasure, being so near, have only wounded him, but he chose to kill him."

MURDER

"By a letter in a St. Louis paper of the 14th, we notice a terrible outrage at Burlington, Iowa. A Mr. Bridgman having had a difficulty with a citizen of the place, Mr. Ross; a brother-in-law of the latter provided himself with one of

Colt's revolving pistols, met Mr. B. in the street, *and discharged the contents of five of the barrels at him: each shot taking effect.* Mr. B., though horribly wounded, and dying, returned the fire, and killed Ross on the spot."

TERRIBLE DEATH OF ROBERT POTTER

"From the 'Caddo Gazette,' of the 12th inst., we learn the frightful death of Colonel Robert Potter. . . . He was beset in his house by an enemy, named Rose. He sprang from his couch, seized his gun, and, in his night clothes, rushed from the house. For about two hundred yards his speed seemed to defy his pursuers; but, getting entangled in a thicket, he was captured. Rose told him *that he intended to act a generous part,* and give him a chance for his life. He then told Potter he might run, and he should not be interrupted till he reached a certain distance. Potter started at the word of command, and before a gun was fired he had reached the lake. His first impulse was to jump into the water and dive for it, which he did. Rose was close behind him, and formed his men on the bank ready to shoot him as he rose. In a few seconds he came up to breathe; and scarce had his head reached the surface of the water when it was completely riddled with the shot of their guns, and he sunk, to rise no more!"

FOUL DEED

"The steamer Thames, just from Missouri river, brought us a handbill, offering a reward of 500 dollars, for the person who assassinated Lilburn W. Baggs, late Governor of this State, at Independence, on the night of the 6th inst. Governor Baggs, it is stated in a written memorandum, was not dead, but mortally wounded.

"Since the above was written, we received a note from

the clerk of the Thames, giving the following particulars. Gov. Baggs was shot by some villain on Friday, 6th inst., in the evening, while sitting in a room in his own house in Independence. His son, a boy, hearing a report, ran into the room, and found the Governor sitting in his chair, with his jaw fallen down, and his head leaning back; on discovering the injury done to his father, he gave the alarm. Foot tracks were found in the garden below the window, and a pistol picked up supposed to have been overloaded, and thrown from the hand of the scoundrel who fired it. Three buck shots of a heavy load took effect; one going through his mouth, one into the brain, and another probably in or near the brain; all going into the back part of the neck and head. The Governor was still alive on the morning of the 7th; but no hopes for his recovery by his friends, and but slight hopes from his physicians.

"A man was suspected, and the Sheriff most probably has possession of him by this time.

"The pistol was one of a pair stolen some days previous from a baker in Independence, and the legal authorities have the description of the other."

RENCONTRE

"An unfortunate *affair* took place on Friday evening in Chartres Street, in which one of our most respectable citizens received a dangerous wound, from a poignard, in the abdomen. From the Bee (New Orleans) of yesterday, we learn the following particulars. It appears that an article was published in the French side of the paper on Monday last, containing some strictures on the Artillery Battalion for firing their guns on Sunday morning, in answer to those from the Ontario and Woodbury, and thereby much alarm was caused to the families of those persons who were out all night preserving the peace of the city. Major C. Gally,

Commander of the battalion, resenting this, called at the office and demanded the author's name; that of Mr. P. Arpin was given to him, who was absent at the time. Some angry words then passed with one of the proprietors, and a challenge followed; the friends of both parties tried to arrange the affair, but failed to do so. On Friday evening, about seven o'clock, Major Gally met Mr. P. Arpin in Chartres Street, and accosted him. 'Are you Mr. Arpin?'

" 'Yes, sir.'

" 'Then I have to tell you that you are a———' (applying an appropriate epithet).

" 'I shall remind you of your words, sir.'

" 'But I have said I would break my cane on your shoulders.'

" 'I know it, but I have not yet received the blow.'

"At these words, Major Gally, having a cane in his hands, struck Mr. Arpin across the face, and the latter drew a poignard from his pocket and stabbed Major Gally in the abdomen.

"Fears are entertained that the wound will be mortal. *We understand that Mr. Arpin has given security for his appearance at the Criminal Court to answer the charge.*"

I will quote but one more paragraph, which, by reason of its monstrous absurdity, may be a relief to these atrocious deeds.

AFFAIR OF HONOUR

"We have just heard the particulars of a meeting which took place on Six Mile Island, on Tuesday, between two young bloods of our city: Samuel Thurston, *aged fifteen,* and William Hine, *aged thirteen years.* They were attended by young gentlemen of the same age. The weapons used on the occasion were a couple of Dickson's best rifles; the distance, thirty yards. They took one fire, without any damage being sustained by either party, except the ball of Thurston's gun passing through the crown of Hine's hat. *Through the intercession of the Board of Honour*, the challenge was withdrawn, and the difference amicably adjusted."

If the reader will picture to himself the kind of Board of Honour which amicably adjusted the difference between these two little boys, who in any other part of the world would have been amicably adjusted on two porters' backs, and soundly flogged with birchen rods, he will be possessed, no doubt, with as strong a sense of its ludicrous character as that which sets me laughing whenever its image rises up before me.

Now, I appeal to every human mind imbued with the commonest of common sense, and the commonest of common humanity; to all dispassionate, reasoning creatures, of any shade of opinion; and ask, with these revolting evidences of the state of society which exists in and about the slave districts of America before them, can they have a doubt of the real condition of the slave, or can they for a moment make a compromise between the institution or any of its flagrant fearful features, and their own just consciences? Will they say of any tale of cruelty and horror, however aggravated in degree, that it is improbable, when they can turn to the public prints, and, running, read such signs as these, laid before them by the men who rule the slaves: in their own acts, and under their own hands?

Do we not know that the worst deformity and ugliness of slavery are at once the cause and the effect of the reckless licence taken by these free-born outlaws? Do we not know that the man who has been born and bred among its wrongs; who has seen in his childhood husbands obliged, at the word of command, to flog their wives; women, indecently compelled to hold up their own garments that men might lay the heavier stripes upon their legs, driven and harried by brutal overseers in their time of travail, and becoming mothers on the field of toil, under the very lash itself; who has read in youth, and seen his virgin sisters read, descriptions of runaway men and women, and their disfigured persons, which could not be published elsewhere of so much stock upon a farm, or at a show of beasts:—do we not know that that man, whenever his wrath is kindled up, will be a brutal savage? Do we not know that as he is a coward in his domestic life, stalking among his shrinking men and women slaves armed with his heavy whip, so he will be a coward out of doors, and, carrying cowards' weapons hidden in his breast, will shoot men down and stab them when he quarrels? And if our reason did not teach us this and much beyond; if we were such idiots as to close our eyes to that fine mode of training which rears up such men; should we not know that they who among their equals stab and pistol in the legislative halls, and in the counting-house, and on the market-place, and in all the elsewhere peaceful pursuits of life, must be to their dependants, even though they were free servants, so many merciless and unrelenting tyrants?

What! shall we declaim against the ignorant peasantry of Ireland, and mince the matter when these American taskmasters are in question? Shall we cry shame on the brutality of those who ham-string cattle: and spare the lights of Freedom upon earth who notch the ears of men and women, cut pleasant posies in the shrinking flesh, learn to write with pens of red-hot iron on the human face, rack their poetic fancies for liveries of mutilation which their slaves shall wear for life and carry to the grave, break living limbs as did the soldiery who mocked and slew the Saviour of the world, and set defenceless creatures up for targets? Shall we whimper over legends of the tortures practised on each other by the Pagan Indians, and smile upon the cruelties of Christian men? Shall we, so long as these things last, exult above the scattered remnants of that stately race, and triumph in the white enjoyment of their broad possessions? Rather, for me, restore the forest and the Indian village; in lieu of stars and stripes, let some poor feather flutter in the breeze; replace the streets and squares by wigwams; and though the death-song of a hundred haughty warriors fill the air, it will be music to the shriek of one unhappy slave.

On one theme, which is commonly before our eyes, and in respect of which our national character is changing fast, let the plain Truth be spoken, and let us not, like dastards, beat about the bush by hinting at the Spaniard and the fierce Italian. When knives are drawn by Englishmen in conflict, let it be said and known: "We owe this change to Republican Slavery. These are the weapons of Freedom. With sharp points and edges such as these, Liberty in America hews and hacks her slaves; or, failing that pursuit, her sons devote them to a better use, and turn them on each other."

José Martí

*Osceola lay down and died in his war paint
because he "did not have the heart to kill
the white man like a bear or a wolf, although
he comes upon us with friendship in one
hand and a serpent in the other."*

Until his heroic death, the Cuban poet and revolutionary José
Martí (1853–1895) was the major interpreter of the United
States to the Spanish-speaking world. Martí was exiled by Spanish authorities in Cuba in the 1870's for his revolutionary work.
He studied in Madrid and traveled to Mexico and Guatemala,
but settled in New York in 1880. Charles Dana invited him to
contribute articles to the New York *Sun*, and there he wrote
about "the other America" (his phrase) of Grant and Jesse
James, of Coney Island and Buffalo Bill. During his fifteen year
exile in America, Martí helped win the sympathy and support
of many Americans to the cause of Cuban independence. "I
shall arouse the world," he told his friends. Martí's essays on

José Martí, *The America of José Martí*, translated by Juan de Onis.
Copyright 1954 by The Noonday Press, Inc., pp. 124–130. Reprinted by permission of Farrar, Straus & Giroux, Inc.

America resound with ambivalence. He was proud to be an "American" of the Western Hemisphere, yet conscious of the need to preserve the integrity of the Latin set deep within him. "The free Antilles," he wrote a few weeks before he died, "will preserve the independence of our America, and the dubious and tarnished honor of the English America, and perhaps may hasten and decide the balance of the world."

Like most foreigners, Martí was especially fascinated by the West. As he explained to his Spanish-speaking readers, the long hair of the buffalo hunters, their clothes of hide and their hunger for the kill were proof that, in America, man and nature were still one: "The strange life men lead in the remote regions of this country," Martí said, "develops in them all the appetites, magnificence, impulses and elegance of the wild beast!" But in this romantic evocation of primitivism, nomadic hunters pursued their prey from steam-driven boats and trains. And while killing beasts they were also fighting Indians. Here was the paradox: Americans, in primitive dress, chased wild animals (and humans) from roaring, iron trains while modern cities grew.

Heroic cowboys and savage Indians played out their mutually distorted roles before millions of vicarious adventurers in the many "Wild West" shows which toured Europe in the nineteenth century. These "shows" (mentioned by Eleanor Marx, below) were transformed in the twentieth century, appearing as novels and movies and finally becoming polyglot television serials like *Gunsmoke* and *Bonanza*. Some more astute foreign critics, however, were appalled by the violence and destruction Americans used to conquer the West. "I have in my pocket," wrote a French visitor, Georges Duhamel (see below), in the 1930's, "several of your small coins [nickels] on which is stamped the word 'liberty.' And what do you see immediately under the word? The figure of a buffalo or an Indian. Oh, irony! They represent two free and spirited races that you have destroyed in less than three centuries."

Replaced, the early settlers might have said, with Benjamin

Franklin. Doctor, printer, inventor, scientist, philosopher, revolutionary, diplomat—Franklin was the most striking American.
Here is his description of some Indians he met on the frontiers
of Pennsylvania:

> They were all drunk, men and women quarrelling and
> fighting. Their dark-coloured bodies, half-naked, seen
> only by the gloomy light of the bonfire, running after
> and beating one another with fire-brands, accompanied
> by their horrid yellings, formed a scene the most resem-
> bling our ideas of hell that could be well imagined . . .

Later the Indians apologized for their behavior but explained
that rum was provided for by "The Great Spirit" who told
them, "Let this [rum] be for the Indians to get drunk with."
Never a man to interfere with the will of the Great Spirit,
Franklin placed rum within the reach of their thirst. "And, indeed," he explained some years later, "if it be the design of
Providence to extirpate these savages in order to make room for
the cultivators of the earth, it seems not improbable that rum
may be the appointed means. *It has already annihilated all the
tribes who formerly inhabited all the seacoast.*"

This confession from Franklin was too much, too tempting,
for D. H. Lawrence, writing in the 1920's. "Moral America!
Most moral Benjamin. Sound satisfied Ben! . . . This, from the
good Doctor with such suave complacency is a little disen-
chanting. Almost too good to be true. But there you are! The
barbed wire fence. 'Extirpate these savages in order to make
room for the cultivators of the earth.' . . . Cultivate the earth,
ye gods! The Indians did that. . . . And they left off there.
Who built Chicago? Who cultivated the earth until it spawned
Pittsburgh, Pa.? The moral issue! Just look at it!" And for what
purpose was this barbarism tolerated? To permit a thriving
life for "white savages," Lawrence said, "with motor cars, telephones, incomes and ideas! Savages fast inside the machine; yet
savage enough, ye gods!"

Martí's account of the Oklahoma Land Rush of 1889 is a
description in microcosm of all the grandeur and pathos of
American civilization as it conquered, occupied and settled the
West. All the greed, cheating, and chaotic violence are brought
to life by his understated prose. The last of nature's reserves on
the continent was finally opened to capitalism and civilization.
"The white invader is rampant in the land of the Indian," Martí
observed. The land itself, however, was without a soul; the
Indians had taken it with them.

Marti returned to Cuba in 1895 during an abortive insur-
rection against colonial Spain. In his last letter, he told friends
of his peculiar duty "to prevent, through the independence of
Cuba, the U.S.A. from spreading over the West Indies and
falling with added weight upon other lands of Our America.
All I have done up to now and shall do hereafter is to that end
. . . I know the Monster, because I have lived in its lair—and my
weapon is only the slingshot of David." A few days later, he
was shot to death while leading a cavalry charge.

———————◆———————

HOMESTEADERS WAIT IMPATIENTLY on the distant prairie for
the stroke of noon on Monday when they will invade the
new Promised Land and stake their claims in the ancestral
hunting ground of the Seminole. They clean their rifles,
pray, and carouse. All along that straining frontier, held in
check only by the vigilance of the troops, one hears the
shouted greetings of the penniless who are about to become
landowners, of the speculators who see a froth of gold, of
the adventurers who live by crime and death. Who will be
the first to arrive? Who will drive the first stake on the plot
that will front the main street? Who will lay claim with the
heels of his boots to the fertile acres? Miles of wagons; a

welter of horsemen; random shots fired in the air; songs and
sermons; taverns and sporting houses; a coffin, followed by a
woman and child; from the four corners of that land
besieged by settlers one cry goes up: "Oklahoma! Oklahoma!"

The white invader is now rampant in the land of the
Indian that was left as if without a soul when Osceola lay
down and died in his war paint with his knife on his breast
because he "did not have the heart to kill the white man
like a bear or a wolf, although he comes upon us like a
bear or a wolf, with friendship in one hand and a serpent
in the other." So spoke Osceola, arrayed in his wampum
belt and feathered head-dress in the hour of death, half his
face painted red and his knife unsheathed. The Seminoles
sold the land to the "Great White Father" in Washington
with the understanding that other Indians or Negro freed-
men might come and live there. Neither Indian nor Negro
ever set foot on it, but cattlemen, who strung fences
through it as if they owned it, and homesteaders who
wanted it for fields to sow and a place to live, and not "so
that these kings of the earth who have friends in Washington can fatten on pure gold." The blood of strife ran where
only the blood of the hunt had flowed before. Federal
troops forced out the trespassing cattlemen and settlers. The
President finally proclaimed the area of the public domain,
and set April 22 as the date for its occupation. Ready, on
your mark! The first to drive the stake claims the land! A
section by law to the first to arrive! After ten years of
work, the railroads, the speculators, those who want to
"grow with the country," those to whom the soil of Kentucky or Kansas has not been kind, those who want finally
to settle down somewhere, who are tired of living on the
move, hungry one day, begging the next, gather on the
borders of the territory where many of them have already
been squatters, raising children and grazing cattle on the
very spot ambition has marked as the best site for the city,

and where the only signs of man now are the ashes of the settlers' cabins, the tracks of the railroad and the red station.

The isolated towns along the frontier fill up with people; horses and wagons soar in price; bronzed faces, of dark and sinister eye, turn up where they were never seen before; there are hand-clasps in the shadows between those vowing aid to one another and death to their rivals. The settlers close in from every side until they are face to face with the cavalry guarding that million acres of free land. There they wait in silence, side by side, with their horses, their covered wagons, their rifles on their shoulders, and their wives beside them. Only the marshals named by the President are allowed within the territory, and persons authorized by the army, such as railroad workers laying track, a newspaperman setting up his press, a hotel man preparing his establishment, and the employes of the land office, where the eager throng must register its claims in orderly turn. But the word is going around that a suspicious number of marshals have entered the territory, that the railroads have hidden people in the underbrush, that the army has certified hotel men who have no hotel, and that the railroad owners have made a bargain with the government so that Guthrie, where the red station stands, will be completely staked out by the time the territory is legally opened.

But they continue to pour in from near and far. Whole towns have migrated. In clusters, in straggling lines, in cavalcades they come, amidst clouds of dust. The silent land stretches, virgin and green, with its grassland and bluffs, surrounded on all four sides by human masses, fenced off only by the flanks of the mounted troops. Burning eyes peer between the flanks. This is how the wilderness has been settled here, and how the wonder called the United States has come into being.

As the entry day approaches, the region is like an entire nation on the move, like a camp on the march, for miles around. There is no fear of the sun or the night, of death or rain. Railroads have extended their tracks into the famed territory; rival communities have sprung up to receive the caravans that come from afar, the horsemen carrying a deck of cards between their teeth, pistols at a hair-trigger, and their queans on the saddle behind them, pilgrim bands of army veterans, farmers, old men and widows.

Arkansas City has torn the awnings from its houses to make beds for the immigrants, and every saw in town is nicked and dulled from cutting up lumber for benches and tables. There is no milk left to sell a pioneer woman who steps down from the wagon where her husband watches over their only possessions—a tent, a stove, a plow, and the stakes with which to establish their claim to the land. There are seventy-five wagons in Arkansas City under lock and key ready to make the dash to Guthrie with the people that crowd its streets, beg, drink whiskey till it runs out of their ears, buy land now, sell it a moment later, and calculate their profit on the transaction. Land not yet owned is selling for two dollars an acre in Oklahoma City where speculators count on their agile rider, who will not hesitate to kill to arrive first and stake a claim. Night is converted into day in Purcell, where a thousand Texas cowboys are roaming the town, and there is not a man without a woman. Pistol shots and drunken guffaws are heard on every side: Heaven help the homebodies in the wagons if they get in their way! The best land to the best rifle! "If they try to stop me with a child, Henrietta, I'll bring him back to you as beefsteak!" The carousing goes on until they fall asleep in their vomit.

The migrating towns, the towns on wheels, roll by toward the frontier. When the horses tire, the men put their shoulder to the wheel. If the men cannot do it alone, their wives get behind the other wheel. The beast's knees buckle, and the strapping son, his belt bristling with knives, kisses and caresses it. Day comes to a close, but not the journey. Now it is a thousand veterans, womanless and in good wagons, seeking land. Now it is a hundred men, with a Negro walking alone at their head. Now a group of cowboys on horseback, in boots and blue shirts, four revolvers in the belt and a Winchester across the saddle, passing the bottle and mouthing oaths. Here come a hundred more, with a woman leading the way. There goes the Widow Dickinson, with three daughters and two rifles bouncing in the wagon. Many wagons carry a sign painted on the canvas: "Land or bust!" One wagon, from which boots stick out from under every flap as thought it were filled with men stretched out, carries this sign: "There are plenty of damn fools like us!" Covered with dust, and with spades on their shoulders, a group of men plod forward under the command of a tall, spare man who is everywhere at once, with a spring in his step and a word of encouragement on his lips, hat pushed back, a few straggling hairs on his chin and two burning coals for eyes, in a faded shirt, and pants made out of an American flag tucked in his boots. Others come at a gallop with two bodies thrown across a saddle: two brothers who killed each other in a knife fight over which had the better "title" to a section that had already been picked out, "nobody knows where." Here comes the great caravan, that of the "old settlers" who had been living in the territory these ten years, headed by the man who pushed the land act through Congress. His voice is martial, his shoulders broad, and he stands six feet in his socks. The troop marches forward a thousand strong, determined to throttle anyone who stands in their way to the land they consider their own, to which they are returning after having been ousted by the cavalry, and where they already have staked their claim. The clouds suddenly pile up and rain comes down in torrents. The wind tips over the wagons and rips off their canvas coverings, and frightened horses bolt from under their riders. The storm passes as quickly as it came, and the caravan proceeds. Here is an entire hotel of tents and folding chairs; here the newspaper press; here a wagon filled with coffins.

Only one day more, only one day to go! Reports of bad doings come in from Purcell and Arkansas City. They say a cowboy was found in the morning impaled with a knife to the saloon table; that fast ponies are being sold at fabulous prices for the hour of entry; that the speculators have joined up with the desperadoes, and the desperadoes with one another, to defend the land they take away from the first arrivals, who will have no defense but that which they carry in their cartridge belt; that some thirty trespassers forded the river and entered the territory through a wood, and surrendered, one with his arm shot away, another with his jawbone shattered, another dragging himself along with a bullet in his belly, to the troops that went to dislodge them from their parapet, from which a youth, whose face could not be seen for the blood, emerged carrying a white flag. But the horses graze peacefully on this side of the frontier, where the best of the settlers are gathered. The people come in their Sunday best from miles around to where an old man with a milk-white beard calls them to services with a cowbell, a soap box serving as his pulpit. The veterans tell how they broke down and cried and hugged each other when they saw the land, and sang and shot off their rifles. A group squats in a circle, chin in hand, listening to the old Negress, Aunty Chloe, who had already raised chickens and kept a dog in Oklahoma before the soldiers put her out, and is now going back to the "land of the Lord" to see if she can find her chickens. Another group is made up of women who have come alone, like the men, to stake a claim for themselves, or to speculate in land they buy from others, like Polly Young, the pretty widow, who has already speculated in Kansas. Some will pool the lands they get and hold with horse and rifle, like the nine girls from Kentucky, who are pledged to work together. Some are going back to their lands, like Nellie Bruce, who hid in the woods with the chickens, when the soldiers put her father off his place, and burned down the cabin he had built so she could teach school. Nanny Daisy is going back to see if anybody has taken down the sign she she left on the homestead which said: "This belongs to Nanny Daisy, who knows her way around, and has two medals for sharpshooting. Beware!" Nanny takes out her medals, mounts bareback, without bit or bridle, slides off the neck or the croup, twirls her pearl-handled revolver, tells how she slapped the judge who tried to kiss her, and recalls her days as a schoolteacher, as a candidate for the post of librarian in Kansas, and as a newspaperwoman in Washington. From around the bend in the road comes the sound of the crack of the whip and a high-pitched, girlish voice: "Ehoe! Hooray! Here we come in calico dresses and shingle bonnets! Ehoe! Hooray! Tommy Barny ran off with Judas Silo's wife! Here is pretty Ella Blackburn, and her three sisters, with no men but these two Colts at my side."

By noon the next day everybody is ready, everybody is silent; forty thousand human beings and not a sound. Those on horseback are crouched forward on their horse's neck; those in wagons, standing with their foot on the footboard, the lines in their hands. Those with spavined beasts are to the rear, so they will not be trampled. The swish of horses' tails driving away troublesome flies is the only sound. A bugle note rends the silence, the cavalry turns aside, and from all sides at once that human torrent pours into the territory, spur to spur, wheel to wheel, without cursing, without talk, all eyes fixed on the dry horizon. From Texas, the horsemen at a dead gallop, firing their

rifles, standing in their stirrups, yelling like mad, and slap-
ping their horses with their hats. From the opposite direction, the ponies from Purcell, running flank to flank,
without yielding their place, without surrendering their
advantage. From Kansas, at full tilt, the heavy, bouncing,
thundering covered wagons on the heels of the riders. Some
stop, unhitch the horses, leave the women with the wagon,
saddle a horse, and overtake the horsemen. They pour into
the valley.

They are lost from sight behind the bluffs, they re-
appear and are lost again, they dismount, three at a time,
on the same acre of land, and face each other, murder in
their eyes. One suddenly reins his horse short, dismounts,
and sinks his knife in the ground. The wagons gradually
come to a halt, and their hidden occupants, the wives and
children, spread out on the prairie, where the father drives
his stakes. They do not climb down, they erupt. The
children roll in the grass, the horses whinny and swish
their tails, the mothers shout distractedly and wave their
arms. One late arrival does not want to surrender his place,
and the father fires his rifle point blank in his face, and
returns to laying out his stakes, kicking the body aside with
his foot to clear the line. The horsemen disappear from
sight in the distance. The torrent continues to pour in.

The railroad station, the tents of the troops, and the
registry office, flying the flag, are in Guthrie, which will
be the principal city. All of Arkansas City and Purcell
moves into Guthrie. The men throw themselves into the
cars like madmen, fighting, punching and biting to keep
their place, tossing out their knapsacks and suitcases to be
among the first arrivals, riding on the roofs of the cars. The
first train pulls out with shouts and hurrahs; the first car is
filled with newspapermen. Few talk; eyes are as big as
saucers. A deer runs by, and is riddled with shots from the
train. "Oklahoma now!" calls a voice and they go out on the

back platform to fire off their guns; they shoot through the window and stand on the seats, shouting and shooting off pistols at each other's feet.

They arrive: they tumble through the windows, they scramble over each other, men and women go down together in a heap: to the office, to get in line! to the office, to file the claim! But the first arrivals find to their amazement that the city is plotted, divided, occupied, with one hundred claims filed in the office, and men clearing brush from the land, with rifles slung over their shoulders and knives in their belts. Treachery! The troops have proved false! The troops have permitted their friends to hide in the underbrush! These names are those of the Federal marshals who are not allowed to take land, but have done so! "People began coming out of the ground at noon," they say in the office. Hurry for what is left! Some carry a sign that says "Bank of Guthrie" which they have to put up two miles from the station when they had planned to put it up right across the street. One gets down on all fours to have a better claim to a lot than one who simply stands on his two feet. One sells a corner lot at five dollars a foot. But how is it that in twenty-five minutes there are corners, avenues, streets, and squares? The truth comes out: there was trickery! The favorites, those hidden in the underbrush, the ones who "came out of the ground," the ones who entered in the guise of marshals and railroad workers, held their meeting at 10 a.m., when, legally, there was no land on which to hold a meeting, and divided up the city, marked out the streets and lots, assigned themselves the best plots, and at twelve noon were placing their privileged signatures in the registry book. Rock-coated lawyers with pistol at the hip go about drumming up suits. "What for, so the lawyers will wind up with the land?"

Bankers offer loans to the settlers in return for mortgages on their property. Those coming from the prairie ride in to register a claim on horses that drop to their knees. Two by two they stand in line, crowding through the door of the registry office where their claims and title to one of the free sections will be recorded. That is one way to obtain land; another, surer but more dangerous, is to occupy it, stake it out, clear it, fence it, take the wheels off the wagon and pitch the tent. "Bank of Oklahoma" it says on one big tent. "Guthrie's First Hotel!" "Rifles for sale!" "Water, a nickel a glass!" "Bread, a dollar a loaf!" Tents everywhere, with banners, signs, gambling tables, and banjos and violins at the door. *"The Oklahoma Herald,* with the announcement of elections for city officers!" The meeting is at four o'clock, and 10,000 men are present. At five o'clock *The Herald* gets out an extra with the list of elected officials.

Sandwichmen parade through the crowds advertising names of carpenters, hardware merchants, and surveyors. One cannot see the ground for the discarded handbills. At nightfall, the red railroad station is a living city. Forty thousand children sleep for the first time on the Oklahoma prairie. A muted sound, like the beating of the surf, is carried by the night wind from the prairie.

The black shadows of those still abroad are thrown against the tents by the light from the fires. All night a light burns in the registry office. All night the pounding of the hammer is heard.

Eleanor & Edward Aveling Marx

The cowboys are as much at the mercy of the capitalist as a New England cotton-worker.

Eleanor Marx (1855–1898) and her lover, Dr. Edward Aveling (1851–1898), went to America in 1886 to raise money for the socialist cause in Europe. "I have spoken on the subject to several people who know America *well*," she wrote to a German comrade a few years earlier, "and all say you would make plenty of money there." The couple arrived in America in September, 1886. A reporter for a local émigré paper described Aveling as looking like a Quaker, "grey travelling costume and a broad, black felt hat." Eleanor had "rich, glossy, black hair,

---

Eleanor and Edward Aveling Marx, *The Working-Class Movement in America* (London, S. Sonnenschein, Lowrey and Co., 1888), pp. 154–65.

dark-brown eyes and a not unlovely, oval face . . . which was covered by a large, white straw hat with a white bow." They began a lecture tour in New York which carried them as far west as Kansas City. In Chicago they visited the condemned men of the Haymarket anarchist bomb case, lectured on Marxian scientific socialism, and Eleanor, as one of the chief translators of Ibsen, played Nora in *A Doll's House* at a local theater. In Cincinnati she and Aveling met a disgruntled cowboy who related the details of his life under the burden of capitalist exploitation on the range. Their *The Working-Class Movement in America* seems to be more her work than his, in style if not in content. They drew much of their material from state factory commission reports. But the most original chapter concerns the cowboy as proletarian.

The Marx-Avelings had a tragic life. Eleanor, the youngest daughter of Karl Marx, was devoted to her father and a fully convinced disciple. In London she knew George Bernard Shaw (who used her life as a model for Jennifer Dubedat in *The Doctor's Dilemma*), Havelock Ellis, Beatrice Webb and many other late Victorians of radical persuasion. Aveling, a trained physiologist, discovered the "free thought" of Annie Besant (and became her lover) and then the principles of the class struggle (and became Eleanor's lover). A contemporary said of him, "Nobody can be so bad as Aveling looks." Marx's collaborator, Frederick Engels, who survived him by a few years, protected Eleanor and defended Aveling, who was accused of fraud by his fellow socialists. Aveling billed various American socialist party organizations for expenses incurred during the American tour and they refused to pay for his luxurious tastes in wine and cigars. Ten years after their American tour, Aveling apparently jilted Eleanor and she committed suicide. He died a few months later.

THE CAPITALIST EXPLOITATION OF THE COWBOYS

THE COWBOYS OF THE WEST have long been objects of interest to Americans. Recent events have made them familiar to the English public. But there is one aspect under which this class of men seem little known to their fellow-countrymen, and are almost wholly unknown to other peoples—that is, in their capacity as proletarians.

Until lately, the cowboy was a "bold, bad man," to most people, generally full of whiskey, and always handy with a revolver; reckless of the lives of others (as well as his own); and with rather vague ideas as to morals, and especially, to the rights of property. Spectators of the "shows" in which he has been exhibited on both sides of the Atlantic have modified their ideas upon this human subject. The modification has been in the recognition of the fact that he is not much worse or better morally than his more civilised fellows. In his manners, as in his physique, the cowboy is, for the most part, considerably the superior of these.

In the present chapter we hope to show the reader what the cowboys themselves have made plain to us: that they are distinctly members of the non-possessing, yet producing, and distributing, class; that they are as much at the mercy of the capitalist as a New or Old England cotton-worker; and that their supposed "freedom" is no more of a reality than his. Furthermore, evidence will be given that the cowboys, as a class, are beginning to recognise these facts, are becoming anxious that the general public should know them, and, best of all, are desirous, through the medium of either the Knights of Labor, or some other working-class organisation, to connect themselves with the laboring masses and with the general movement of that class against the tyranny of their employers.

Our first acquaintance with these facts was made in a curious way at Cincinnati. Some delightful German-American friends, in their anxiety to show us all the sights of the city, lured us into a dime museum. The chief attraction at this show, pending the arrival of Sir Roger Tichborne—who came the next week, who was not seen and who did not conquer—was a group of cowboys. They were sitting in groups of twos and threes on little raised platforms, clad in their picturesque garb, and looking terribly bored. Presently, a spruce gentleman, in ordinary, commonplace garments, began to make stereotyped speeches about them in a voice metallic enough for stereotyping. But, mercifully, he stopped short at one platform, and told us that a Mr. John Sullivan, alias Broncho John, would take up the parable.

Then a cowboy of singularly handsome face and figure, with the frankest of blue eyes, rose and "spoke a piece." To our great astonishment he plunged at once into a denunciation of capitalists in general and of the ranch-owners in particular. We were struck both by the manner and the matter of this man's talk. It had the first, second, and third qualifications for oratorical success—earnestness. Broncho John evidently knew what he was talking about, and believed in what he said. The gist of his speech is embodied in the next to last paragraph. To that need only be added John's appeal to the newspapers of the East—that they should do what the Western ones were afraid or unwilling to do: state clearly the case of the cowboys, their complaints, and their demands.

There are some 8,000 to 10,000 cowboys (this is Broncho John's estimate, and is considerably below the actual number), and "no class is harder worked, . . . none so poorly paid for their services." The reason why they are so poorly paid and hard worked is simple enough.—"They have no organisation back of them," while their employers have "one of the strongest and most systematic and, at the same time, despotic unions that was ever formed to awe and dictate to labour." The conditions under which the cowboys work are such that organisation is immensely difficult, in many cases well-nigh impossible. They are dispersed over miles upon miles of huge plains and desolate wastes, a few here and a few there, so that concerted action seems almost out of the question. Yet so many are "awakened to the necessity of having a league of their own" that a Cowboy Assembly of the Knights of Labor or a Cowboy Union is sure to be started in the near future. Meanwhile, the fact that such a league is desired by the cowboys is significant enough, and even more significant is their employers' fear of any such combination. One means by which the bosses hope to ward it off is by issuing "orders" that the men "must not read books or newspapers." Small wonder the cowboys regard such an "order" as "tyrannical in the extreme!" We found a pathetic example of the belief of the cowboys in a movement of some sort in Broncho John's conviction that a return of Blaine (as President) would mean that "all the thieving would go on," while the election of Henry George* would "make a change."

As to the actual work and wages of the cowboy—the work is necessarily extremely arduous and dangerous. For some six to eight months in the year—i.e., the working time on the plains—he has not only to be in the saddle from morn to night, but often the whole night through as well. To look after these huge Western herds of cattle, to keep a cool head during stampedes and "milling" is no small matter. "I have been with a party," says John Sullivan, "when we were obliged to ride two hundred miles before we got the cattle under control. In all that time not one of

---

* [Henry George, the Single-Tax theorist, was the leader of a national reform party. In 1886 he was defeated in the New York mayoralty campaign. GES]

us took a moment's rest or a bite to eat." While getting the cattle across streams "milling" often occurs, i.e., the beasts take fright and swim round and round and in every direction but that of the shore. As a consequence "many a good cowboy has been drowned," and it is not "uncommon for a party to spend three weeks or a month in getting a herd of four thousand cattle across a stream." There are also innumerable dangers to face from bands of marauders, Indians, and prairie fires. And, into the bargain, the herd must not only be delivered safe and intact, but they must have increased in weight since leaving the ranch. "The rule is, the cowboy must fatten the cattle on the trail, no matter how thin he may grow himself."

For such work as this the ranchers, who expect their employees to risk their very lives in looking after the stock, pay the best paid of the cowboys—twenty-five dollars a month. Moreover, the cowboy has to outfit himself, except for his horses, which belong to the ranchers, and a cowboy's outfit is very expensive. He must have a heavy fur hat, Mexican "chafferals" (leggings), a "slicker" (oilskin coat), a good saddle, a "quirt" (a heavy whip some three feet long), spurs, revolver, specially made boots, etc., etc. In all, this costs him about one hundred forty-five dollars. But the cowboys who cannot afford such an outlay at the start are supplied by the ranchers, who give them goods of a kind that barely last through a season. For these "supplies" the rancher deducts fifteen dollars a month out of a cowboy's wages. Indeed, so inferior is the outfit, that it has constantly to be renewed, and thus the cowboy remains constantly in debt.

From climatic and other conditions, it is almost impossible for cowboys to obtain any employment during the "off-time." These men must therefore keep themselves and their families on the one hundred twenty to one hundred fifty dollars that can be earned in the year. Nor is this the only difficulty with which the cowboys have to contend. Black-listing is apparently not peculiar to the East of America. It seems to flourish even in the Wild West, and the cowboy is as much its victim as the cotton-worker. "It may easily be seen then," says Broncho John, "that the cowboys have a serious struggle against actual want, and such is the system of the Ranchers' Society they dare not protest. Experience has taught them that to ask for an increase in wages means immediate discharge. But that is not the worst of it. The moment a man is discharged by any member of the Ranchers' Society his name is sent to every other member, the name is written in the books of each ranch and a black mark placed opposite it. This is called 'black-listing' the cowboy. He might as well leave the country at once."

But perhaps the greatest injustice, the most flagrant piece of robbery, perpetrated by these large ranch owners, and one which affects both settlers and cowboys, is that of "repleving" cattle. To "repleve" is wild-western for seizing all unbranded cattle. Lately, the right to do this has been claimed by the Association of Ranchers under the Maverick Law. A settler or cowboy gets a few head of cattle; in time these increase. A few years ago he could sell them to the Association or some other traders at "fair market price." But this did not suit the ranchers. Just as they—to use Broncho John's words—are "grinding out" the settlers from the land which they have opened up; just as the "road agent" is ousting the settler from the little homestead he has raised—so the ranchers want all the cattle—and take it! Any unbranded animal is claimed by them. Against this iniquitous proceeding two men—settlers we believe— named Cooper and Leineberger, tried to protest. They refused to give up cattle which was their property.

The Association (The Wyoming Stock Growers) instituted an action against them (in 1884) for infringement of the Maverick Law. The defendants' counsel pleaded that, while the law was in force in that State, it was against the Constitution of the United States. Judge Parks would give no decision at all, and Judge Corn gave his decision in favour of the Association. Thereupon Cooper and Leineberger appealed to the Supreme Court, with what result we have been, so far, unable to learn. For such cases as this never get into Eastern papers, and the Western ones mostly fear to touch them. The press, like everything else, is under the terrorist regime of the ranchers. Meantime, "repleving" goes on merrily, and the small settlers, robbed of their little stock, become cowboys and the wage-slaves of the ranchers, who are all staunch upholders of the sacred rights of property.

Knut Hamsun

*If a man emerges in that democratic mob
who believes in anarchism as the eventual,
most ideal form of society, this man is* too
free—the Americans hang him!

"My lopsided view of the land of Philistines," the Norwegian
writer Knut Hamsun (1859–1952) said of his *The Cultural
Life of America*, "is violently oppositional." Written after two
visits to America in the 1880's, *Cultural Life* created a mild
scandal among the literary circles of Scandinavia. Hamsun,
though born into a poor farmer's family, had an aristocratic flair
for the beauty and excellence best cultivated by an élite. America was the land of mass culture best exemplified by that common jokester, Mark Twain. Hamsun attacked him as naive, a
victim of the democratic way of life.

Knut Hamsun, *The Cultural Life of Modern America*, edited and
translated by Barbara G. Morgridge. Copyright © 1969 by the
President and Fellows of Harvard College. (Cambridge, Harvard
University Press, pp. 104–13, 142–46.)

Although the book was consciously sensational—Hamsun was a young writer on the make and he meant to stir the genteel literary worlds of Denmark, Sweden and Norway—it contains one of the most evocative portraits of America during the Haymarket bomb case. German and American anarchists in Chicago were accused of throwing a dynamite bomb into a crowd of police during a labor rally on May 4, 1886. After a fraudulent trial conducted by a corrupt judge and a fixed jury, eight anarchists were convicted, seven sentenced to be hanged. Eventually one committed suicide, three served prison terms and four were hanged. All were innocent.

The prominent Danish literary critic, George Brandes, called *Cultural Life* "disjointed, cutting, humorously exaggerated, striving after effect and, as a rule, achieving the effect." Hamsun defended his bias when his book appeared in Scandinavia. "My book is tolerably interesting," he said, "for it is different from other books on America." Years later, then established as the celebrated author of *Hunger*, Hamsun dismissed his tirade as "a youthful work. It has ceased to represent my opinion of America."

CONCEPTS OF FREEDOM

FOR A LONG TIME it has been common journalistic practice here at home to use American freedom as an illustration of what freedom is and ought to be. The gentlemen of the press know so little what they do! The Liberals boast on principle; the Conservatives protest out of habit—an incessant clip-snip which only in the rarest instances builds on personal experience.

Just drawing together the casual impressions mentioned

thus far, we find that American *intellectual* freedom has manifested itself as follows: it punishes a newspaper for admitting that Congress has committed a piece of parliamentary stupidity; it forces a commonschool pupil to beg Jesus for forgiveness because he has thrown paper wads in an arithmetic period; it rebukes an author by boycotting him because he has exposed some of the humbug connected with American female virtue; it silences another author because his books show signs of European influence; it puts a thirty-five percent import duty on modern culture; it mutilates Zola's books and refuses to tolerate them in bookstores;* it prohibits a painter from depicting shepherds that are not all buttoned up; it attacks Sarah Bernhardt's honor because this artist, as a human being, has loosened a button —just these few instances chosen at random give a fairly good idea of the nature of American intellectual freedom.

If we now turn to *social* freedom, a couple of those features already noted will also serve to illustrate it: for example, it is a civic duty to clap for George Washington's name; people can with impunity fire nutshells and cigar butts at a man in a public place because he does not go into raptures at the sound of that name; an immigrant very frequently has to deny his foreign origin if a Yankee is to hire him; at the same time that a few thousand African half-apes were freed, more than a million white children were held in legally protected slavery; finally, a woman without money or title does not have access to certain American homes. It is a trifle naïve to set such freedom up as a model for freedom in general: it is conditional freedom.

In the first place, freedom in America is very disproportionate and inharmonious—like everything else in the country. You notice immediately that it is not the product of a gradual, progressive development but in many areas

* In October it finally became unlawful to import *La Terre* "by reason of its immorality."

simply the result of precipitous congressional decision. It has no form; it is without balance or continuity. Life is so free in America that you can shoot a man down on the open street for having cursed in a shop when a lady was present, but life is not so free in America that you can spit on the floor where you please or go with a lighted cigar— that is not true! American freedom is just as ridiculously exacting and restrictive about little things as, indeed, according to the Constitution it is generous and liberal about big things. When, for example, an immigrant goes ashore in New York, his knife is taken from him immediately—a knife that he wears in a sheath and uses for shredding his pipe tobacco; but he is allowed to carry a revolver in both hip pockets if he wants to, for the revolver is the national murder weapon.

Furthermore, freedom in America is not always voluntary but often compulsory, a freedom dictated by law. Congress sits and makes laws governing how free the individual is obliged to be instead of simply determining how free he may *not* be. You come up against a number of instances of freedom that are dictated by law in America. Washington's birthday is thus a prescribed public holiday that each year disrupts school instruction far more than any religious holiday; but on that day you are obliged to be free. In 1868 a writer bobbed up in the republic who wrote that he believed in monarchy; the man's name was Fred Nicolls and his book was called *Thoughts*. Things did not go well for that man; he had not felt obliged to be free. His treatment by the newspapers and at public gatherings was such that he felt he could take a trip down to Mexico with a clear conscience—and he has never returned. Behold, even a man's thoughts are required to contain a certain measure of American freedom; otherwise he finds that he has an errand in Mexico. In addition to this freedom dictated by law, there is the kind of compulsory freedom that these patriotic people have prescribed for themselves. You can be certain that a merchant who does not close his shop on the Fourth of July has to pay for it in one way or another; a man seated in a theater who fails to lose his head over George Washington's name also has to pay for it. A foreigner does not feel unconditionally free right there in America—his tastes and opinions are dictated to him, and he simply has to acquiesce or take the consequences. He is faced with the despotism of freedom—a despotism that is all the more intolerable because it is exercised by a self-righteous, unintelligent people. In America no distinction is made between freedom and democracy; in order to maintain a compact democracy, freedom is willingly sacrificed. That noble, ardent craving of the individual for freedom is wounded in many different ways. By undermining all individual yearning for freedom in its citizens, America has finally managed to create that horde of fanatic freedom automatons which make up American democracy.

Last of all, there are great, open holes in American freedom which, even in formal terms, is greatly inferior to conditions in several other countries. This is particularly true of those areas in which religious stupidity and patriotic fanaticism operate hand in hand. I want to tell you about an important and characteristic instance of American intellectual and social freedom that is both accurate as an example and illustrative as a picture—an instance that will at the same time begin to explain the spirit pervading American legal justice.

The following paragraph occurs in the proposals for restricting immigration: "Socialists, anarchists, and nihilists are forbidden to land . . . because these people stir up the American working population and make it dissatisfied with wages. America is not the place for socialistic propaganda." The truth is, America is not the place for cultural and sociopolitical development; it stands where it stood on that

blessed day of national independence. Mention the word
anarchism in America, and a man with an ordinary, average
American education crosses himself immediately. He con-
ceives of anarchism as dynamite simply, nothing but
dynamite. That anarchism is a scientific theory, a doctrine
which even halfway sensible people profess, is beyond him;
he cannot stand to hear a word about it. Anarchism is
dynamite; anarchists are to be hanged! Here is a gaping
hole in American freedom, a hole held open by just that
thickskulled democracy whose control of freedom in
America is absolute. During the great anarchist trial in 1886,
the hole quite simply widened into an abyss. At the time,
people of every social class—from those who by some
stroke of luck had made millions on wheat swindles to those
who could not read or write their own names—that is, all
Americans went around and privately condemned these
seven anarchists to death. Had they read a word about what
anarchism was? Not one in a hundred, not one in a thousand; they simply knew that these seven were *charged* with
having thrown a bomb. That was sufficient! This is the
nature of American freedom. It demands just the right
degree of liberalism from the individual, no more, no less.
Toward those who overstep the bounds in any direction it
is as intolerant as a medieval despot. It is too conservative to
budge one step; today it remains standing where it stood two
hundred years ago. Time has not altered its forms one iota.
For it is a democracy fixed by law. If a writer turns up who
believes in monarchy, this writer is not free enough—the
Americans run him out of the country; if a man emerges
in that democratic mob who believes in anarchism as the
eventual, most ideal form of society, this man is *too* free—
the Americans hang him! Whatever is more or less than
George Washington's exceedingly simple mind could grasp
is punished by exile or loss of life. Such is American freedom—a freedom not for the individual, the person, but
freedom *en masse* and for all.

Recently the following notice appeared in America: "At last there is some prospect that the heroes of the Haymarket are to receive a lasting testimonial of their gallant conduct on that eventful May night. The model of the Haymarket monument was recently completed by the sculptor [...] and will soon be sent to New York to be cast in bronze. The statue will be eight feet high [. . .] and will represent a patrolman defending the law, and is reported to be a remarkably artistic piece of work. It is about time that the efforts to obtain a suitable memorial [. . .] materialized, and, although no monument can represent the debt of gratitude the people of Chicago owe to the men who lost their lives in defense of the law, still it is well that the people are to have a memorial to remind them of that occasion."

As for that occasion, however, the truth is this: in the first place it is the most recent major instance of American freedom, its nature and substance; it is also the most eloquent example of genuinely American legal proceedings. On May 4, 1886, an unseen hand threw a dynamite bomb at a large public gathering in Chicago's Haymarket Square, killing five policemen and injuring two.* No one knows who the perpetrator was; he may have been a cabman, a minister, or a congressman just as well as an anarchist. During the investigation—I mention this in passing—it was virtually ascertained that the authorities themselves had arranged to have a policeman throw the bomb in order, at a single stroke, to establish grounds for complaint against the leaders of the anarchists. But they simply took seven of the leading anarchists at random for these seven victims of the bomb. Five of the seven were condemned to death for the five that died as a result of the bomb, and two were sentenced to life imprisonment for the two who were only injured by the bomb. An eye for an eye! A tooth for a

* The others who were injured on the same occasion were immediately disregarded by the authorities.

tooth! A practical and exceedingly American justice! One
of the anarchists who was hanged, Parsons, was not even at
the Haymarket the evening the bomb was thrown. "Well,"
they answered him, "but aren't you an anarchist?" "Yes!"
said Parsons.

This is the way those free Americans respond to ideas:
they hang them. From the moment Editor [August] Spies
made public his shocking descriptions from the coal districts
in Ohio, he was a dangerous man who bore watching, a
marked man foredoomed to death. And no sooner are the
seven idealists cold in their nooses than the mob of freedom-
loving Americans throughout Yankeeland raises a monument in memorial to the great patriotic deed of hanging
ideas. And the newspapers thought it was about time
it was done . . .

CRIME AND THE JUDICIAL SYSTEM

IT IS IMPOSSIBLE to obtain a more comprehensive or truer
illustration of social freedom and the American judicial
system than the case of the anarchists. In all its revolting
brutality, it characterizes to perfection the state of American society from top to bottom. It shows us a people that
for the most part is made up of Europe's lowest types,
going around and condemning to death the country's most
intelligent men of ideas because they profess beliefs that
the howling mob does not understand a syllable of. It shows
us how the American courts, openly bribed and under the
influence precisely of the demanding, ignorant mob, make
the innocent take the blame for the guilty. Finally, it shows
us which crimes are particularly frightening in that land of
America—those crimes that do not occur every day, those
that the mob is incapable of understanding—the crimes of
ideals. The mere charge of political crimes was enough to
fell these seven men, whereas crimes of a simpler, cruder,

and therefore more readily understandable nature do not cause any stir. A murder committed in an entryway with the intent to rob, a congressman's unconcealed pillage in the national forests year after year, the cleverly devised land frauds of a railroad baron, the unprecedented bank swindles in New York of President Grant and his son-in-law—for such crimes it is possible in America to come to terms with the proper authorities on payment of a given assessment and in consonance with one's financial means. But the penalty for advocating social ideas in opposition to the despotic freedom of democracy is death.

It is indicative of the American judicial system that it is quite powerless when faced with fraud of any magnitude. Not because the country has no laws prohibiting fraud or because it is impossible to detect crimes over there, but because the courts can be bribed to an absolutely incredible extent. It is also indicative of the entire outlook of the American people, both their interests and their ways of thinking, that major frauds elicit their admiration, not to mention their sympathy. The ability to put over a smart swindle is regarded as an expression of Yankee ingenuity; the newspapers remark that it was very neatly done. Nor are the laws stringent in this respect; American criminal law is conceived in the "spirit of compromise." A couple of very recent happenings, chosen at random, will explain what I mean.

Six days before I left America the last time, a bank teller in New York stole $200,000 from his till. Was he apprehended? No. Where did he go? To Canada. Is he still there? He is still there. Last November 14, the owner of the Valparaiso Bank in Omaha disappeared; his name was Scoville. He made off with $300,000 more than was his, and he had managed it in the following manner: To the securities that were payable to his bank Scoville had appended certain additions—a practice that apparently oc-

curs only in local American finance—so that the securities
were now worth as much as twice their original value;
thereafter Scoville deposited these securities in a couple of
major banks that he was in the habit of drawing on and
drew out the money. Then he disappeared. Where did he
go? To Canada. Is he still there? He is still there. Canada
is a safe place, a sanctuary; no scoundrel can be appre-
hended in Canada—there is no extradition agreement between Canada and the Union. Scoville is safe. After a train
ride lasting a day and a night he found himself in a country
where American criminal law could not reach him. What
did the United States do now? The United States now did
what it has always done on such occasions; it acted and
operated in accordance with the "spirit of compromise."
The United States sent a detective to Canada with instruc-
tions to negotiate with the swindler! If he turned over two
thirds of his loot, Scoville would get to keep a third for
himself. "And go free?" asked Scoville. "Come back and
go free!" America answered its beloved son. Scoville was
just about ready to go along with this, but then he had
second thoughts. "I'll have to talk with my wife," says he.
And the detective, who doubtless also has a wife, could
readily understand that, when it was a question of $300,000
for a man, he had to talk with his wife. Accordingly Scoville
talked with his wife. "No!" says his wife. And there was
simply no mistaking that what she said was no. So that was
the message the detective had to take back with him. Mrs.
Scoville, who was almost the same as Mr. Scoville, had said
no to America.

Now how was this business taken in the Union? It was
shrugged off, forgotten for new swindles of the same kind,
swindles toward which America acted in the very same
fashion, in accordance with the very same "spirit of compromise." But the newspapers ran headlines about this
splendid expression of the ingenious Yankee mind; they

said a couple of times that it was neatly done, very neatly done. Then the whole thing died away.

Just as American laws are severe and inflexible when it comes to political crimes, so they are mild and indulgent when it comes to those brutal crimes, those simple peasant sins that every cunning prairie farmer is able to commit. An acquaintance of mine is the publisher of an anarchist paper—a paper the United States Post Office refuses to be contaminated by. The *Police Gazette*, published in New York, is the most contemptible sheet in the world, an organ almost exclusively devoted to the most shameless crimes in the Union: murder, adultery, rape, incest, fistfights, robberies, and swindles, often accompanied by lewd drawings printed on rose-colored paper—this sheet is handled by the United States Post Office. The *Police Gazette* has sixty thousand subscribers; it is found in hotels, barbershops, and clubs; it gets the Americans' undivided attention. It talks about crimes that everyone can understand—the simple-minded sins that any prairie farmer is able to commit with a brick.

When a foreigner starts digging into American crime statistics and attending American court sessions, he is astonished at how unusually crude and purposeless the crimes are in America. He gets the feeling increasingly that he is in a country that is not modern even in its crimes. In a hundred of one hundred and one instances, he looks in vain for some sign of sophistication, of, let us say, intelligence in these crimes; he finds that they do not resemble modern crimes so much as the misdoings he has read about from bygone ages. In America a great deal of cleverness is displayed in the implementation of a crime, but in most cases the purpose of the crime, its motive, its basis and idea, are simply proof of the brutish instincts of this backward people whom a disproportionate and inharmonious freedom is unable to control. Take a crime that is common to all

countries—fraud, by which I mean forgery, a higher order
of theft—forgery has quite a different character in America
than in other countries (with certain exceptions here as
elsewhere). Thus here at home forgery generally has its
origin in a bad financial situation, but only in a very few
instances does American forgery have its origin in a really
critical financial situation—as everyone knows who has
more or less kept up with the history of crime over there.
No, forgery in America has its origin first and foremost in
the Americans' insane craving for money salted away—
even the smallest sum—that is, economic self-sufficiency,
invincibility. A bank teller does not go off to Canada with
the till because he is poorly paid; he gets a yearly salary of
between 12,000 and 25,000 crowns. He goes off to Canada
with the till because he cannot stand to look at the money
he handles without possessing it himself, because his American blood prods him into stealing it, because *without* this
money he is just an ordinary bank teller, because *with* this
money he steps into the economic nobility—which is
America's nobility. He is an American; he likes to throw
money around, to be nicely dressed, to wear rings and gold
trinkets, to eat at hotels, to be in demand in a small prairie
town. This is the only ambition he has, and in order to
satisfy this rather low-slung ambition he will stop at nothing;
at last it drives him to forgery. There is nothing intelligent
about his crime: he robs the till, takes a seat on the Erie
express, rides a day and a night, and steps out in Canada as
an American nobleman.

This cheap commonness characterizes all of America's
crimes. Let a foreigner listen carefully to the sessions in an
American city hall to see if he can find some hint of loftiness
in the misdeed, let him really struggle to find even one element of refinement in the blue police reports—almost always he does so in vain. If one examines a nation's crimes
as rationally as one examines the other phenomena of life,

one is finally faced with the discovery that even in its crimes
the country is outdated and outdone. It is not even modern
in its transgressions. They are those committed by the
Indians and the first Dutch pioneers. People scalp the first
man that comes along, they blow up a bank in order to get
pocket money for candy, they rip open the stomach of
five-year-old children and rape them, they rob a poor devil
of a day laborer simply to lay hands on his money—every
single day the American newspapers are brimming over
with accounts of the brutish instincts that belong to this
free people. American crimes are even without formal elegance; sin in that country is characterized by a gory shame-
lessness that has parallels only in the very distant past; it is
even without any elements of nobility or purpose. Such a
crime as the anarchists were accused of was bound to cause
a commotion in such a country! And it did, too. Every well-
bred hero who knew his ABC's shouted "crucify!" Democratic old maids—of both sexes—bought pictures of the
anarchists and "hanged" them in their windows. Shopkeepers advertised as follows: "Because we are *for* the
anarchists' being hanged, business is so good that we can
afford to sell our well-known blue Rio for nine cents a
pound."

And not one in a hundred knew what anarchism was,
not one in a thousand. You see, it cannot automatically be
assumed that the Americans are the enlightened people we
here at home go around imagining them to be. . . .

CONCLUSION

BUT IN ALL OF AMERICA is there not an *elite*, a select society
of intellectuals, a court of the intellect, a salon, a class, a
coterie, cultivated individuals, noble minds?

America is two hundred years old. For one hundred of
these years America was completely undeveloped; in the

next hundred, good people started coming from Europe—
fine people, hardworking thralls, creatures of brawn, bodies
whose hands could clear land and whose minds could not
think. A generation passed; more and more good people
came by square-rigger to Quebec—now and then a bank-
rupt cafeowner and now and then a pietistical minister
followed them. Time passed; a schooner headed into Baltimore with thirty-three thralls on board, five bankrupts,
and one manslayer. Time passed; a barque glided into Portsmouth's harbor; it held a hundred thralls, a thousand pounds
of pastors, a half dozen murderers, fourteen forgers, and
twenty thieves. Then one night a merchantman slipped into
New Orleans, one night so dark and still, a merchantman
so full of wares; it came from the upper Nile and it had
seventy blacks in its cargo. They were put ashore; these
were creatures of brawn, Negroes from Niam-Niam, whose
hands had never cleared land and whose minds had never
conceived a thought. And time passed; people came to the
land in great, great streams; steam was invented to propel
them across the ocean; they flooded Boston, they pushed
into New York. Day after day after day great masses of
people poured into the prairie kingdom—people of all races
and tongues, good people without number: bankrupts and
criminals, adventurers and madmen, ministers and Negroes
—all members of the pariah race from the entire earth.

And not a noble mind among them.

Among this population, from these individuals America
had to establish a cultural elite . . .

The country prospered. There was gold in Nevada and
California, silver and oil in Pennsylvania, iron, copper,
mercury, and lead in Montana, coal in the Allegheny
Mountains, in Ohio, Kentucky, and Virginia; there was
farming and cattle raising, logging and plantations, fishing
and trapping. The sun was hot and the soil rich; fruit
ripened on the smallest trees and grass grew on the open

road. The good people from every corner of the earth thrived in this new kingdom; they mated and had offspring, enjoyed life, waded in food up to their knees, and ate between three and four times as much as in the old country. And from the thralls came patriots.

From these patriots, among these good people America had to develop its cultural elite . . .

How did they go about it? Now there was no culture in the country; good people are not born noble, and when good people later develop into patriots, they become very smug human beings. America's most cultivated minds, the loftiest of them, just those outstanding men who should have been the start of an intellectual elite in the country, placed, out of the smugness of their hearts, a thirty-five percent duty on the importation of culture—in order to create an elite in their own country. On January 1, 1863, they made the Negroes masters over the Southern freeholders; they took these creatures of brawn from Niam-Niam into their families and gave them their sons and daughters in marriage—in order to beget an elite class of intellectuals!

It is unfair to expect an elite in America; it is more than unreasonable to demand an elite in a country which, when considered as a nation, is purely an experiment and whose people, starting with innate deficiencies, have been fostered in a climate of patriotic hostility to all that is unpatriotic. If one is not born noble in mind and spirit, one must either be ennobled by foreigners or else never be ennobled. Among Americans there is no yearning *beyond* the stars; no more is asked of them than that they be well-born Yankees whose goal is mediocrity, that is, political democracy. In them there is no demanding desire for an aristocracy of the mind, an intellectual sultanate. If there were an aristocratic court of the intellect, why then is it silent in all the realms of the spirit? Where is the class, the coterie, the salon?

But America does have great minds, does it not? Have I perchance gone and forgotten those twenty-one poets included in an encyclopedia, those seven historians, eleven painters, two literary historians, two theologians, one General Grant, one Henry George? I have not gone and forgotten these geniuses. I have not forgotten them on a single page . . .

In the fifties there were signs of an intellectual elite in two of the oldest Southern states, but the war came and uprooted it before it was established. Since then it has not shown itself. From that time on, the nation's blood was democratically mixed with that of the Negro, and intelligence sank rather than rose. Cohabitation with the blacks was foisted upon the people. Inhumanity stole them away from Africa where they belong, and democracy transformed them into civilized citizens against the entire order of nature. They have leaped over all the intermediate stages between voracious rat eater and Yankee. Now they are used as preachers, barbers, waiters, and sons-in-law. They have all the rights of a white man and take all the liberties of a black. A Negro is and will remain a Negro. If he shaves a man, he grabs him by the nose as his own blessed grandfather grabbed at a crocodile leg along the Nile; if he serves a meal, he sticks his shiny thumb into the soup all the way up to his elbow. There is no use in rebuking him for his slightly uncivilized manner of doing things. If you are not rudely answered back, the African democrat will at least tell you in an insulted voice to "mind your own business!" And then you have to hold your tongue; the discussion is at an end. Still, if you are right, and you are sitting there with two big fists, then you swallow your food with little appetite. Of course, it would be another matter if you had expressly ordered soup with thumbs.

The Negroes are and will remain Negroes, a nascent human form from the tropics, creatures with entrails in their heads, rudimentary organs on the body of a white society.

Instead of founding an intellectual elite, America has established a mulatto studfarm; therefore one might be justified in seeking an intellectual elite in countries where there are greater chances for its existence than in America. It does not necessarily follow, because there is an elite in every established land with a long history and a richly varied contemporary culture, that there is also an elite in a newly discovered land with no national history and an old, effete culture. One cannot reasonably demand more of an intellectual elite in America than what the clergy has fashioned in four generations. What there is, is situated in Boston. It operates quietly; it shatters no worlds and shakes no earths.

IF, THEN, it is unreasonable to demand culture of the Americans because their temperament and social organization largely preclude it, it is surely excusable in part that they have no culture. However, you do not risk life and limb by quietly mentioning this; it is safest to remain completely silent. The inexperienced person who makes excuses for America's cultural barrenness in the presence of an American will be asked on the spot to come and make something of it—just come on! So the Americans are not completely blameless when they reject all foreign guidance purely because of their thin-skinned egotism; one has to search far into the past to find a nation that has kept its cultural life that barren simply because of jealous national vanity. There is reason to doubt progress that comes gradually, step by step—the small improvements and minor special reforms that are fought for today only to be totally obliterated by the next generation; so instead one can only put one's faith in the great chess moves, the mighty revolts of individual geniuses who suddenly thrust mankind forward for several generations. But what then if the time is not ripening for a historical revolt, if the ground is not being prepared for the shoots of intellectual possibility in a country? If, on the contrary, the land is being put by, fenced in, left standing with wild vegetation and weeds in profusion? An overgrown national park, a vast wonder of a park! It is every American's primary mission in life to be a patriotic citizen of the great prairies rather than to become a mature individual within the entire human race. This feeling has penetrated and colored all their notions from the cradle on; only by being an American is one truly a human being. Therefore, not one doubter can be found in that whole wide country—a seeker of the light, a rebellious spirit who could kick over the traces, fall out of step, take the first deliberate misstep to the miserable and foolish pipings of the penny whistles. Everyone goes merrily along amid loud hurrahs, without ever looking around . . .

A world of shouting and steam and great groaning stamping machines; a kingdom of that world with people from every zone, from the whites of the north to the apes and intellectual mulattoes of the tropics; a land with light, fertile topsoil and a preserve of primordial spaces.

And black skies . . .

Paul Bourget

*If two horsemen saw one another at five
miles' distance on the prairie, each would
turn in the opposite direction. Strange desert,
which man sought to make still more deserted, and where he dreaded nothing but his
own kind!*

Charles Joseph Paul Bourget (1852–1935) wrote a series of
articles for the New York *Herald* giving his impressions of an
American tour in 1893. A French writer of distinction, Bourget
covered the United States and its social and political contradictions with elegance and flair. His notes on America were popular in Europe because his descriptions included rich dialogues
with people from all over the country: "the Lower Orders,"
"Down South," in prisons (Blackwell's Island and the Tombs)
and insane asylums. Bourget was uncommonly credulous; he
believed almost everything bad or contradictory or portentous.
His message was quite clear: a revolution was coming, perhaps
not of classes, but surely one between ethnic groups.

Paul Bourget, "A Cowboy's Story," *Outre-Mer* (New York,
Charles Scribners Sons, 1895), pp. 250–58, 264–66.

The following selection is from a tale told to Bourget by a French expatriate, "Raymond," who tried to settle "out West" with an English fellow-adventurer.

———————◆———————

OUR EXCITEMENT increased as we drew near to the mountains and entered the great forests of Douglas pines. The first spring flowers were peeping through the grass. Transparent running waters gushed out everywhere from fissures in the quartz. The sky was blue and high above our heads; and besides, we were drawing near to Custer City, the town of whose magnificence Johnson had been boasting ever since we set out. We were looking forward to it as the Hebrews to the Promised Land. Many a year has passed since then, years of bitter struggle which count double and triple. Not one of their sensations has effaced the intense strain of expectancy of that April afternoon when our worthy friend led us up a hill at a gallop, that he might proudly point us to the end of our hard pilgrimage. He checked his horse, made signal to us to do the same, and extending his arm he said:

"There is Custer City."

I looked, my heart beating hard with hope. Why should I blush to own to one moment of cowardice, the only one that I knew in all my prairie life? Tears that I could not restrain suddenly gushed from my eyes—tears not of hope, but of despair, tears wrung from me by atrocious disappointment, the sudden collapse of all my high dreams.

A wretched mining-camp lay on the other side of the valley, more miserable than the poorest hamlet in the Alps. And it was to live there, in one of those hovels, in this remote corner of the world, to struggle there, to die there, perhaps, that I had left three thousand leagues behind me our little château in Dauphiny, with its three square towers and its square donjon, and in the château my mother, my sisters, everything that I loved and that loved me!

So, under a glorious sunset, at the foot of Mount Calamity Jane, the "tenderfoot" Raymond died, on his first arrival from Europe. And in his place arose the cowboy Sheffield—so named because of his knife-blade face—he who wrote these memoirs.

About a month later I was quietly breakfasting in Miller's bar-room, situated in the principal street—Main Street—when a well-known miner, Big Browne, began to quarrel with Eddie Hutts, a cowboy who had left his ranch.

Both drew their revolvers and fired at the same moment. Browne fell stone dead. His opponent's ball had gone through his head. But his ball had taken me square in the jaw, breaking the bone, and stopping near the artery. Miller, who professed a particular esteem for Browne, has often, since then, tried to excuse his friend, with the plea that the unfortunate man had taken a few too many "corpse revivers" that morning. The Americans have a jolly lot of names for the various alcoholic mixtures with which they delight to poison themselves: "a widow's smile," "a sweet recollection," "an eye opener." The most potent of all was the one used by Miller, the "corpse reviver." There was some irony in the circumstance, since the intemperance of that brute Browne nearly caused two deaths, his own and mine.

I had sprung up when I found myself wounded, but I had not strength to take a step. Everything seemed to turn around me, and I fell as if struck down by a blow. Consciousness quickly returned, with that sort of lucid and unavailing attention that we have in dreams. I was lying on the ground near Browne's dead body. I could have touched it by reaching out my hand. Half a score of faces, all automatically moving in the act of chewing tobacco, were gazing curiously upon me, without any one thinking of coming to my aid. My blood was still flowing upon the floor, and I was suffering cruelly. I asked for a priest, but I spoke in French and no one understood me. For that matter, the nearest was a hundred and fifty miles away, and what need had I of a priest, to die like Browne? One more or less doesn't count on the prairie.

Seeing that not one of the men around me so much as shifted the quid in his cheek, so indifferent were they to my appeal, I began to shout, or rather to gurgle, the names of Herbert and Johnson. Within a quarter of an hour my friends both arrived, accompanied by an ill-favored personage in a frock coat, with a ten days' beard, a battered silk hat, a white necktie streaked with dirt, and diamond studs shining in his frayed shirt. This was the celebrated Dr. Briggs, the principal physician in the Black Hills, a somewhat skilful surgeon, though even the Americans thought him "rather fond of the knife, you know." He was usually drunk at ten in the morning, but by good luck he was now sober. I had abundant leisure to note the details of the picturesque dilapidation of his costume; for having caused me to be laid upon the billiard table he began to probe the wound, very gently, I must admit, while drops of tobacco juice fell from his lips upon my face.

"Well!" he concluded, with a coolness hardly reassuring. "The gentleman has had a lucky escape. The ball has just grazed the artery. The bones will soon knit, but, as to the ball, if he lets it remain it will by degrees wear through the artery, and will suddenly burst sometime, causing internal effusion and sudden death. If he prefers to have me remove it, I can try, but I will answer for nothing. It is for him to choose."

Herbert translated this redoubtable diagnosis. I mentally performed my act of contrition and said that the ball was to be removed. Before probing the wound, Briggs had cleared the room of every one except Herbert and Johnson. He now called by name six of the men who were standing around the door, who ranged themselves, grave and indifferent, around the billiard table.

"Why?" I asked Herbert, who was still acting as interpreter.

"Well," replied Briggs, "these gentlemen are the first citizens of the town, and they will testify that it is no fault of mine if death occurs during the operation."

With these words I fell asleep under the sickish odor of chloroform. When I awoke, I had a great slit in my throat and the ball in my hand. The best citizens disappeared, enchanted at having had this little morning "excitement." The doctor received three hundred dollars.

A month later my jaw was well, but I had lost so much blood that it was some weeks before I recovered strength. As to Briggs, meeting him three years later at Rapid City, at the time of a hotly contested election, he dragged me up to the platform, exhibited me and my scar to fifteen hundred loafers, and secured a brilliant victory over his opponent. It appeared that I was his sole living witness to a successful operation!

This sample of the manners and customs then reigning in Custer City will convince you that this abode of idleness, intemperance, and assassination did not keep us long. For that matter, we could hardly make a living there. The smallest necessaries of life were horribly dear, as in all mining towns. For example, at Custer it never occurred to any one to ask change for a nickel. The five-cent piece was the unit of expediture. It is hard to conceive of the ravages which such trifles made in small incomes like ours. We resolved, therefore, to return to our original plan, and select a ranch, a wide pasturage, watered by living streams, where we could devote ourselves to horse breeding.

We had the luck to find almost immediately such a place

as we sought, and we named our little establishment
Lance-Head, because in digging the foundations of our
house we found an iron point, which had no doubt dropped
many years before from some Indian's arrow. With roughly
hewn beams, ill-planed boards, and wooden pegs—nails
were scarce in those parts—we managed to put up a sort
of barrack for ourselves and a stable for our horses. This
work cost us no less than six months' labor, during which
we were too busy to concern ourselves with the ranch itself.
Now calculate: a fortnight's voyage, five days in New
York, seven on the railway, two weeks on the prairie, come
to more than a month. A month of expectation, a month of
illness, a month of convalescence, make three months. Add
to this six months devoted to our wretched little building,
and you have nearly a year since we left our homes—
Herbert's in Derbyshire and mine in Dauphiny. And in
the course of this time I had nearly died, we had impaired
our joint capital, and sole acquisition was this "log-house,"
this hut built with our own hands!

And we held this property only on condition of defending it. The stream and pasturage had belonged to a
former proprietor, Bob, a well-known horse thief, called
"Yorkey Bob," from his native city. This rascal, by abandoning this property, had forfeited all his rights in it. That,
however, was no reason why he should not undertake to
fleece the new occupants; and, in fact, having returned to
Custer City, he loudly proclaimed in Miller's "saloon":

"I shall soon settle up with those two European tenderfeet. I'll teach them to enter upon my succession before my
death!"

This reassuring remark was reported to us by Dr. Briggs,
who lavished visits upon us. When my "savior," as he freely
called himself, had given us this so-called evidence of
sympathy, Herbert and I looked at one another. Each read
in the other's eyes desire to mount at once and be the first

to settle accounts with this saloon bully. On the prairie one soon comes to this theory of legitimate defence—to attack first and not be attacked. Fortunately, we did not yield to this impulse of preventive indignation. Herbert had the presence of mind to concoct a test which should forever safeguard us from all threats of this kind. He took aim at an unconscious pigeon that was cooling on the roof of the stable fifty feet away, and brought it down with his revolver.

"You may tell Yorkey Bob what you have seen," he said to Briggs, "and add that if ever I meet him, wherever it may be, in a bar-room, in the street, or on the prairie, I shall do as much for him."

He turned his back upon the doctor. This worthy stood for a moment as if nonplussed, then spat at a distant point. It is the American token of profound impression. I have always thought that his purpose in coming had been to propose to the new proprietors, in the name of the old, a good and firm treaty of alliance, cemented by hard cash. However that may be, Herbert's pistol-shot and his little remark sufficed to discourage this intention. But for two whole months we were on the alert, sleeping out of doors every night for fear of a surprise. As to precautions by day, we could not have taken more. The times were so troubled that if two horsemen saw one another at five miles' distance on the prairie, each would turn in the opposite direction. Strange desert, which man sought to make still more deserted, and where he dreaded nothing but his own kind! This was the time when the Deadwood mail was looted about once a month, the time when the carriage of the Lead City receiver, notwithstanding its escort of six horsemen, was held up, and the one hundred and fifty thousand dollars that it contained—seven hundred and fifty thousand francs in gold bars—dispersed to the four corners of Dakota and Wyoming. A flood of adventurers, the scum of all countries and all races, had overwhelmed Deadwood, where a new lead of gold had just been discovered. Human life, which the Yankees like to say is "very cheap" among them, was really so cheap that to live in the Black Hills was to be on campaign every day and every hour. One soon adapts oneself to conditions that appear so extraordinary. It is surprising how soon one becomes accustomed to the thought of a violent death. It is the other death—by illness—with which the imagination can never reconcile itself, at least mine cannot.

As for Yorkey Bob, he no doubt thought differently from me on this subject, for he took great care, after the proof of address given by Herbert, to keep clear of the two tenderfeet from Europe. It was written that he should be killed, but in a different manner. He again stole so many cattle in the neighborhood of Custer City and near us, that the cowboys determined to rid the town of so dangerous a character. One evening, when he was quietly drinking in Miller's bar-room, a treacherous cowboy lassoed him from behind, and threw the end of the cord to a horseman who was waiting outside. The latter set off at full speed, and Bob was strangled in a few seconds. He had instinctively seized his left revolver (he carried one on each side), and through all the frightful consciousness of that mad flight across the plain his fingers never loosed their hold. It was necessary to break them to get the weapon from him. We happened by accident to be present at this last episode of our enemy's death. I cannot better explain to you the metamorphosis which this first awful year had wrought in us than by telling you that we remained indifferent to this summary execution.

Bob was regretted by one person only, a woman thief who kept a hotel at Custer City, and whose lover he was. This creature had a dexterity with the rifle of quite another sort than that of Herbert. I have seen her, not once but ten times, pierce a gourd at a hundred paces, sending her ball through a hole already prepared for the cork, without even grazing its edges. In every room of her hotel you might see the following inscription, written up with her own hand in enormous red letters:

"Don't lie on the bed with your boots on. Don't spit on the blankets. Be a man."

She had committed many murders, and with her man's clothes and her continual oaths she was a fit companion for Bob, whom she would certainly have avenged if she had known his assassins. But enterprises of this nature were always carried on with masked or muffled faces, as I have already said with regard to train robberies. For that matter, you can learn as much from the newspaper reports. This summary justice was more potent than legal justice as we afterward knew it, with its judges and lawyers, costing much more than executive committees such as the one which rid us of Yorkey Bob. And take it all in all, the second sort of justice was much less just.

As for the Indian, he is the cowboy's enemy only when the war hatchet is dug up. This came near being the case a few months after our arrival. The foreman of one of the ranches had sown the prairie with quarters of venison filled with strychnine, to poison the coyotes. Two Sioux ate one of them, and died in frightful convulsions. Happily, the foreman was the friend of Sitting Bull, the hero of the massacre of General Custer and his cavalry regiment. The chief kept his tribe from rising. They used to be very useful neighbors to us at the time when the county tax was levied. We would drive three-quarters of our cattle into the Reservation, and could then, in all honor, declare only a very small number of animals.

I shall later explain to you how this apparently unhandsome conduct was only a too legitimate way of escaping legalized robbery. The Indians obligingly lent themselves to this stratagem, having themselves much to suffer from the thefts of government agents. And besides, their dread is not the free cavalier, who lives on the prairie as they do, but the colonist and the engineer. I knew Sitting Bull well, myself, who, by the way, having given himself up, received a house from the United States. He always slept before the door, outside, and had never slept under a roof. I happened to be with him, on a hill, the first time the whistle of a locomotive resounded among the echoes of the Black Hills. He looked long at the strange machine, then he squatted upon the ground, his head in his hands. Two hours afterward, coming back to the place, I found him in the same posture.

"Sitting Bull is old," was his sole reply to my questions. "He would be with his fathers, on the other side of death."

It was impossible for me to get another word from him that night. Did he divine that these two rails, crossing the prairie as far as the eye could reach, must bring to his tribe, in this last remote refuge of their independence, civilization, and in its train a certain end? I think so.

He was a great chief, and his wish was not long delayed. He was killed in the uprising of 1891, and I wish him all peace "on the other side of death." When I think of the Indians I knew in those days, his gaunt face, with its long jaw, comes first before me, and that of a young woman, a Ute, whom I met with her husband in the outskirts of Salt Lake City. They asked me for tobacco, and devoured my cigarettes, wrappers and all. The brave, displeased with his wife, was proposing to kill her in some retired spot. In fact, she never reappeared. Although I did not then suspect the Ute's design, I have always reproached myself for not having continued my explorations in their company, either by goodwill or by force. The thought of it did cross my mind in a sort of presentiment. I should doubtless have saved the life of that poor child. Her sad face, with its great, gentle eyes, resigned in advance, has followed me for years.

$\mathcal{M}$. I. Ostrogorski

*You collect your impressions and you real-
ize what a colossal travesty of popular institutions you have just been witnessing.*

Moisei Iakovlavitch Ostrogorski (1854–1919), the son of an
assimilated Russian Jewish family, was born in Grodno and
educated in law at St. Petersburg. He studied in Paris at the
Libre des Sciences Politique and there began a long and detailed comparative history of British and American political
parties which was written in French and translated into English
in 1902. His observations on American politics were derived
from many visits here in the 80's and 90's; he was particularly
entranced by the Free Silver campaign of 1896. Ostrogorski
was attending a peace congress in London when the Russian

M. I. Ostrogorski, *Democracy and the Organization of Political
Parties* (New York, The Macmillan Company, 1902), Volume II,
pp. 263–69, 275–79, 576–77. Translated from the French by Frederick Clarke.

Revolution of 1905 broke out; he returned to St. Petersburg, where he served in the first Duma as a member of the liberal Constitutional Democratic party. He left the party with the dissolution of the Duma, becoming an independent. He returned to Russia again during the March Revolution of 1917. His fate after the Bolshevik seizure of power in October of that year is not known. He died in 1919.

Ostrogorski was the first serious and imaginative student of the theory and power of mass parties in democratic cultures. His work had an enormous influence on such sociologists as Max Weber and Robert Michels. Many of his ideas anticipated the theories of David Riesman. And some of the still influential generalizations of Tocqueville were modified or rejected by Ostrogorski in his *Democracy and the Organization of Political Parties*.

As a moderate revolutionary against autocratic despotism, Ostrogorski looked at America as both a student and a potential disciple. He knew and hoped that Russia would change soon; that some form of middle-class democracy would be established. In America he found political machines; bosses; corruption; influence peddling; mediocrity in office and hysteria in the electorate; special-interest lobbying and bureaucratic self-aggrandizement. All this was due to the debasing role of political parties which were developed to thwart, to control, to exploit the true and best interests of a free people. "To the low types which the human race has produced," Ostrogorski sighed, "the age of democracy has added a new one—the politician . . . [who possesses] a motley soul . . . made up of innumerable pettinesses, with but one trait to give them unity—cowardice."

His essay below is drawn mainly from the Democratic national convention of 1896, when William Jennings Bryan, the "Boy Orator," stampeded the party and propelled himself into the presidential nomination with his dynamic "Cross of Gold" speech.

ALL THE STATES ARE INVITED, in alphabetical order, to introduce their aspirants.

These champions are carefully selected beforehand from among those delegates who are most conspicuous for their eloquence, as well as for their influence. The principal spokesman of each aspirant makes the nominating speech in his favor, then another delegate, or several delegates, second the nomination in less elaborate speeches; and so on until the list of the states and of the aspirants is exhausted. It is only when all these torrents of eloquence have ceased to flow that the voting begins. The nominating speeches are looked on as the aesthetic treat and the *pièce de résistance* of the entertainment. The eulogium of the aspirant is generally pompous and bombastic; it tries to be at once persuasive and affecting. It dwells on the aspirant's special chances of being elected if he is adopted as a candidate; it tells the story of his life, beginning with the days of his childhood and his youth. If they have been full of toil and hardship, so much the better: that will melt the hearts of the audience. If he has had to go barefoot for want of shoe leather, that is a real godsend; the people, "the plain people," will recognize in him "one of themselves," and the others will share this feeling out of democratic snobbery.

The speaker who eulogizes him never considers himself under any restriction in the choice of terms for glorifying him; the speech teems with the most extravagant epithets and with metaphors of extraordinary boldness. The orator lays under contribution the poets, mythology, modern history, ancient history, and that of Rome in particular. Daniel Webster, who had to touch up President Harrison's inaugural speech, said afterwards: "It was a very stiff job. I killed no less than fourteen Roman consuls." It appears that these consuls have left issue. At the Democratic convention of 1896 a candidate was introduced in these terms: "We give you another Cicero—Cicero to meet another Catiline." Another candidate, a farmer from the West, was put forward as "that illustrious statesman and patriot, that Tiberius Gracchus"; and the speaker adjured the convention to vote for the American Gracchus "by the ashes of your ancestors; by the memories of your great and venerated dead; by the love which you bear to your children; by the duty which you owe to posterity; in the name of all that men hold sacred." In the majority of cases, the authors of these impassioned appeals know perfectly well that their clients have not the faintest chance of obtaining a majority in the convention, and all the delegates and the public are aware of it too; but the grand specimen of eloquence is none the less delivered and listened to with conviction, for, as in the theater, if the actors and the audience did not look as if they believed that it has all really happened, there could be no play at all.

It is remarkable, as illustrating the psychology of the American elector, that for more than sixty years, from the date at which one finds the prototype of the nominating speech, the national convention style of eloquence has not changed, amid the incessant progress of American society. I subjoin, as a matter of record, the text of that speech, delivered at the Democratic convention of 1835, in favor of the candidature of R. M. Johnson to the Vice-Presidency (the candidate for the Presidency, Martin Van Buren, was marked out by the all-powerful will of Jackson, and it was useless to recommend him by harangues of the delegates):

WHO IS HE? If, Mr. President, you could transport yourself to the "Far West," you would find upon one of her green and sunny fields, surrounded by the implements of husbandry, a personage whose plain and simple garb, whose frank and cordial and unostentatious bearing, would tell you that he had sprung from the people—that he was still one of them, and that his heart, in all its recollections, its hopes and its sympathies, was blended with the fortunes of the toiling millions. But, sir, his seared and shattered frame and limping gait would tell you, too, that the story of his life was not confined to a mere recital of household hospitalities or neighborhood charities. That story is no legend of obscure or doubtful authenticity; it lingers not alone in the kindly bosoms of friends, but every tongue in the Republic can give it utterance, and the brightest pages of your country's history have caught luster from its glowing record. When this nation was agonizing and bleeding at every pore, when war had desolated with fire and sword your northern frontier, and the best blood in the land had been vainly spilt upon its plains, he left the warm halls of Congress for the bleak winds of the Canadas; and, waiting for no summons of the recruiting officer, he rallied about him the chivalry of his state, and dashed with his gallant volunteers to the scene of hostilities, resolved to perish or to retrieve the national honor. With daring impetuousity he pursued and overtook the enemy—threw himself like a thunderbolt of war into the thickest of the fight—fought hand to hand and eye to eye with the Briton and his savage myrmidons—poured out his blood like water —triumphed and returned home with the richest trophies of the campaign. Sir, his deeds rely not for recollection or blazonry upon musty records, nor yet upon caucus or convention addresses; they have been spoken in the thunders of victorious battles, they have been written upon the hacked and broken armour of his country's invaders. His life has been one of unfaltering, unswerving devotion to freedom and to the people. The people "love him because he first loved them." His popularity rests upon no calculation of political chances. It is not seated in the arithmetics, but in the deep and ardent affections of his country. . . .

His fame, like that of our venerated chief magistrate, spreads everywhere—alike in the wilderness and with "city full," penetrating into the far valleys, climbing to the hill tops, and reaching in its kindling, animating influences every log cabin beyond the mountains. . . . There is a voice from the great valleys of the West; from all her cities and cottages. There is a voice from the East, from the North, and the South; there is a voice from the fields of the husbandman, from the workshops of the mechanic, from the primary assemblies of the people, from the conventions of neighborhoods and states, calling aloud for the elevation of the war-worn soldier, this tried and uncorruptible patriot, this advocate of the destitute and downtrodden, this friend to freedom and to man. Such, sir, is Richard M. Johnson.

LET US NOW TURN to a nominating speech made at a recent convention. I take the conventions of 1884 at random. Here is an address delivered at the Republican convention in favor of a candidate who obtained thirteen votes out of eight hundred thirteen. After having sketched the history of the Republican party and of its glories, the speaker narrates the life of the aspirant:

X. WAS BORN IN NORTH CAROLINA. He draws from Southern blood and Southern soil and Southern skies the generous chivalry of a nature that abhors cant and hypocrisy and falsehood, and feels the stain like a wound. Thirty-four years ago he came, a poor, barefooted, penniless boy, to the rugged soil of Connecticut, where breathing its free air, listening to its free speech, and taught in its free school, he laid the foundation of a manly character and life in principles which are as enduring as Connecticut's everlasting hills. . . .

The fierce light that beats against a presidential candidate will explore his record in vain, and he will come out brighter from the blaze. His life is gentle, and the elements are so mixed in him that nature might stand up and say to all the world "This is a man." . . . . If he is nominated, all elements can support him, for he is a radical conservative and a conservative radical; a friend of Garfield and a friend of Grant. Sir, if he should be nominated, it would ensure you Connecticut by a ten thousand majority. It would weld together with fervent heat the dissensions in New York. It would blaze through the state of Garfield, that daughter of Connecticut, more beautiful than her mother.

It would carry the Southern states, for he is the only candidate that this party would have named who was born on Southern soil. It would please all parties and all professions, for he is a lawyer, editor, soldier, statesman, orator. It would take the people, for he is what the people all love —God Almighty's noblest work, an honest man. Such a nomination would sweep from the storm-beaten coast of the Atlantic to the Golden Gate of the peaceful sea. With him elected in vigor of his life and plenitude of his powers, beloved at home and respected abroad, with our free institutions and our imperial domain, we should need no Bartholdi statue standing at the gateway of commerce with uplifted torch to typify the genius of liberty enlightening the world, but our history under a Republican President, administered upon a Republican policy, would of itself bear witness to all times, and to all people, that America is the greatest, freest, most prosperous country upon which the sun in his course has ever looked down.

THE ELOQUENCE OF THE SPEAKERS, however great it is or appears to be, only produces its full effect when accompanied by the more or less noisy manifestations with which the audience greets the speeches and the names of the presidential aspirants who form the subject of them. Every speech is interrupted and brought to a close by more or less frantic shouts; being looked on as a criterion of the aspirant's popularity, these outcries impress the delegates, make the weak hesitate, and sometimes decide the wavering. The campaign managers of each aspirant, therefore, considering these manifestations as a card in their game, procure them by means of a paid claque, judiciously distributed over the enormous hall. This is the last and the most impressive act of the "boom" organized on behalf of the aspirant; inside the convention building the boom becomes an apotheosis. As soon as the aspirant's name is uttered, the delegates who support him and the paid applauders jump up on their seats and break into cheers or other less articulate cries, which are immediately taken up by a more or less considerable section of the crowd. The latter are only too ready to make a row, they have almost a physiological need of this relief; it is enough for the claque to give the signal for them to go into convulsions. If the aspirant is a favorite, a very popular man, whom the forecasts place in the first flight for the presidential race, the delirium reaches an indescribable pitch of intensity. Hardly has the speaker pronounced his name when his portrait, which has been held in reserve, is hoisted aloft and carried about the hall, every one is on his legs, shouting, screaming, tossing hats and handkerchiefs into the air, waving small flags and open umbrellas. It is a sort of pandemonium or Bedlam. If one could imagine a crowd of fifteen thousand persons all attacked at once with St. Vitus' dance, one would obtain a faint idea of the scene presented by the convention.*

The chairman with his hammer is quite helpless, it is

---

* A well-known American journalist and ex-diplomat has hit on another simile to give an idea of the uproar which he witnessed on a similar occasion at a convention: "Imagine all the hogs ever slaughtered in Cincinnati giving their death squeals together."

in vain that he tells the band to play in order to tranquilize the assembly; a duel begins between the orchestra, which energetically strikes up the "Star-Spangled Banner," and the yelling crowd; now and then a few sounds from the instruments are audible, but they are instantaneously drowned by the shouting. The orchestra tries to play "Dixie," or "The Girl I Left Behind Me"; it is of no avail, the crowd refuses to listen. The paroxysm is at its height. Here a delegate takes off his coat, hoists it on a walking-stick, and, waving it with both hands, begins to dance, probably in imitation of King David dancing before the Ark. Another enthusiast, at the further end of the hall, creates a precedent himself by taking off his boots and waving them one on an umbrella and the other on a stick. The crowd does not stop until compelled by fatigue, by exhaustion. Spectators who know what is coming have taken out their watches from the very beginning, like certain travelers at the entrance of a long tunnel. The duration of the uproar, carefully noted down, is not only of importance for the effect of *the* moment; it is formally placed on record, and later on people will point out that the uproar for McKinley did not last more than twenty-two minutes, that is to say two minutes less than that with which Blaine was honored.

The series of panegyrics of the aspirants continues, each has his more or less well-sustained boom; but all at once a slight incident renews the uproar of a short time back. The speech on behalf of a much-talked-of aspirant is at an end, but his boom, which has been started in the regulation way, flags, and his adherents are pained to see that it is about to die out when it has hardly begun. At this point, however, a young woman in one of the galleries, dressed entirely in white, stands up, shouts out the name of the aspirant at the top of her voice, seizes two small flags, and whirls them round like windmills with her bare arms. Her cries and her gestures attract the attention of the adjoining groups, then of others, and, finally, of the whole meeting; and the fifteen thousand persons, adherents as well as opponents of the aspirant in question, greet his youthful admirer with unearthly shrieks, which last for several minutes. The delegates of the aspirant's state go to fetch the intrepid damsel, and, under their escort, with a heavy banner adorned with the aspirant's likeness in her hand, she marches in triumph across the hall in the midst of the raving crowd; she is hoisted over the partition which separates the seats of the delegates from those of the public, and is invited to take her place among the delegates. The whole meeting, delegates as well as the public, yells its loudest—they are all glad to be able to enjoy another fit of hysterics. The most astonished person of all is the heroine of the incident, which she has brought about quite unwittingly; she only obeyed a voice from within, like Joan of Arc.

During the roll-call of the states the adherents of the various aspirants applaud and utter shouts of delight as soon as a delegation announces that it votes for their man. When the result of the ballot is proclaimed, an explosion of enthusiasm, often ending in a grand uproar, greets a rise in the total of votes obtained by an aspirant. If the rise is accentuated at the following ballots, the crowd of delegates and spectators becomes delirious. More or less unearthly shrieks, cries of animals, hats thrown into the air, red umbrellas opened, flags and banners frantically waved, start the pandemonium afresh. The standard of the state to which the aspirant in question belongs, planted in front of the seats of its delegates, is pulled up, and in a twinkling it is surrounded by the standards of several other states, which salute it, and all form a procession, which marches several times round the hall along its unencumbered passages. The sitting is practically interrupted; it is impossible to proceed to a new ballot; in vain does the chairman cry out to the secretary in a stentorian voice, "Call the roll"; the delegations do not answer, it is not worthwhile. At the next ballot, the hero of this manifestation has perhaps lost some votes, and the star of another aspirant has suddenly risen; with the fickleness that belongs to crowds, the convention, forgetting the man whom it cheered barely half an hour back, rushes madly after the new momentary favorite of fortune.

The uncertainty as to the final result continues down to the ballot in which an aspirant who already holds a good position is reinforced by an important group of delegates, who give up their aspirant or aspirants. This change of front, which soon grows like an avalanche, constitutes the "crisis" or "break," and raises the excitement of the audience to its highest pitch. With nerves strained to the utmost, the public awaits the dramatic moment from the second ballot onward, and says to itself on each occasion: "It will come this time." This moment sends a thrill of anticipation through the politicians of the convention and causes them a violent emotion, in which they indulge with a feeling of delight. As soon as the "break" takes place, the whole assembly has an epileptic fit, stamping on the floor, yelling, carrying round standards in a procession, etc., in the way with which we are familiar. The politician whose influence has brought about the break will, of course, be in good order with the candidate when the latter has become President; he can count upon an embassy or some other "good thing."

As soon as the result of the last ballot is announced, the champion of one of the defeated aspirants proposes to the convention to make the nomination of their fortunate rival unanimous. The motion is carried, a grand uproar of the regulation kind, with the war-dance of the standards, greets the happy event, the band strikes up "Hail to the Chief," and the assembly goes mad for half an hour or so.

At last, after a session of several days, the end is reached;

the convention adjourns *sine die*. All is over. As you step out of the building you inhale with relief the gentle breeze which tempers the scorching heat of July; you come to yourself; you recover your sensibility, which has been blunted by the incessant uproar, and your faculty of judgment, which has been held in abeyance amid the pandemonium in which day after day has been passed. You collect your impressions, and you realize what a colossal travesty of popular institutions you have just been witnessing. A greedy crowd of office-holders, or of office-seekers, disguised as delegates of the people, on the pretense of holding the grand council of the party, indulged in, or were the victims of, intrigues and maneuvers, the object of which was the chief magistracy of the greatest Republic of the two hemispheres—the succession to the Washingtons and the Jeffersons.

With an elaborate respect for forms extending to the smallest details of procedure, they pretended to deliberate, and then passed resolutions settled by a handful of wire-pullers in the obscurity of committees and private caucuses; they proclaimed as the creed of the party, appealing to its piety, a collection of hollow, vague phrases, strung together by a few experts in the art of using meaningless language, and adopted still more precipitately without examination and without conviction; with their hands upon their hearts they adjured the assembly to support aspirants in whose success they had not the faintest belief; they voted in public for candidates whom they were scheming to defeat. Cut off from their conscience by selfish calculations and from their judgment by the tumultuous crowd of spectators, which alone made all attempt at deliberation an impossibility, they submitted without resistance to the pressure of the galleries masquerading as popular opinion, and made up of a claque and of a raving mob which, under ordinary circumstances, could only be formed if the inmates of all the lunatic asylums of the country had made their escapes at the same time. Here this mob discharges a great political function; it supplies the "enthusiasm" which is the primary element of the convention, which does duty for discussion and controls all its movements. Produced to order of the astute managers, "enthusiasm" is served out to the delegates as a strong drink, to gain completer mastery over their will. But in the fit of intoxication they yield to the most sudden impulses, dart in the most unexpected directions, and it is blind chance which has the last word.

The name of the candidate for the presidency of the Republic issues from the votes of the convention like a number from a lottery. And all the followers of the party, from the Atlantic to the Pacific, are bound, on pain of apostasy, to vote for the product of that lottery. Yet, when you carry your thoughts back from the scene which you have just witnessed and review the line of Presidents, you find that if they have not all been great men—far from it —they were all honorable men; and you cannot help repeating the American saying: "God takes care of drunkards, of little children, and of the United States!"

How is it that the people have allowed themselves to be despoiled in this fashion? How has it been possible to get the better of this American nation which has presented the admirable spectacle of a creative force, of an indomitable energy, of a tenacious will that has no parallel? The explanation is a simple one: the people have expended all their moral strength in the material building-up of the commonwealth. In that new world which was a mine of untold riches for whoever cared to work it, material preoccupations have engrossed the American's whole being. He has thrust back all other considerations or has subordinated them to their objects. The desperate race for wealth has absorbed the citizen and has not left him time to attend to the public welfare; it even encouraged his want of public spirit, and converted it almost into a virtue.

W. T. Stead

I discussed with policemen, saloon keepers, gamblers and keepers of houses of ill fame what Christ would think of the poisonous, fiery and venomous city of Chicago!

Chicago was considered the geographical center and symbolic heart of America. Towards the end of the nineteenth century, the city earned world-wide fame for its corruption and vice, its dirt and squalor. Tourists were proudly shown the stockyards, the rambling parks and the Water Tower, the only major structure to survive the Great Fire in 1871. But the city was known also for its blatant subversion of the democratic process. Officials thrived on bribery. Violence in the streets was notorious. During the years of Prohibition, the gangsters of Al Capone turned America's Second City into an urban battlefield; the bloodshed televised during the Democratic national convention in 1968 sustained the city's reputation.

W. T. Stead, *If Christ Came To Chicago* (London, Chapman and Hall, 1893), pp. 244–60.

The English reformer and publicist William Thomas Stead (1849–1912) published a detailed assault on the city in 1893, calling it *If Christ Came to Chicago*. Stead took the Victorian ideal of Christianity and imposed it upon the Sodom and Gomorrah of North America. He was a determined, muck-raking journalist with transatlantic ambitions. In England he once served three months in jail for dealing in pornography during one of his vice crusades. Chicago's comic genius Finley Peter Dunne, who knew Stead, may well have had him in mind when he had "Mr. Dooley" say that "Vice is a creature of such heejous mien that th' more ye see it the betther ye like it." Stead died on his way to a peace congress in America. He went down on the Titanic.

———◆———

THE SCARLET WOMAN

A LEADING MEMBER of the Knights of Labor said the other day that the Americans as a nation no longer believed in God. They worshiped, he said, three things, first gold, secondly women, thirdly children. I wish I could have found more proofs of their devotion to women and to children in their laws. The statutes made and provided for the protection of young girls are in many states a very grim and ghastly commentary upon the traditional respect of the Americans for their women.

In some states it is true the law has been amended—largely under the influence of the same cyclone of moral indignation which raised the age of consent in England in 1885 from thirteen to sixteen, but in many others the law is still in a condition to be a disgrace to heathendom. The legislatures of Delaware, of Wisconsin, and other states in the following list would seem to be composed of Yahoos rather than of Christian citizens of a republic founded by the descendants of the Puritans. The age of consent—the technical term used to denote the number of years that a girl must have lived before she is regarded by the law as competent to consent to her own seduction—varies all over the Union. I quote here the black list of dishonor from a table compiled by the *Philanthropist* from official returns:

AGE OF CONSENT

Delaware	7 years	Kentucky	12 years
Texas	10 "	Indiana	12 "
Idaho	10 "	Wisconsin	12 "
South Dakota	10 "	Virginia	12 "
Carolina, North	10 "	West Virginia	12 "
" South	10 "	Louisiana	12 "
Georgia	10 "	Iowa	13 "
Alabama	10 "	New Hampshire	13 "
Minnesota	10 "	Tennessee	13 "
Colorado	10 "		

These are the worst states in the Union from this point of view. There are others nearly as bad. Seventeen states fix the age of consent at fourteen and two at fifteen. Six follow the English rule and place the age of consent at sixteen. Florida, the most southern of all the states, raises it to seventeen, while Kansas and Wyoming place it at eighteen.

The time is coming when such laws as those which practically hand over innocent and unsuspecting girl children of seven and ten to twelve to be the lawful prey of brutes in human shape if they can but get their consent—forsooth—to something of which they know nothing until it is too

late, will be regarded with as much shame and indignation
as the Fugitive Slave Law. Certainly as long as these states
persist in leaving defenseless maidenhood without the protection of law, the vaunts about American chivalry and high
regard for women and children sound as hollow as did the
Declaration of Independence in the old slave states.

The increase in the number of young women in America who make their living as clerks, shop girls, teachers and
other callings which take them away from home, has not
been accompanied by increased safeguards for their protection. Young children are employed as cash girls in Chicago
at a much earlier age than would be permitted in Europe,
and in more than one of the great stores ugly stories are
current of wages being fixed at a rate which assumed that
they would be supplemented by the allowance of a
"friend." The recurrence of this worst feature of Parisian
shops in the Far West is a much more painful phenomenon
than the appearance of the familiar figure of the street-
walker. In one of the largest of the dry goods stores in
Chicago, the head of the dress-making department, now
happily discontinued, was the manager of a house of ill-
fame down the levee. She is said to have found the combination very convenient, as she recruited in one establishment by day for assistants in the other at night. These
things are only too well known to the unfortunate victims,
but as public exposure would add the last drop to their
bitter cup, they suffer in silence. The Missions and Refuges
which receive the shattered wrecks of lost womanhood
know only too well how deadly is the system by which the
daughters reared in American homes are lured to their
doom. Another lost illusion is the belief that American girls
are trusted with knowledge instead of being kept in that
cruel ignorance which is confounded with innocence. It is
not the case. If legal protection has been peremptorily
denied American girls by the men who monopolize the

legislative function, neither are they delivered from the dangers of ignorance by their mothers. No disability of sex stands in the way of the timely performance of the most necessary duty which maternity ever imposed upon woman. But even that is denied the American girl. Anna B. Gray, M.D., writing in the February number of *New Occasions*, a monthly magazine edited by Mr. B. F. Underwood and published at Chicago, on "Ignorance at the Price of Depravity," bears testimony on this point that is worth nothing. She writes:

> I have given years of attention to the subject, and have arrived at this much of knowledge. In nine out of every ten cases of seduction, the woman in America has erred through affection, not passion; that instinct of common humanity, most highly developed in women, to please the beloved, but chiefly through *ignorance*. They feel no passion; they are totally ignorant of its signs in others, even if they feel, they are in equal ignorance of what it means. While that much lauded ignorance prevents any thought of evil, the result is that before they know they have arrived within sight of it they have crossed the threshold of sin.
>
> I have not arrived at my conclusions hastily nor do I state them lightly. I have talked with all sorts and kinds of women from the common prostitute to the purest matron, from the girl who committed suicide when told of the consequences that would follow her error, to those whose sins never became known, and this is my sure conviction. The commonest, and largest factor in the seduction of unmarried women is unadulterated ignorance. Ignorance of any love less innocent than that which teaches her to clasp a baby in her arms, caress its tender limbs, smother it with kisses, and half crush its life out in a passion of tenderness. If she won-

ders at the fervor of the caresses bestowed upon her,
they mean no more to her than those she so freely
bestowed upon her baby brother or sister.

If any good is to be done in dealing with this saddest
of all social maladies it must be done betimes. Prevention
is a thousand times better than cure and many thousand
times easier. The chief difficulty that stands in the way of
frank sensible speech on such subjects between parent and
child is the absurd prudery which in the old days led
American matrons to put frills round their piano legs and
which quite recently led an American girl to call legacy
limbacy, in order to avoid the improper first syllable. A
prudish silence with ignorance as the necessary result lands
many an innocent girl in Fourth Avenue. This is a subject
upon which an ounce of fact is worth a pound of theory.
The facts are indisputable. The keepers of houses of ill
fame who reap the harvest of these blighted lives are
authorities on this point. Take for instance the evidence of
Mrs. Vina Fields, who next to Carrie Watson is the best-
known madame in Chicago. Vina Fields is a colored woman
who has one of the largest houses in the city. During the
Fair she had over sixty girls in the house, all colored, but
all for white men. Now she has not more than thirty or
forty. She has kept a house for many years and, strange
though it may appear, has acquired the respect of nearly all
who know her. The police have nothing to say against
her. An old experienced police matron emphatically declared that "Vina is a good woman," and I think it will
be admitted by all who know her that she is probably as
good as any woman can be who conducts so bad a business.
I had a talk with her about it one afternoon and some days
after she wrote me a long letter upon this subject. She says:

> The present state of affairs results from the want of
> proper knowledge regarding self. When cultivation of

self is made universal, a better condition is possible, and
not until then. The cause for prostitution will continue
until it is made honorable for the sexes to seek knowledge of self and their duties toward each other. The
most important things of human life ought to never
make an honest educated man or woman blush. It is
ignorance that causes shame and all this distress. Let the
causes of life and common things be more understood
and the greater things will take care of themselves, in
private matters between man and woman the same as in
other things.

Therein Vina spoke wisely and well. The result of not
teaching young people the truths of physiology at home is
that they usually acquire them abroad when it is too late.

Vina Fields is a very interesting woman. She is now
past middle age. She has made a moderate competence by
her devotion to her calling and she prides herself not a little
upon the character of her establishment. The rules and
regulations of the Fields house, which are printed and
posted in every room, enforce decorum and decency with
pains and penalties which could hardly be more strict if
they were drawn up for the regulation of a Sunday school.
In it the ladies are severely informed that even if they have
no respect for themselves, they should have for the house.
She is bringing up her daughter, who knows nothing of the
life of her mother, in the virginal seclusion of a convent
school, and she contributes of her bounty to maintain her
unfortunate sisters whose husbands down South are among
the hosts of the unemployed. Nor is her bounty confined to
her own family. Every day this whole winter through she
has fed a hungry, ragged regiment of the out-of-work.
The day before I called, two hundred and one men had had
free dinners of her providing. She had always given the
broken victuals away, she said, but this year the distress

had been so great she had bought meat every day to feed the poor fellows who were hunting jobs and finding none.

"What brings your girls here?" I asked. "Passion, poverty, or what?"

"Misery," she answered quietly. "Always misery. I don't know one who came that was not driven here by misery. Unhappy homes, cruel parents, bad husbands. Misery, always misery. I don't know one exception."

On this subject Vina wrote me afterwards at some length. And I cannot do better than quote this homily on home, the duty of making home happy—although few, perhaps, would be prepared to listen to such a discourse from the colored keeper of a house of ill fame.

It is not necessary to go to houses of prostitution to find the cause that places girls there. All you have to do is to investigate the homes of the people. These women called prostitutes come from these homes from every grade of life, from the upper classes as well as the others; and I am sorry to say that they give a good percentage to this class, as the daughters are educated to an idle, frivolous life. As a rule the marriage policy does not work very charmingly, and only a few succeed in obtaining comfortable homes, the balance have to find shelter wherever they can, and as houses of ill fame are open to this class of woman—they prefer it to dying and starving on the street; many of them find it more pleasing and preferable to their married lives. These women are no more lustful than their sisters in other positions in life. They simply have not been successful in marrying at home, and as many, very many do not know how to do any kind of work, they come here.

The only remedy for prostitution will be to educate woman in the value of home life.

It is natural only for man to provide. He cannot

make a home alone. It is absolutely necessary that there be the mother and wife, and as girls enter into the most important condition of life without any previous culture or consideration of the new life that they enter, as a rule, there will be failure, and more is to pity than to blame for the results. The men from necessity are forced to houses of prostitution. Why? Because the women are uneducated in the business of becoming wife and mother, and they, as a rule, know nothing about the formation of a new home; that is left to chance. Is it any wonder that there is trouble and ruin all around us? Do you think that there is even a single instance where a young girl leaves her mother today to form a new home, that she is taught by that mother to believe that the grandest and best work of women is to be able to produce a grand, noble woman or man; and that to do this her home must be a heaven, and that it rests with her, more than all things else, whether her home is a heaven or hell? The great cry of today is the advancement of woman—that means for all to make a grand rush for outside employment, other than home work. While the husbands and sons are walking the streets idle the mother and sisters are earning the living, and by so doing, the homes from necessity are dirty and the younger children uncared for or left with ignorant nurses, and this state of affairs makes the women tired and fretful, the husbands, when they have money, naturally seek the house of ill fame, as wives are too tired from work or devoting their time to society, to give husbands even a pleasant word. Yes, I say, the only way out of this trouble is to teach girls the value of home, and when women in a mass elevate their homes and make them all that the word implies, that is, clean, homelike and cheerful; their kitchen the cleanest and most cheerful room in the house, and their parlor for use of the family instead of strangers; the houses of ill fame will have to shut up shop. They will have to close for want of patronage.

When this is made the highest ambition of girl's life, to be a possessor of a model home by her own virtues; and the boys, by mother, are taught to value a good woman; they will then think it an honor to keep those homes clean and wear a bright smile for husband and little ones, and will then know the value of a clean calico dress, a gingham apron for work and a white apron for eyes of father and dear children. There is not a man living that would not prefer a dear little home to "a wandering, no-account, haphazard life."

Another typical scarlet woman of Chicago is Carrie Watson, whose brownstone house in Clark Street has long been one of the scandals of Chicago. She was there before the fire and is there still. She does not have quite as many girls as Vina Fields, but they are white and not colored, and as she is at the head of her shameful profession prices run higher. Business is carried on openly enough, with carriages standing at the door at all hours of the night waiting for the "gentlemen" inside. Carrie Watson and Lame Jimmy, her violin player, are a typical Chicagoan pair. Lame Jimmy acquired an unenviable notoriety this year, for at his annual benefit ball one of the best-known police officers in Chicago was shot dead in the midst of the orgy. Lame Jimmy's benefit is one of the saturnalian nights of the Levee when all the professional forces of debauchery are let loose to disport themselves in a Music Hall, with the assistance of the police, as the above incident shows. Carrie Watson herself has made a fortune out of her trade in the bodies of her poorer sisters. She is the exploiter, the capitalist of her class, for the same conditions reproduce themselves every-where. In the brothel as in the factory the person at the top carries off most of the booty. Carrie Watson is a smart woman, said to be liberal in her gifts to the only churches in her neighborhood, one a Catholic just across the way and the other a Jewish synagogue which local rumor asserts is run rent-free owing to Carrie's pious munificence. This is probably a slander but its circulation is significant as proving that Carrie Watson can be all things to all men. She is emphatically a smart woman, and cynical as might be expected. Prostitution is to her the natural result of poverty on the part of the woman and of passion on the part of the man. She regards the question from the economic standpoint. Morals no more enter into her business than they do into the business of bulls and bears on the stock exchange. Girl clerks and stenographers, she says, are often unable to earn salaries to keep them in clothes, to say nothing of the numberless relations who are often dependent upon their labor for a livelihood. If they have youth, health and good looks, they can realize these assets at a higher price down Clark Street or on Fourth Avenue than at any other place in the city. Women who are desperate go to Carrie Watson and her class as men go to the gaming hell in the hope of recouping their fortunes. The misfortune of it is that women can almost always secure their stakes at first, whereas the gambler quite as often as not is deterred by an initial failure. Few people realize that a young and pretty woman can make more money for a short time by what may be called a discriminate sale of her person than the ablest woman in America can make at the same age in any profession. But as life's enchanted cup but sparkles near the brim so the profits of that life are of very short duration. When the bloom is off the rose, a very rapid process of degradation sets in which ends in the lock hospital, the jail or the drunkard's grave.

Carrie Watson agrees with Vina Fields in believing that girls do not take to the life from love of vice, neither do they remain in it from any taste of debauchery. It is an easy, lazy way of making a living, and once they are started either by force, fraud or ill luck there is no way of getting back. They have to go through with it to the bitter end. They bury the memories of the past by drinking the waters of that temporary Lethe which men call strong drink, and quiet their conscience by the thought that after all they are not worse than the highly respectable men who visit them and that they are able by suffering these things to help relations who would otherwise often be in very great straits. Carrie Watson, for instance, says that almost every girl in her house has three to four persons depending on her who share with her the wages of sin.

The peculiar temptation of a woman is that her virtue is a realizable asset. It costs a man money to indulge in vice, but for a woman it is money into pocket. This temptation has naturally greatest force when work is scarce, and when sickness is in the house. Even if they have a living wage in ordinary homes, these periods of stress and strain break them down.

"I lived at home," said a girl in a house of ill fame, "and had a mother and a sister to support on five dollars a week. One time, however, my mother got ill and I could not get the necessary medicine for her. Then some young man whom I knew in the street and who came quite frequently to my counter to buy goods, offered me a good deal of money if I would go with him to an assignation house. I wanted the money for my mother and so I went. Having gone once I went again until I gradually drifted into a house of prostitution."

The keepers of houses always deny indignantly the accusation that they recruit their establishments with unwilling volunteers. They profess to detest "greenhorns." They prefer experienced women well broken to the work, etc., etc. All the same there are many who are only too glad to obtain young simpletons whom they can fleece even if they cannot, as is sometimes the case, realize heavily upon them for rum. One well-known procuress, Mrs. Davis, was arrested twelve months ago for one of these offenses, but she escaped. Criminals "who have a pull" can usually escape in Chicago. And procuresses, of necessity, "stand in," with the police, whom they subsidize for permission to live.

Cabmen in Chicago are frequently the active agents of the houses of ill fame. If they find a pretty girl who has not enough money to pay her fare they can usually raise the money by delivering her at a sporting house. That this is done may seem incredible, but it was not merely admitted but even complained of by keepers of houses, who being overstocked objected to the practice of an imposition. One madame on Fourth Avenue told me that on three occasions last year she had received consignments in this fashion. She did not want the girls so she handed them over to the Annex to Harrison Street police station. If only any one will take the time and trouble to watch some of the depots and houses of prostitution on Plymouth and Custom House, places in the "Levee" district, and those on Dearborn Street and Armour Avenue in the vicinity of Twenty-second Street, they will realize the sad state of affairs.

An ex-police reporter in this city said recently: "I have to my knowledge had four distinct cases of cabmen taking young girls who had just arrived in the city and engaged him to drive them to a hotel, to a house of ill fame. In each of the cases the girls were only saved by police interference, and yet no effort was made to punish the guilty driver of the vehicle in which the girls had been driven to the houses where they were found."

When once a young girl is ensnared there is very little chance of her escaping. The police report that twenty per cent of the girls between fourteen and eighteen reported missing are never heard of. Those zealous A.P.A.* emissaries who work themselves up into a fever heat of indignation

---

* [American Protective Association, a large and noisy anti-Catholic society which flourished in the 1890's. GES]

and of passion because of more or less imaginary narratives of the way in which convents are used to imprison unwilling maidens, would find a more profitable field for their emotions in contemplating the underground railway by which keepers of houses of ill fame move girls out of the way. After a girl has been ruined in one town, especially if there is any trouble, she is exchanged for a safer girl in another city. A case of this kind, which can be vouched for, occurred about a year ago. L. M., a girl of eighteen, came to Chicago from a well-known city in the western part of New York. While here she was seduced under a promise of marriage and taken to a house of ill fame on South Clark Street. Meanwhile she had ceased writing to her parents, and they, fearful that she had met with an accident, communicated with the police here. She was located soon afterwards, but before the authorities could arrest her she was sent to Council Bluffs, Iowa. A few weeks later another girl arrived at the South Clark Street resort to take the place of L. M. Strange to say, she *had come from the same house* in Council Bluffs to which her fallen sister had been sent. Her story was also on the same line with that of the deported girl.

In places of amusement, the Park Theater is an outrage as it has been and is being conducted. The whole theater is an exhibition which would be more in place in Sodom and Gomorrah than in Chicago. The proprietors, it is said, make friends of the powers which be by subscribing to the funds of both parties. Whether that is so or not I cannot say. As a matter of fact it is but the antechamber to a lupanar. The moral level of its stage is below that of a decently conducted sporting house. The Midway dance was one of its standing attractions long after it had been banished from Boston and New York. Although the manager lied to me like a Trojan on the only occasion when I visited the place, I had no difficulty in obtaining trustworthy information as to the orgies which have given an evil fame to the wine room. In a book called *In Darkest Chicago* it was stated that dancing by naked women was one of the regular performances of this theater after the play concluded. That, however, I think, is no longer true, the only difference, however, being that when the women dance the cancan in the Park they pay such homage to decency as is implied in the wearing of a single garment which enhances rather than interferes with the obscene suggestiveness of the performance. An outward semblance of decency could be secured by canceling their license whenever their decorations or entertainments violated the municipal standard of decency. There is no necessity for making that standard extreme or Puritanical, but in a civilized city the goatlike gambols of Satus might be forbidden. It would be too much no doubt to expect certain classes, including some of the most respectable so-called citizens, to comport themselves like human beings, but they might certainly be compelled to preserve the natural decency of an ordinary brute beast. The unnatural and worse than bestial performances which are carried on in certain places in Chicago well known to the police ought to land a considerable number of persons in Joliet for the rest of their natural lives. Offenses which in England a very short time ago sent men to the gallows and still entail penal servitude are among the sights of Chicago which are not interfered with by the police, because it is held by large wholesale houses, so the story runs, that it is necessary for them to have certain amusements for their country customers. Entertainers are attached to the large wholesale houses, and when the country customer comes in to make his purchases the entertainer personally conducts him round the sights of the town. As Mayor Hopkins remarked when discussing the gambling houses, it is surprising how many merchants in this city approve of their existence for the sake of their country customers. They say that the first night a country customer comes to town he is taken to the theater; next he is taken round to the questionable resorts, and on the third night he insists upon going to the gambling hells. The questionable resorts to which the Mayor referred as occupying the country cousin's second night may be said to be run, if not under the patronage of the police, at least with their cognizance. A friend of mine who made the round was personally escorted by a detective. When the police and the large wholesale houses and country cousins are in collusion to support unnatural crimes which the good people of Chicago fondly imagined existed only in the corruption of the later Roman Empire, it is obvious that the moral reformer has a very uphill task before him.

Lepel Henry Griffin

America is the country of disillusion and disappointment. I can think of none except Russia in which I would not prefer to reside.

After retiring from the Anglo-Indian imperial bureaucracy, Sir Lepel Henry Griffin (1838–1908) visited America in the 1880's and wrote a series of bitter reports which were collected in book form as *The Great Republic* (1884), a title chosen more for its facetiousness than its accuracy. Griffin's friend the distinguished literary critic and essayist Matthew Arnold had toured America earlier in search of "civilization," and he too had found none. "What human nature . . . demands in civilization," Arnold wrote, "is best described by the word *interesting*. . . . Do not tell me only, says human nature, of the magnitude of your industry and commerce; of the beneficence of your institutions, your freedom, your equality; of the great

Sir Lepel Henry Griffin, *The Great Republic* (London, Chapman and Hall, 1884), pp. 1–2, 6–7, 17–20, 22–30, 150–55.

and growing number of your churches and schools, libraries and newspapers; tell me also if your civilization—which is the grand name you give to all this development—tell me if your civilization is *interesting*." It was not. Arnold sympathized with English gentlemen like Griffin who found America so barren of "the comforts and conveniences" of life. "For men of his kind," Arnold suggested, "men who have been at the public schools and universities, men of the professional and official class, men who do the most part of our literature and our journalism, America is not a comfortable place of abode."

Griffin and Arnold continued the nineteenth-century English tradition of both playful and vigorous condescension to everything cultural in America. And Mrs. Trollope's famous judgments—"I do not like their principles, I do not like their manners, I do not like their opinions"—were echoed towards the end of the century by Oscar Wilde. During a lecture tour, Wilde ascended the Rockies to give "readings" to a group of miners in what he was told was the richest town in the world, Leadville, Colorado. Since the men were "working in metals," he lectured them, naturally, "On the Ethics of Art" by rendering passages from the *Autobiography of Benevenuto Cellini*. "They seemed much delighted," Wilde said, "but I was reproved by my hearers for not having brought him with me. I explained that he had been dead for some little time which elicited the inquiry: 'Who shot him?' " Just before his performance at the local theater, a first act preceded Wilde. Two men accused of murder were tried *and* executed on the stage before a large crowd. That drama seemed quite in keeping with the tone of the whole country. Even the local dance hall provided Wilde with "the only rational method of art criticism" he had ever seen. Over the hall's piano was a notice:

PLEASE DO NOT SHOOT THE
PIANIST.
HE IS DOING HIS BEST.

The cultural knowledge of the Western American was infinitesimal. A rich, grubby miner sued a railroad company because a plaster cast of the Venus de Milo, ordered all the way from Paris, arrived without the arms. "What is more surprising still," Wilde added, this "patron of the arts" won his case and damages.

Excessive democracy, Griffin complained, was the cause of this cultural desolation. The suffrage had been extended even to the newly freed Negro, who was as fit for the vote, Griffin said, "as the monkeys he closely resembles." A gentleman of high sensibilities, as well as a racist of vulgar prejudices, Griffin would not live in such a place. Appropriately, he chose as the motto for his screed Shakespeare's "The Commonwealth of Athens has become a forest of beasts."

IF, THEN, THERE BE THOSE, like myself, who believe that no greater curse could befall England than for her to borrow political methods, dogmas and institutions from America, there seems every reason why such should explain the grounds, good or bad, for their belief, with which American travel may have furnished them. The good in American institutions is of English origin and descent; what is bad is indigenous, and this she now desires to teach us. But Britannia, who, since her daughter has become independent and carried her affections elsewhere, has escaped the dreary *rôle* of chaperone, may surely refuse invitations to see Columbia dance, in fancy dress, to the tune of Yankee Doodle, and may plead her age and figure when asked to learn the new step. There are doubtless in English politics and society many evils and anomalies—privileges which cannot be defended, wrongs and injustice and misery which must be redressed and relieved; but, nevertheless, the English constitution, with its ordered and balanced society from the throne to the cottage, is the symbol and expression of liberty in the world. Republican institutions have had a trial for a hundred years, and, so far as outsiders can judge, their failure is complete. France under a Republic has become a by-word in Europe for weakness and truculence abroad, and financial imbecility and corruption at home; while America, which boasts of equality and freedom, does not understand that, with the single exception of Russia, there is no country where private right and public interests are more systematically outraged than in the United States. The ideal aristocracy, or government of the best, has in America been degraded into an actual government of the worst, in which the educated, the cultured, the honest, and even the wealthy, weigh as nothing in the balance against the scum of Europe which the Atlantic has washed up on the shores of the New World.

Whether the discovery of America by Columbus has been of advantage or loss to the so-called civilised peoples of the Old World would form an interesting thesis for discussion. When we remember the gentle and refined races of Mexico and Peru trampled beneath the gross feet of Pizarro, Cortes, and the Inquisition; or regard the savage picturesqueness of the Indian tribes that wandered over the North American continent, cruel, brutal, and happy, uninjured by and uninjuring Western culture, we cannot but look with some doubt and hesitation at America of today, the apotheosis of Philistinism, the perplexity and despair of statesmen, the Mecca to which turns every religious or social charlatan, where the only god worshipped is Mammon, and the highest education is the share list; where political life, which should be the breath of the nostrils of every freeman, is shunned by an honest man as the plague; where, to enrich jobbers and monopolists and contractors, a nation has emancipated its slaves and enslaved its freemen; where the people is gorged and drunk with materialism, and where wealth has become a curse instead of a blessing.

America is the country of disillusion and disappointment, in politics, literature, culture, and art; in its scenery, its cities, and its people. With some experience of every country in the civilised world, I can think of none except Russia in which I would not prefer to reside, in which life would not be more worth living, less sordid and mean and unlovely.

THE BIG THINGS OF AMERICA

AN ENGLISH CHARACTERISTIC, strongly developed and even grotesquely caricatured in America, is the love of big things which is, after all, a failing akin to virtue, and which will guide America into fair pastures when adversity and Mr. Matthew Arnold shall have chastened and purified Philistia. At present, Americans are satisfied with things because they are large; and if not large, they must have cost a great deal of money. One evening, at the Madison Square Theatre, an American observed to me, "That is the most expensive drop-scene in the world." It was a glorified curtain of embroidery, with a golden crane and a fairy landscape, and might justly have been claimed as the most beautiful drop-scene in the world; but this was not the primary idea in the Yankee mind. The two houses most beautiful architecturally in the Michigan Avenue at Chicago were shown to me as half-a-million-dollar houses. A horse is not praised for his points, but as having cost so many thousand dollars; a man, who certainly may possess no other virtue, as owning so many millions. The habit of making size a reason for admiration is less jarring to an educated taste than that of making money the standard of beauty and virtue.

Full in front of the White House at Washington, as a

warning to all future Presidents to avoid the penalties which
attach to patriotism, a column of white marble is slowly
rising to the memory of Washington. It is intended eventually to appear as an obelisk of six hundred feet, "the highest structure ever raised by man, excepting the Tower of
Babel." Whether the design, which would seem to have
been framed in the spirit which brought confusion on the
builders of its prototype, will ever be completed it is impossible to say. The cornerstone was laid thirty-five years
ago, and something more than half the destined height has
been already reached. Colonel Casey, in charge of the work,
promises its early completion; but if America continues to
depart from that standard of free and honest administration
which the high-minded, chivalrous, and clean-handed
founder of the Republic set up, it would seem that for very
shame the monument will be left unfinished, to symbolise
as the tower of a shot manufactory or a cotton-mill, the
triumph of industrial enterprise rather than of successful
patriotism. In no case will it possess any interest beyond its
size. Many nations have begged or stolen obelisks from
Egypt to decorate, with dubious taste, their capitals. Half
a dozen may be found in odd corners in Rome; London,
and Paris, and New York have each their trophy; and modern imitations have been raised in cemeteries and on battle-
fields in memory of those whom the affection of friends or
the gratitude of nations have not thought worth an original
design. But the obelisk is a monolithic feature in Egyptian
architecture proportional to and in harmony with surround-
ing buildings, and never placed by itself. On the banks of
the Potomac, and to the memory of the most distinguished
American, this gigantic obelisk, although embellished with
three large windows and a patent elevator for country
visitors, is incongruous and absurd. When the next saviour
of his country shall have liberated America from the tyranny
of rings and monopolists, as much heavier than that of

George III as were the scorpions of Rehoboam compared with the whips of his father, a grateful people must logically raise a pyramid, greater than that of Cheops, to his memory.

The only sight which, in American eyes, disputes the pre-eminence of the Chicago slaughter-yards is Niagara, and there may be some who would unhesitatingly assign it the palm. Its chief beauty consists in its being the largest waterfall in the world, with greater capacity than any other for producing by water-power those manufactured abominations which, as American fabrics or novelties, are gradually debasing the taste of the civilised world. Its one drawback is that the left bank of the Niagara river being English territory and the main body of the fall being situated therein, Americans are unable to claim a monopoly in this natural marvel for the States. It is fortunate for posterity that the Canadian English have control over the finer portion of the Niagara scenery, as this alone protects it from such ruin as vulgarity and greed combined can bring on nature. On a small island, midway across the American fall, the authorities of the State of New York—whose names I would hand down to eternal infamy were I not convinced that, being New York officials, they are already as infamous as it is possible for officials to be—have permitted the erection of a papermill, hideous in its architectural deformity, and blighting with a curse the beauty of Niagara. It is not possible to describe the effect that this building has upon a sensitive visitor. The outrage on good taste is so extreme, and the state of nervous irritation induced by the unconscious vandalism of the American people is so acute, that I am disposed to consider a visit to Niagara a source of more pain than pleasure. This mill is the outward and visible sign, blazoned voluntarily to the world, of American Philistinism. The Boston journals may announce the advent of the millennium of good taste; Messrs. James and Howells and White may set forth their poor platitudes to prove the cultured and refined sentiments of their countrymen; but the Niagara papermill raises its tall chimney high above the everlasting roar of the torrent to give them all the lie.

Nor is this the only outrage on good taste at Niagara. The torture of the paper mill ceases with the daylight, and its presence may be forgotten. The traveller then, in frantic search for an emotion, may hope to wander alone to the edge of the avalanche of waters, and there commune with such soul as waiters, rival touts, and coachmen may have allowed him to retain. In the solemn moonlight the wonderful pageant seems more weird and mysterious than ever. But what is this new and unknown effect of the moonbeams? Is it—yes, it is—the coloured limelight, red, green, and blue, thrown upon the hoary fleece of Niagara by American cockneys! In sheer disgust and exasperation the traveller turns his back on the insult and retires sulkily to bed. I remember, some years ago, arriving at Naples in the evening with two ladies who had never seen Vesuvius, and, as the volcano was in eruption, I anticipated great pleasure in showing them the glorious spectacle. Darkness fell, and the red lines of the molten rivers of lava burnt into sight, and the sullen clouds above the crater turned to crimson. But suddenly a long line of bright points of light appeared from the observatory along the crest of the mountain. These were lamps of electric light, which the Neopolitan municipality, who would make a profit out of the Day of Judgment if it were possible, had set up to guide visitors along a wire tramway to the summit. If I remember rightly, the work was afterwards destroyed by the lava, and I sincerely trust its promoters and constructors were burnt with it. But the disgust with which I saw those electric lights degrading the most majestic of nature's phenomena to the level of Cremorne or Mabille was repeated in my heart as I looked upon the limelights at Niagara.

The manner in which Americans permit their most

beautiful scenery to be spoiled by the rapacity of vulgar advertisers, notifying their respective swindles on rocks and stones and trees, or by the erection of the most commonplace or ugly buildings in most incongruous situations, is hardly to be explained except on the supposition that the long and absorbed contemplation of the dollar has destroyed any popular appreciation of natural beauty. The question is one of great psychological interest, and some obscurity, for the deepest love of nature and the fullest delight in natural beauty fill the works of such American poets as Bryant and Longfellow, and dignify the obscene ravings of Walt Whitman. Yet on what reasonable ground can we account for the Niagara paper mill? It is not that the love of freedom in the States is so keen that the individual right of the manufacturer to erect his building over the waterfall cannot be safely disputed. The whole argument of this book is to show that such cannot be the explanation, since individual right is not regarded in America when opposed to the wishes or prejudices of the majority, or of that minority which, by impudence and audacity, has usurped the prerogatives of the majority. Democracy is everywhere tyranny; in the same sense and only differing in degree from that socialistic tyranny which Mr. Herbert Spencer has made the text of his latest warning. If the New York people thought the Niagara paper-mill the outrage on decency which it is, they would sweep it away without a thought of the individual rights which they well know have been acquired by bribing the State officials. It would almost seem that the sense of beauty was so faint in Americans that the desecration of beautiful scenery excited no sensation of annoyance in their minds.

. . . . .

THERE IS ONE LEGACY of the [civil] war, in the negro vote, which will only become more intolerable by the lapse of time, for the reason that the African race is extremely prolific, and, under existing conditions, may be expected to increase more rapidly than any other element of the heterogeneous mass of American citizens. The position of the negro is anomalous and embarrassing. Without referring to the multiplied researches of the Anthropological Society on the capacity of the African races, it may generally be asserted that the negro is as fit for the franchise as the monkey he closely resembles. He has one or two good qualities and many bad ones. He makes a very good waiter if in firm hands, but is usually spoilt by American familiarity, which in his small mind breeds contempt, so that the head waiter at a restaurant gives himself more airs than an English duke. For any occupation requiring higher intellectual powers than blacking boots or waiting at table the vast majority of negroes are unfit. A few of the best struggle into the professions and there fail, though I remember at Washington some cases of partial success; while one coloured female lawyer of much vivacity roundly declared, during the recent civil rights discussion, that the negroes were the superior race in America. Since the war they have largely increased, and now number some six millions of uneducated and unimprovable persons, as useless for the purposes of civilisation as if they were still wandering naked through the African jungle. Slavery is an accursed thing, but it is rather as degrading the higher race of slaveholders than as brutalising the slaves that it must be condemned. There is no more natural equality among races than individuals, and imperial peoples have to use up some of the weaker and poorer in their political manufactories. The Nemesis of slavery was not exhausted in the civil war. Its evil fruits are still to be gathered by the American people, who have in their midst this ever-growing mass of savagery which they hate and despise, and to which they were compelled to give the rights of citizenship. For although it sounds well to speak of the war as the protest of the North against slavery, the emancipation of the slaves was never intended by the Americans. They then cared for the negroes no more than now, when they would be delighted to carry the whole race to the middle of the Atlantic and sink them there. The North was driven into war, much against its will, by the threats, the insults, and the hostile acts of the South. Abraham Lincoln, in his inaugural address as President, repeated and emphasised his former declaration that "he had no purpose, directly or indirectly, to interfere with the institution of slavery in the States where it existed." And when the war was over and the victory won, he was far too shrewd to desire to admit the negroes to the franchise. This fatal measure was taken in sheer self-defence to swamp the Southern vote, which would otherwise have restored the intolerable situation previous to the war. Since that day the miserable negro has been the tool and sport of every party; now petted, now kicked; his strong limbs and feeble brain at the service of any demagogue who might best know how to tickle his vanity and arouse his passions. If he were other than himself he would be a fit object for compassion; but he is of too low a type to be unhappy, and is probably the only man who laughs today in America.

Few days pass without the newspapers recording lynchings in Southern or Western states, generally with indifference, often with approval. In October last, within two or three days, I noted several such cases which attracted no particular attention. In one, in North Carolina, a negro, in a quarrel with a white man named Redmond, shot him dead. Campbell, the negro, was arrested. The same night a band of thirty masked men took him from the jail and hanged him to a tree, doing their work so quickly, and it may be supposed so entirely with the connivance and consent of the jail officials, that the occurrence was not known till Campbell's body was found dangling from the tree at daylight.

"Everything" (says naively the local newspaper) "is quiet now." A day or two before, what the journals call "an effective but unusual punishment" was inflicted upon a negro of the name of Lewis Wood, who had been convicted of outraging a young coloured girl. The mob waited at the Edgerly station for the train conveying the prisoner, dragged him a short distance from the line, chained him to a tree, covered him with pine knots and chips, and burnt him to death. About the same day at Lafayette, Indiana, an old man named Jacob Nell, who had confessed to the murder of a young girl, Ada Atkinson, was with difficulty saved from the mob. The crime seemed to me so motiveless that, in England, a verdict of acquittal on the ground of insanity would have been probably given: but the mob were excited and demanded blood. The local paper observed calmly that the mob appearing to have no leader, "it was probable that the law would be allowed to take its course." Whether the old maniac was torn to pieces or hung I cannot say. I did not follow his fortunes further. Such cases are too common in America to excite more than a passing interest. The inveterate dislike to the negro on the part of the white population in the Southern states is shown very clearly in these outrages. The assault or the manslaughter committed by a white man is often passed over altogether by the community. The unfortunate negro, whose passions are strong and uncontrolled by education or self-respect, has no such immunity, and is ruthlessly strung up by Judge Lynch, or sometimes, as we have seen, burnt alive.

As these lines are passing through the press, I notice in the American telegraphic intelligence the following announcement:—"A negro who had brutally murdered a woman near Austin, Texas, was chased and captured. He was taken to the scene of the crime by a lynching party of one hundred, and confessed his guilt. He was then roasted to death." The confession extorted under such circumstances

was probably worth neither more nor less than those wrung
from the victims of the Inquisition previous to an *auto-da-fe*.

"It will be noticed," writes the New York *Tribune*,
"that the privilege of becoming furious because one of
their race has been killed by one of the other is strictly
reserved to the whites. The negroes are expected to be
serene, if not grateful, when negroes are killed by
whites."

Last September I was in Cheyenne, Wyoming, a day or
two after a lynching had occurred, and I inquired into its
circumstances from some of the townsmen who had assisted
at the ceremony. So far as I remember, the victim was
accused of having murdered a man whom he had met camp-
ing in the prairie, who had invited him to share his meal,
and whom, when sleeping, he killed and robbed. The crime
was an atrocious one, though whether the accused were
guilty can be never known, for, having been arrested, he
was lodged in the lockup, whence the good citizens, fearing
that he might escape punishment, through the uncertainty
of the law, incontinently took him, without any resistance
on the part of the officials, and hanged him to a telegraph
pole in the principal street. One of my informants was a
young man employed in a large dry-goods store, who as-
sured me that, although he took his gun, he only attended
the execution in the character of a spectator. The self-
constituted judges and executioners were, he said, the most
respectable inhabitants of the town, shopkeepers and merchants. The hangman was a telephone clerk, and as,
mounted on a ladder, he drew the rope, already round the
victim's neck, to the top of the pole, he put the end to his
ear and shouted "Hullo," in telephonic fashion, attracting
the attention of the person at the other end of the line.
This brutal witticism was received with great laughter by
the crowd, though it may have been less appreciated by the

condemned, who was straightway launched into eternity. No one of the Cheyenne people to whom I spoke seemed in any way ashamed of the occurrence. The murderer, they said, would have escaped punishment if he had been sent for trial, and their procedure, if less regular, was more certain and just than that of the courts. Now we may allow, for the sake of argument, that this hanged man was guilty, though of this there can exist no legal proof; and, further, that his execution was due to the fear that, if regularly tried, he would escape proper punishment. Yet to a person who has been privileged to live in a civilised country, where the passions of the mob are held in control by the firm and impartial administration of the law, the respectable citizens of Cheyenne, which is a wealthy, prosperous town, with churches, banks, hotels, and daily newspapers, seem little removed from savages. If the people of Wyoming or any other state desire a pure administration of justice, they can obtain it. The remedy is in their own hands. The judges are not appointed by the Government, but elected by themselves: the juries who acquit murderers are their own friends and comrades, and the defeat of justice is due to their own low standard of public morality.

Hugo Munsterberg

The foreigner cannot see these charming American girls without a constant feeling that there is something unhealthy in their nervous make-up, an over-irritation, a pathological tension.

Hugo Munsterberg (1863–1916) was a professor of psychology at Harvard in the days before Freudian theories captured the discipline. Born and trained in Germany, Munsterberg wrote a number of books on the American character as he saw it evolve before and after the turn of the century.

The revolt of American women in the Gilded Age, foreigners remarked, was not merely aimed at *equality* of the sexes; it demanded feminine superiority in all things on heaven *and* earth. W. H. Dixon (*The New America*, 1878) believed the "Women's Party" a peculiarly American development, since it brought together the spiritual and the mundane. These women, Dixon said, do not want "either chivalry or courtesy"

Hugo Munsterberg, *American Traits* (Boston and New York, Houghton, Mifflin and Company, 1901), pp. 140–72.

from men: "They claim the sovereign rule." The rationale for this war begins with the first principle of physical superiority.

> Woman is the more perfect being, later in growth, finer in structure, grander in form, lighter in type . . . the one being allied to the cherub and seraph, the other to stallion and dog. What man is to the gorilla, woman is to man.

Females have more organs than man and "organs are the representatives of power." What are these additional "organs"? "Two magnificent sets of structure which concern the nourishing of life."

> Her bust has a nobler contour, her bosom a finer swell. Her voice is sweeter, her ear quicker. Her veins are of brighter blue, her skin is of purer white, her lips are of deeper red.

Her brain of course is larger, of higher quality. Nature works, it was claimed, in true Darwinian fashion, "through an ascending series," and woman is the step beyond man towards angelic life. "He is the lord of the earth, while she is a messenger from heaven." Women were the saving hope of a spiritual revival which could rescue civilization from Mammon. "He" must toil and save so that "she" may "dispense and enjoy," a higher intelligence turning his material gifts into use and beauty. . . . "One sex is the cultivator, the other a reconciler. . . . Man conquers the soil, Woman mediates with God." God always intended this to be. The Bible, written by males, distorts the authentic story of creation: "Peter and Paul put women under men." Feminine superiority was clearly established in all living things, "from the female mollusk to the New England lady."

Elizabeth Denton defended the claims of women back through the annals of history and into the arts, poetry and science. Shakespeare says nothing of woman "that is to her credit, or to his own"; Ophelia is drawn as a fool; and while Shake-

speare makes suitable amends with Portia, by characterizing her
as "sensible, courageous, brilliant and without vanity," Miss
Denton knew "a hundred American women who are better
than she." Even the great Darwin, who should have known
better, suggests that the rudimentary "mammae" are the ruins
of old organs in men. Actually, these "mammae" are "the
germs of new organs" which in time will permit man to come
into closer resemblance with "female functions." Science, too,
is wrong, like history and art. But what is science? "Just what
man knows—man, who knows nothing; and who is only a
grade higher in the scale of being than a chimpanzee."

The following chapter on women is famous for its reitera-
tion of the "nervous" theme regarding Americans in general,
and Munsterberg's worried predictions about the effeminisa-
tion of the culture.

———————◆———————

I TAKE FOR GRANTED that no American girl loses in attractive-
ness by passing through a college, or through other forms
of the higher and the highest education. But we have only
to look at the case from the other side, and we shall find
ourselves at once at the true source of the calamity. The
woman has not become less attractive as regards marriage;
but has not marriage become less attractive to the woman?
And long before the freshman year did not the outer influences begin to impel in that direction? Does it not begin
in every country school where the girls sit on the same bench
with the boys, and discover, a long, long time too early,
how stupid those boys are? Coeducation, on the whole unknown in Germany, has many desirable features—it
strengthens the girls; it refines the boys; it creates a comrade-
ship between the two sexes which decreases sexual tension

in the years of development; but these factors make, at the same time, for an indifference toward the other sex, toward a disillusionism, which must show in the end. The average German girl thinks, I am sorry to say, that she will marry any one who will not make her unhappy; the ideal German girl thinks that she will marry only the man who will certainly make her happy; the ideal American girl thinks that she can marry only the man without whom she will be unhappy, and the average American girl approaches this standpoint with an alarming rapidity. Now, is not the last a much more ideal point of view? Does it not indicate a much nobler type of woman—the one who will have no marriage but the most ideal one, as compared with the other, who in a romantic desire for marriage takes the first man who asks her? But in this connection, I do not wish to approve or to criticise; we may pospone that until we have gathered a few more facts and motives. Coeducation is only one; a whole corona of motives surrounds it.

Coeducation means only equality; but the so-called higher education for girls means, under the conditions of the American life of today, decidedly not the equality, but the superiority of women. In Germany, even the best educated woman—with the exception once more of the few rare and ambitious scholars—feels her education inferior to that of the young man of the same set, and thus inferior to the mental training of her probable husband. The foundations of his knowledge lie deeper, and the whole structure is built up in a more systematic way. This is true of every one who has passed through a gymnasium, and how much more is it true of those who have gone through the university! Law, medicine, divinity, engineering, and the academic studies of the prospective teacher are in Germany all based essentially upon a scholarly training, and are thus, first of all, factors of general education—powers to widen the horizon of the intellect. All this is less true in America: the lawyer, the physician, the teacher, the engineer, obtain excellent preparation for the profession; but in a lower degree his studies continue his general culture and education; and the elective system allows him to anticipate the professional training even in college. And, on the other side, as for the businessman who may have gone through college with a general education in view—how much, or, better, how little of his culture can be kept alive? Commerce and industry, finance and politics absorb him, and the beautiful college time becomes a dream; the intellectual energies, the factors of general culture, become rusty from disuse; while she, the fortunate college girl, remains in that atmosphere of mental interests and inspiration, where the power she has gained remains fresh through contact with books. The men read newspapers, and, after a while, just when the time for marriage approaches, she is his superior, through and through, in intellectual refinement and spiritual standards. And all this we claim in the case of the man who has had a college education; but the probability is very great that he has not had even that. The result is a marriage in which the woman looks down upon the culture of her husband; and, as the girl instinctively feels that it is torture to be the wife of a man whom she does not respect, she hesitates, and waits, and shrinks before the thought of entering upon a union that has so few charms.

And can we overlook another side of the delightful college time? No noise of the bustling world disturbed the peace of the college campus; no social distinctions influenced the ideal balance of moral and intellectual and aesthetic energies: it was an artificial world in which our young friends lived during the most beautiful years of their lives. Can we be surprised that they instinctively desire to live on in this peculiar setting of the stage, with all its Bengal lights and its self-centered interests? They feel almost unconsciously that all this changes when they marry, when they are mistresses of a household—a situation which, perhaps, means narrowness and social limitation. They feel that it would be like an awakening from a lofty dream. There is no need to awake; the life in the artificial setting of remote ideals can be continued, if they attach themselves, not to a husband and children, but to clubs and committees, to higher institutions and charity work, to art and literature; if they remain thus in a world where everything is so much more ideal than in that ungainly one in which children may have the whooping-cough. . . .

The college studies do not merely widen the horizon; they give to many a student a concrete scholarly interest, and that is, of course, still truer of the professional training. The woman who studies medicine or natural science, music or painting, perhaps even law or divinity, can we affront her with the suggestion, which would be an insult to the man, that all her work is so superficial that she will not care for its continuation as soon as she undertakes the duties of a married woman? Or ought we to imply that she is so conceited as to believe that she is able to do what no man would dare hope for himself; that is, to combine the professional duties of the man with the not less complex duties of the woman? She knows that the intensity of her special interest must suffer; that her work must become a superficial side-interest; that she has for it but rare leisure hours; and no one can blame her, however much she may love her own home, for loving still more the fascinating work for which she was trained.

All these tendencies are now psychologically reinforced by other factors which have nothing to do with the higher education as such, but are characteristic of the situation of the woman in general. The American girl, well or carelessly educated, lives in the midst of social enjoyments, of cultured interests, of flirtations, and or refinements—what has she to hope at all from the change which marriage brings?

Well, the one without whom her heart would break may have appeared—there is then no use of further discussion. But it is more probable that he has not appeared, while she, in the meanwhile, flirts with half a dozen men, of whom one is so congenial, and another such a brilliant wit, and the third such a promising and clever fellow; the fourth is rich, and the fifth she has known since her childhood, and the sixth, with the best chances, is such a dear, stupid little thing! What has she really to gain from a revolution of her individual fate? Is there anything open to her which was closed so far? . . .

But the American girl has not only no new powers to expect; she has in marriage a positive function before her, which she, again unlike her European sister, considers, on the whole, a burden—the care of the household. I do not mean that the German woman is enraptured with delight at the prospect of scrubbing a floor; and I know, of course, how many American women are model housekeepers, how the farmers' wives, especially, have their pride in it, and how often spoiled girls heroically undertake housekeeping with narrow means, and that, too, much more often than in Germany, without the help of servants. And yet, there remains a difference of general attitude which the social psychologist cannot overlook. The whole atmosphere is here filled with the conscious or unconscious theory that housework is somewhat commonplace, a sort of necessary evil which ought to be reduced to a minimum.

The general American tendency to consider housework as a kind of necessary evil, which as such cannot appeal to those who have free choice, is not less evident in the lower strata of the community. The conviction of every American girl that it is dignified to work in the mill, but undignified to be a cook in any other family, would never have reached its present intensity if an anti-domestic feeling were not in the background. Exactly the same tendency appears, therefore, when work for the parents is in question. The laborer's daughter has, of course, not such a complete theory as the banker's daughter; but that it is dull to sit in the kitchen and look after the little sister, she too knows. In consequence, she also rushes to the outside life as saleswoman, as industrial laborer, as office worker: it is so exciting and interesting; it is the richer life. The study of the special cases shows, of course, that there are innumerable factors involved; but if we seek for the most striking features of woman's work, here and abroad, from a more general survey of the subject, it would seem that the aim of the German woman is to further the interests of the household, and that of the American woman to escape from the household. . . .

I have mentioned merely mental factors which are to be taken into account in their subconscious cooperation against family life; but the mental strain and excitement to which young girls are subjected, and the lack of social restraint, the constant hurry, and, above all, the intellectual over-tension must influence the nervous system, and the nervous system must influence the whole organization of that sex which nature, after all, has made the weaker one. The foreigner cannot see these charming American girls without a constant feeling that there is something unhealthy in their nervous make-up, an over-irritation, a pathological tension, not desirable for the woman who is preparing herself to be the mother of healthy children. The vital statistics tell the whole story. The census of 1890 showed that there were born per thousand of the whole population in Prussia 36.6, in Massachusetts 21.5; and this diminished birth rate is still much lower in the native families here than in those of foreign birth—the Irish or Swedish or German.

If we will consider this social background, this general social situation, we shall perhaps see the problem of higher education from another point of view; we shall begin to feel that under these conditions, which in themselves work so clearly against the home, it must be doubly dangerous to reinforce those tendencies in woman's higher education which, as such, impel toward a celibacy of spirit; and we foreigners ask ourselves then instinctively, "Is the woman question really solved here in the most ideal way?"

The American system injures the national organism, not only because it antagonizes the family life, and thus diminishes the chances for the future bearers of the national civilization, but it has, secondly, the tendency to feminise the whole higher culture, and thus to injure the national civilization itself.

It is not true that men and women can do the same work in every line. Earnestness certainly the women have. However large the number of those who may meet their public duties in a spirit of sport or amusement or ennui, the majority take these duties seriously; and the college girl especially comes home with a large amount of earnestness in the cause of reform and of the higher functions of the national life. The only misfortune is that earnestness alone is not physical energy, that good will is not force, that devotion is not power. But her lack of physical power and strength would be less dangerous to the undertaking if her intellectual ability were equal to that of the man. But here the social psychologist can feel no shadow of a doubt that neither coeducation nor the equality of opportunities has done anything to eliminate those characteristic features of the female mind which are well known the world over, and which it is our blessing not to have lost. The laws of nature are stronger than the theories of men.

To express the matter in a psychological formula, on which the observations of all times and all nations have agreed: in the female mind the contents of consciousness have the tendency to fuse into a unity, while they remain separated in the man's mind. Both tendencies have their merits and their defects; but, above all, they are different, and make women superior in some functions, and man superior in some others. The immediate outcome of that feminine mental type is woman's tact and aesthetic feeling, her instinctive insight, her enthusiasm, her sympathy, her natural wisdom and morality; but, on the other side, also, her lack of clearness and logical consistency, her tendency to hasty generalization, her mixing of principles, her undervaluation of the abstract and of the absent, her lack of deliberation, her readiness to follow her feelings and emotions. Even these defects can beautify the private life, can make our social surroundings attractive, and soften and complete the strenuous, earnest, and consistent public activity of the man; but they do not give the power to meet these public duties without man's harder logic. If the whole national civilization should receive the feminine stamp, it would become powerless and without decisive influence on the world's progress. . . .

If we keep up an artificial equality through the higher development of the present day, American intellectual work will be kept down by the women, and will never become a world power. . . .

That such effemination makes alarming progress is quickly seen if we watch the development of the teacher's profession. I have seldom the honor of agreeing with the pedagogical scholars of this country, but, on this point, it seems to me, we are all of the same opinion: the disappearance of the man from the classroom, not only of the lower schools, but even of the high schools, is distinctly alarming. The primary school is today absolutely monopolized by woman teachers, and in the high school they have the overwhelming majority. The reason for this is clear: since the woman does not have to support a family, she can work for a smaller salary, and thus, as in the mills the men tend more and more toward the places for which women are not strong enough, in the schools, too, female competition

must, if no halt is called, bring down salaries to a point
from which the supporter of the family must retreat. It
would be, of course, in both cases better if the earnings were
larger, and more men were thus enabled to support families,
while in the schoolroom, as in the mill, the female competitor brings the earnings down to a point where the man
is too poor to marry her—a most regrettable state of affairs. But the economic side is here not so important as the
effect on civilization. Even granting, what I am not at all
ready to grant, that woman's work, preferred because it is
cheaper to the community, is just as good as man's work,
can it be without danger that the male youth of this country, up to the eighteenth year, is educated by unmarried
women? Is it a point to be discussed at all that "nascent
manhood requires for right development manly inspiration,
direction, and control"? Where will this end? That very
soon no male schoolteacher of good quality will survive is
certain, but there is no reason to expect that it will stop
there. We have already today more than sixty per cent of
girls among the upper high school classes, and this dis-
proportion must increase. Must we not expect that in the
same way in which the last thirty years have handed the
teacher's profession over to the women, the next thirty
years will put the ministry, the medical calling, and, finally
the bar, also into her control? To say that this is not to
be feared because it has never happened anywhere before
is no longer an argument, because this development of our
schools is also new in the history of civilization. There was
never before a nation that gave the education of the young
into the hands of the lowest bidder.

We know that in Paradise, Eve followed the seducing
voice of the serpent, and ate the fruit from the tree of
knowledge, and gave of it unto Adam. The college-bred
Eve has no smaller longing for the apple of knowledge; but
the serpent has become modern, and his advice has grown

more serpent-like than ever: "Eat of the apple, but give not unto Adam thereof." The Bible tells us that when they both ate, they were cast out from Paradise, but saved the race. However it may be with the modern paradise, the race will be saved only on the condition that Adam receive his share of the fruit. Listen not to the serpent, but divide the apple!

Maxim Gorky

*Everywhere is toil, everything is caught up
in its whirlwind, everybody obeys the will
of some mysterious power hostile to man and
to nature. A machine, a cold, unseen, unreasoning machine, in which man is but an
insignificant screw!*

The failure of the Russian Revolution of 1905 sent many people
into exile and frustration. Maxim Gorky (1868–1936), a famous
writer with ties to some of the more extreme revolutionaries,
wrote of the pain he suffered in being pushed out of his native
land. "If a tooth could feel after being knocked out, it would
probably feel as lonely as I did. . . . 'Everything is lost,' people
said, 'they have crushed, annihilated, exiled, imprisoned everybody!'. . . . I often felt as if a pestilential dust were blowing
from Russia." The winds of expulsion drew him to Italy and
then, in 1906, to America. "The land of Liberty!" he said to
himself as his boat entered New York harbor, gliding past the
great Statue of his dreams. Once ashore, he awoke to a nightmare.

Maxim Gorky, "The City of Mammon," *Appleton's Magazine*,
(New York), Volume 8 (1906), pp. 177–82.

Gorky acquired world fame before the turn of the century with his brilliant short stories and his play *The Lower Depths.* A socialist committed to the revolutionary overthrow of the Tsar and autocracy, Gorky became a close friend of Lenin and other Bolsheviks, helping the party with funds and prestige in the desperate years before 1917. Lenin tolerated certain "ideological deviations" in Gorky because of personal affection and respect for his work. After the Revolution, Gorky interceded with Lenin to save various intellectuals from the executioners in the Bolshevik secret police. But his quarrels with the Soviet regime continued and in 1921 he exiled himself, this time from Soviet Russia, and lived in Italy until 1933 when he returned home. His great friend Lenin was now dead and in his place was Stalin, who was once described to Gorky by Lenin in 1913 as "a wonderful Georgian" and an expert on the "nationalities question." Again during the purges of the 30's, as he had done in days of 1917, Gorky tried to save writers and friends from prison and death. Stalin warned him that the Revolution was quite prepared to sacrifice its "great names," which included, no doubt, Gorky himself. But he continued to oppose Stalin's harshness and in 1936 the "wonderful Georgian" ordered him poisoned to death.

THE CITY OF MAMMON
MY IMPRESSIONS OF AMERICA

A GRAY MIST hung over land and sea, and a fine rain shivered down upon the somber buildings of the city and the turbid waters of the bay. The emigrants gathered to one side of the steamer. They looked about silently and serious, with eager eyes in which gleamed hope and fear, terror and joy.

"Who is this?" asked a Polish girl in a tone of amazement, pointing to the Statue of Liberty. Some one from
the crowd answered briefly: "The American Goddess."

I looked at this goddess with the feelings of an idolater,
and recalled to mind the heroic times of the United States
—the six years' War of Independence, and that bloody
struggle between the North and the South which the
Americans formerly used to call "The War for the Abolition of Slavery." Before my memory flashed the brilliant
names of Thomas Jefferson and of Grant. I seemed to hear
again the song of John Brown, the hero, and see the faces
of Bret Harte, Longfellow, Edgar Allan Poe, Walt Whitman, and all the other stars on the proud American flag.

Here then is the land about which tens of millions of
people of the Old World dream as of the Promised Land.
"The Land of liberty!" I repeated to myself, not noticing
on that glorious day the green rust on the dark bronze.

I knew even then that "The War for the Abolition of
Slavery" is now called in America "The War for the Pre-
servation of the Union." But I did not know that in this
change of words was hidden a deep meaning, that the
passionate idealism of the young democracy had also become covered with rust, like the bronze statue, eating away
the soul with the corrosive of commercialism. The senseless
craving for money, and the shameful craving for the power
that money gives, is a disease from which people suffer
everywhere. But I did not realize that this dread disease
had assumed such proportions in America.

The tempestuous turmoil of life on the water at the
foot of the Statue of Liberty, and in the city on the shore,
staggers the mind, and fills one with a sense of impotence.
Everywhere, like antediluvian monsters, huge, heavy steam-
ers plow the waters of the ocean, little boats and cutters
scurry about like hungry birds of prey. The iron seems
endowed with nerves, life and consciousness. The sirens

roar as if with voices of the mythic giants, the angry mouths send forth their shrill whistles that lose themselves in the fog, anchor chains rattle, the waves splash.

And it seems as if all the iron, all the stones, the wood and water, and even the people themselves are full of protest against this life in the fog, this life devoid of sun, song, and joy, this life in the captivity of hard toil. Everywhere is toil, everything is caught up in its whirlwind, everybody obeys the will of some mysterious power hostile to man and to nature. A machine, a cold, unseen, unreasoning machine, in which man is but an insignificant screw!

I love energy. I adore it. But not when men expend this creative force of theirs for their own destruction. There is too much labor and effort, and no life in all this chaos, in all this bustle for the sake of a piece of bread. Everywhere we see around us the work of the mind which has made of human life a sort of hell, a senseless treadmill of labor, but nowhere do we feel the beauty of free creation, the disinterested work of the spirit which beautifies life with imperishable flowers of life-giving cheer.

Far out on the shore, silent and dark "skyscrapers" are outlined against the fog. Rectangular, with no desire to be beautiful, these dull, heavy piles rise up into the sky, stern, cheerless, and morose. In the windows of these prisons there are no flowers, and no children are anywhere seen. Straight, uniform, dead lines without grace of outline or harmony, only an air of cold and haughty presumption imparted to them by their prodigiousness, their monstrous height. But in this height no freedom dwells. These structures elevate the price of land to heights as lofty as their tops, but debase the taste to depths as low as their foundations. It is always so. In great houses dwell small people.

From afar the city looks like a huge jaw with black, uneven teeth. It belches forth clouds of smoke into the sky, and sniffs like a glutton suffering from overcorpulency.

When you enter it you feel that you have fallen into a stomach of brick and iron which swallows up millions of people, and churns, grinds, and digests them. The streets seem like so many hungry throats, through which pass, into some unseen depth, black pieces of food—living human beings. Everywhere, over your head, under your feet, and at your sides is iron, living iron emitting horrible noises. Called to life by the power of gold, inspirited by it, it envelops man in its cobweb, deafening him, sucking his life blood, deadening his mind.

The horns and automobiles shout aloud like some giant ducks, the electricity sends forth its surly noises, and everywhere the stifling air of the streets is penetrated and soaked with thousands of deafening sounds, like a sponge with water. It trembles, wavers, and blows into one's nostrils its strong, greasy odors. It is a poisoned atmosphere. It suffers, and it groans with its suffering.

People walk along the pavements. They push hurriedly forward, all hastily driven by the same force that enslaves them. But their faces are calm, their hearts do not feel the misfortune of being slaves; indeed, by a tragic self-conceit, they yet feel themselves its masters. In their eyes gleams a consciousness of independence, but they do not know it is but the sorry independence of the ax in the hands of the woodman, of the hammer in the hands of the blacksmith. This liberty is the tool in the hands of the Yellow Devil—Gold. Inner freedom, freedom of the heart and soul, is not seen in their energetic countenances. This energy without liberty is like the glitter of a new knife which has not yet had time to be dulled, it is like the gloss of a new rope.

It is the first time that I have seen such a huge city monster; nowhere have the people appeared to me so unfortunate, so thoroughly enslaved to life, as in New York. And furthermore, nowhere have I seen them so tragicomically self-satisfied as in this huge phantasmagoria of stone, iron, and glass, this product of the sick and wasted imagination of Mercury and Pluto. And looking upon this life, I began to think that in the hand of the statue of Bartholdi there blazes not the torch of liberty, but the dollar.

The large number of monuments in the city parks testifies to the pride which its inhabitants take in their great men. But it would be well from time to time to clean the dust and dirt from the faces of those heroes whose hearts and eyes burned so glowingly with love for their people. These statues covered with a veil of dirt involuntarily force one to put a low estimate upon the gratitude felt by the Americans toward all those who lived and died for the good of their country. And they lose themselves in the network of the many stoned buildings. The great men seem like dwarfs in front of the walls of the ten-story structures. The mammoth fortunes of Morgan and Rockefeller wipe off from memory the significance of the creators of liberty— Lincoln and Washington. Grant's tomb is the only monument of which New York can be proud, and that, too, only because it has not been placed in the dirty heart of the city.

"This is a new library they are building," said someone to me, pointing to an unfinished structure surrounded by a park. And he added importantly: "It will cost two million dollars! The shelves will measure one hundred and fifty miles."

Up to that time I had thought that the value of a library is not in the building itself, but in the books, just as the worth of a man is in his soul, not in his clothes. Nor did I ever go into raptures over the length of the shelves, preferring always the quality of books to their quantity. By quality I understand (I make this remark for the benefit of the Americans) not the price of the binding, nor the durability of the paper, but the value of the ideas, the beauty of the language, the strength of the imagination, and so forth.

Another gentleman told me, as he pointed out a painting to me: "It is worth five hundred dollars."

I had to listen very frequently to such sorry and superficial appraisement of objects, the price of which cannot be determined by the number of dollars. Productions of art are bought for money, just as bread, but their value is always higher than what is paid for them in coin. I meet here very few people who have a clear conception of the intrinsic worth of art, its religious significance, the power of its influence upon life, and its indispensableness to mankind.

To live means to live beautifully, bravely, and with all the power of the soul. To live means to embrace with our minds the whole universe, to mingle our thoughts with all the secrets of existence, and to do all that is possible in order to make life around us more beautiful, more varied, freer and brighter.

It seems to me that what is superlatively lacking to America is a desire for beauty, a thirst for those pleasures which it alone can give to the mind and to the heart. Our earth is the heart of the universe, our art the heart of the earth. The stronger it beats, the more beautiful is life. In America the heart beats feebly.

I was both surprised and pained to find that in America the theaters were in the hands of a trust, and that the men of the trust, being the possessors, had also become the dictators in matters of the drama. This evidently explains the fact that a country which has excellent novelists has not produced a single eminent dramatist.

To turn art into a means of profit is, under all circumstances, a serious misdemeanor, but in this particular case it is positive crime, because it offers violence to the author's person and adulterates art. If the law provides punishments for the adulteration of food, it ought to deal unmercifully with those who adulterate the people's spiritual food.

The theater is called the people's school; it teaches us to feel and to think. It has its origin in the same source as the church, but it has always served the people more sincerely and truly than the church. While the government has been able to make the church subserve its own interests, it has never been able to enslave the theater. "The Sunken Bell" of Hauptmann is a liturgy of beauty and of thought, as are many of the plays of Ibsen, Shakespeare, and Aeschylus. The exploitation of the theater by capital ought not to be permitted by people who are interested in the development of the spiritual forces of the country.

But perhaps the Americans think that they are cultured enough? If so, they are easily in error. In Russia such an attitude is observed among the students in the fifth class of the gymnasium, who, having learned to smoke tobacco, and read over two or three good books, imagine themselves to be Spinozas.

A twelve-story building and a Sunday newspaper weighing ten pounds are certainly great. It is but hollow grandeur, however, the vast number of people in the building and the large array of advertisements in the paper notwithstanding. Without ideas, there can be no culture.

The first evidence of the absence of culture in the American is the interest he takes in all stories and spectacles of cruelty. To a cultured man, a humanist, blood is loathsome. Murder by execution and other abominations of a like character arouse his disgust. In America such things call forth only curiosity. The newspapers are filled with detailed descriptions of murders and all kinds of horrors. The tone of the description is cold, the hard tone of an attentive observer. It is evident that the aim is to tickle the weary nerves of the reader with sharp, pungent details of crime, and no attempt is ever made to explain the social basis of the facts.

To no one seems to occur the simple thought that a nation is a family. And if some of its members are criminals, it only signifies that the system of bringing up people in that family is badly managed. Cruelty is a disease; interest manifested in it is also an unhealthy symptom. The more that interest is developed, the more crime will develop.

I will not dwell on the question of the attitude of the white man toward the negro. But it is very characteristic of the American psychology that Booker T. Washington preaches the following sermon to his race:

"You ought to be as rich and as clean outwardly as the whites; only then will they recognize you as their equals." This, in fact, is the substance of his teachings to his people.

Having a dollar in one's pocket, wearing a frock coat, cleaning the teeth every day, and using soap—all this is still not quite sufficient to make a cultured man. Ideas are wanted also. Respect for one's neighbor is necessary, no matter what the color of his skin may be; and a whole lot of such trifles without which the difference between a human being in a frock coat and an animal with his woolly skin is difficult to discern. But in America they only think of how to make money. Poor country, whose people are occupied only with the thought of how to get rich!

I am never in the least dazzled by the amount of money a man possesses; but his lack of honor, of love for his country, and of concern for its welfare always fills me with sadness. A man milking his country like a cow, or battening on it like a parasite, is a sorry sort of inspiration. How pitiful that America, which they say has full political liberty, is utterly wanting in liberty of spirit! When you see with what profound interest and idolatry the millionaires are regarded here, you involuntarily begin to suspect the democracy of the country. Democracy—and so many kings. Democracy and a "High Society." All this is strange and incomprehensible.

All the numerous trusts and syndicates, developing with a rapidity and energy possible only in America, will ultimately call forth to life its enemy, revolutionary socialism, which, in turn, will develop as rapidly and as energetically.

But while the process of swallowing up individuals by capital, and of the organization of the masses is going on, capitalism will spoil many stomachs and heads, many hearts and minds.

Speaking of the national spirit, I must also speak of the morality of the nation. But on that subject I have nothing interesting to say. That side of life has always been a poser to me. I cannot understand it; and when people speak seriously about it I cannot help but smile. At best, a moralist to me is a man at whom I wink from the corner of my eye, and drawing him aside whisper in his ear:

"Ah, you rascal! It isn't that I am a skeptic, but I know the world, I know it to my sorrow."

The most desperate moralist I have come across was my grandfather. He knew all the roads to heaven and constantly preached about them to everyone who fell into his hands. He alone knew the truth, and he zealously knocked it into the heads of the members of his family with whatever he happened to get ahold of. He knew to a dot everything that God wanted, and he used to teach even the dogs and cats how to conduct themselves in order to attain eternal happiness. But, with all that, he was greedy and malicious, he lied constantly, was a usurer, and with the cruelty of a coward—a trait common to each and every moralist—he beat his domestics, on every spare and unsuitable occasion, with whatsoever and howsoever he desired.

I tried to influence my grandfather, wishing to make him milder. Once I threw the old man out of the window, another time I struck him with a looking-glass. The window and the looking-glass broke, but Grandpa did not get any better. He died a moralist. Since that time I regard all discourses on morality as a useless waste of time. And, moreover, being from my youth up a professional sinner, like all honest writers, what can I say about morality?

Morality seems to me like a secret vessel tightly cov-

ered with a heavy lid of bias and prejudice.* I think that in
that vessel are concealed the best recipes for a pure and
ethical life, the shortest and surest road to eternal happiness. But beside that vessel, as guardians of its purity, people
stand always who do not inspire my confidence, although
they arouse my envy by their flowery appearance. They
are such smug, round, lardy creatures, so well satisfied with
themselves, and standing so firmly on their feet, like veri-
table mileposts pointing the way to the salvation of the
soul. However, there is nothing wooden about them except their hearts. They are as elastic as the springs in a
sumptuous equipage, as the tires of a high-priced automobile.

I wish it to be understood that in thus speaking of
moralists I do not mean those who think, but only those
who judge. Emerson was a moralist, but I cannot imagine a
man who, having read Emerson, will not have his mind
cleared of the dust and dirt of worldly prejudices. Carlyle,
Ruskin, Pascal—their names are many, and the books of
each of these work upon the heart like a good brush. But
there are people who, being born scoundrels, act as if they
were the world's attorneys.

Man is by nature curious. I have more than once lifted
the lid of the moral vessel, and every time there issued from
it such a rank, stifling smell of lies and hypocrisy, cowardice
and wickedness, as was quite beyond the power of my nostrils to endure.

I am willing to think that the Americans are the best
moralists in the world, and that even my grandpa was a
child in comparison. I admit that nowhere else in the world

* [Gorky was attacked in the American press for bringing his
mistress with him. "Gorky Brings Actress Here as 'Mme. Gorky,' "
a headline ran. Mark Twain accused him of violating the "customs"
of America, thereby tarnishing the cause of all revolutionary opponents of Russian despotism. "The man might just as well have
appeared in public in his shirt-tail," Twain remarked. GES]

are there to be found such stern priests of ethics and morality, and, therefore, I leave them alone. But a word about
the practical side. America prides itself on its morals, and
occasionally constitutes itself as judge, evidently presuming
that it has worked out in its social relations a system of conduct worthy of imitation. I believe this is a mistake.

The Americans run the risk of making themselves ridiculous if they begin to pride themselves on their society.
There is nothing whatever original about it; the depravity
of the "higher classes of society" is a common thing in
Europe. If the Americans permit the development of a
"high society" in their country, there is nothing remarkable
in the fact that depravity also grows apace. And that no
week passes without some loud scandal in this "high society" is no cause for pride in the originality of American
morals. You can find all these things in Europe also. There
is perhaps less hypocrisy in these matters on the other side
of the Atlantic, but the depravity exists all the same, and
to scarcely a lesser degree. These are the common morals
of the representatives of the "high society," a cosmopolitan
race, which, with the same zeal, defiles the earth at all its
points.

I must mention the fact that in America they steal
money very frequently, and lots of it. This, of course, is
but natural. Where there is a great deal of money there
are a great many thieves. To imagine a thief without money
is as difficult as to imagine an honest man with money. But
that again is a phenomenon common to all countries.

But enough! It is an unpleasant subject, and has not
Edgar Allan Poe said once, "Keep telling a thief that he is
an honest man, and he will justify your opinion about him."

I put Poe's statement to the test, by taking a man
strongly persuaded of his honesty and convincing him of
the opposite. Results proved that the great fact was always
right. Hence I infer that we must treat people mildly and

gently. It is not important how they treat me, but how I treat them. The individual elevates society, the individual corrupts it.

You think this is a paradox? No, it is the truth.

A magnificent Broadway, but a horrible East Side! What an irreconcilable contradiction, what a tragedy! The street of wealth must perforce give rise to harsh and stern laws devised by the financial aristocracy, by the slaves of the Yellow Devil, for a war upon poverty and the Whitechapel of New York. The poverty and the vice of the East Side must perforce breed anarchy. I do not speak of a theory; I speak of the development of envy, malice, and vengeance, of that, in a word, which degrades man to the level of an antisocial being. These two irreconcilable currents, the psychology of the rich and the feeling of the poor, threaten a clash which will lead to a whole series of tragedies and catastrophes.

America is possessed of a great store of energy, and therefore everything in it, the good and the bad, develops with greater rapidity than anywhere else. But the growth of that anarchism of which I am speaking precedes the development of a socialism. Socialism is a stage of culture, a civilized tendency. It is the religion of the future, which will free the whole world from poverty and from the gross rule of wealth. To be rightly understood, it requires the close application of the mind, and a general, harmonious development of all the spiritual forces in man. Anarchy is a social disease. It is the poison produced in the social organism by the lack of healthy nourishment for his body and soul. The growth of anarchism requires no intellectual basis; it is the work of the instinct, the soil on which it thrives is envy and revenge. It must needs have great success in America, where social contrasts are especially sharp and spiritual life especially feeble.

Impurities in the body come out on the surface as

running sores. Falsehood and vice, now festering and spreading in society, will some day be thrown up like streams of lava, suffocating and drowning it if it betimes heed not the life of the masses corrupted by poverty.

But, methinks, I, too, am turning moralist. You see the corrupting influence of society.

The children in the streets of New York produce a profoundly sad impression. Playing ball amidst the crash and thunder of iron, amidst the chaos of the tumultuous city, they seem like flowers thrown by some rude and cruel hand into the dust and dirt of the pavements. The whole day long they inhale the vapors of the monstrous city, the metropolis of the Yellow Devil. Pity for their little lungs, pity for their eyes choked up with dust!

The care taken in the education of children is the clearest test of the degree of culture in any country. The conditions of life with which children are surrounded determines most certainly the measure of a nation's intellectual development. If the government and society employ every possible means to have their children grow up into strong, honest, good, and wise men and women, then only it is a government and a society worthy of the name.

I have seen poverty aplenty, and know well her green, bloodless, haggard countenance. But the horror of East Side poverty is sadder than everything that I have known. Children pick out from the garbage boxes on the curbstones pieces of rotten bread, and devour it, together with the mold and the dirt, there in the street in the stinging dust and the choking air. They fight for it like little dogs. At midnight and later they are still rolling in the dust and the dirt of the street, these living rebukes to wealth, these melancholy blossoms of poverty. What sort of a fluid runs in their veins? What must be the chemical structure of their brains? Their lungs are like rags fed upon dirt; their stomachs like the garbage boxes from which they obtain their food. What sort of men can grow up out of these children of hunger and penury? What citizens?

America, you who astound the world with your millionaires, look first to the children on the East Side, and consider the menace they hold out to you! The boast of riches when there is an East Side is a stupid boast.

However, "there is no evil without a good," as they say in Russia, country of optimists.

This life of gold accumulation, this idolatry of money, this horrible worship of the Golden Devil already begins to stir up protest in the country. The odious life, entangled in a network of iron and oppressing the soul with its dismal emptiness, arouses the disgust of healthy people, and they are beginning to seek for a means of rescue from spiritual death.

And so we see millionaires and clergymen declaring themselves socialists, and publishing newspapers and periodicals for the propaganda of socialists. The creation of "settlements" by the rich intellectuals, their abandonment of the luxury of their parental homes for the wilds of the East Side—all this is evidence of an awakening spirit; it heralds the gradual rise in America of the human life. Little by little people begin to understand that the slavery of gold and the slavery of poverty are both equally destructive.

The important thing is that the people have begun to think. A country in which such an excellent work as William James's *Philosophy of Religion* was written can think. It is the country of Henry George, Edward Bellamy, Jack London, who gives his great talent to socialism. This is a good instance of the awakening of the spirit of "human life" in this young and vigorous country suffering from the gold fever. But the most irrefutable evidence of the spiritual awakening in America seems to me to be Walt Whitman. Granted that his verses are not exactly like verses; but the feeling of pagan love of life which speaks in them, the high estimate of man, energy of thought—all this is beautiful and sturdy. Whitman is a true democrat, philosopher; in his books he has perhaps laid the first foundation of a really democratic philosophy—the doctrine of freedom, beauty, and truth, and the harmony of their union in man. More and more interest in matters of the mind and the spirit, in science and art—this is what I wish the Americans with all my heart. And this, too, I wish them, the development of scorn for money.

After all that I have said, I am involuntarily drawn to make a parallel between Europe and America. On that side of the ocean there is much beauty, much liberty of the spirit, and a bold, vehement activity of the mind. There art always shines like the sky at night with the living sparkle of the imperishable stars. On this side there is no beauty. The rude vigor of political and social youth is fettered by the rusty chains of the old Puritan morality bound to the decayed fragments of dead prejudices.

Europe shows evidence of moral decrepitude, and, as a consequence of this, skepticism. She has suffered much. Her spiritual suffering has produced an aristocratic apathy, it has made her long for peace and quiet. The spiritual movement of the proletariat, carrying with it the possibility of new beauty and new joy, arouses in the cultured classes of European society nothing but dread for their peace and their old comfortable habits.

America has not yet suffered the pangs of the dissatisfied spirit, she has not yet felt the aches of the mind. Discontent has but just begun here. And it seems to me that when America will turn her energy to the quest of liberty of the spirit, the world will witness the spectacle of a great conflagration, a conflagration which will cleanse this country from the dirt of gold, and from the dust of prejudice, and it will shine like a magnificent cut diamond, reflecting in its great heart all the thought of the world, all the beauty of life.

America is strong, America is healthy! And although

even a sick Dostoevsky is more needful to the world than rich, healthy shopkeepers, yet we will trust that the children of the shopkeepers will become true democrats; that is to say, aristocrats of the spirit. For it is much pleasanter to live if you treat people better than they deserve. Is it not?

H. G. Wells

Three unfortunate Negroes were burned to death, apparently because they were Negroes. It was a sort of racial sacrament. The edified Sunday-school children hurried from their gospel-teaching to search for souvenirs among the ashes, and competed with great spirit for a fragment of charred skull.

Before he came to America in 1906, the English writer Herbert George Wells (1866–1946) had an international reputation for such brilliant science-fiction novels as *The Time Machine* and the *War of the Worlds*. In the 1900's he turned from writing about fantasy and became active in the social and economic movements of Britain, an interest which led him to Fabian socialism. An iconoclast in both his personal life as well as his intellectual enthusiasms, Wells, always retained a fascination for technology and utopias. The American critic H. L. Mencken said of him that "No other contemporary writer has said so many things worth hearing, though maybe not worth heeding."

H. G. Wells, *The Future in America: A Search After Realities* (New York, Harper and Brothers, 1906), pp. 185–202.

America drew Wells to it because it seemed the beginning of man's technological future, a living, machine-run civilization. Wells was appalled by the social misery, the technological refuse of society. But in one remarkable chapter of his critical report, *The Future in America*, Wells compared the hopes of two black leaders of the day: the moderate Booker T. Washington and the radical militant young activist Dr. W. E. B. Du Bois. The future, he said, was with Du Bois. In his mock obituary, published in 1936, Wells wrote of himself: "He had a flair for what is coming." His thoughts on Blacks in 1906 were sorrowful but precise glances into the American fate.

———————◆———————

I

I AM AWARE how intricate, how multitudinous, the aspects of this enormous question have become, but looking at it in the broad and transitory manner I have proposed for myself in these papers, it does seem to present many parallel elements. There is the same disposition towards an indiscriminating verdict, the same disregard of proportion as between small evils and great ones, the same indifference to the fact that the question does not stand alone, but is a part, and this time a by no means small part, in the working out of America's destinies.

In regard to the colored population, just as in regard to the great and growing accumulations of unassimilated and increasingly unpopular Jews, and to the great and growing multitudes of Roman Catholics whose special education contradicts at so many points those conceptions of individual judgment and responsibility upon which America relies, I have attempted time after time to get some answer from the Americans I have met to what is to me the most obvious of questions. "Your grandchildren and the grand-children of these people will have to live in this country side by side; do you propose, do you believe it possible, that under the increasing pressure of population and com-petition they should be living then in just the same relations that you and these people are living now; if you do not, then what relations do you propose shall exist between them?"

It is not too much to say that I have never once had the beginnings of an answer to this question. Usually one is told with great gravity that the problem of color is one of the most difficult that we have to consider, and the conversa-tion then breaks up into discursive anecdotes and state-ments about black people. One man will dwell upon the uncontrollable violence of a black man's evil passions (in Ja-maica and Barbados colored people form an overwhelming proportion of the population, and they have behaved in an exemplary fashion for the last thirty years); another will dilate upon the incredible stupidity of the full-blooded negro (during my stay in New York the prize for oratory at Columbia University, oratory which was the one redeem-ing charm of Daniel Webster, was awarded to a Zulu of unmitigated blackness); a third will speak of his physical offensiveness, his peculiar smell which necessitates his social isolation (most well-to-do Southerners are brought up by negro "mammies"); others, again, will enter upon the pain-ful history of the years that followed the war, though it seems a foolish thing to let those wrongs of the past domi-nate the outlook for the future. And one charming South-ern lady expressed the attitude of mind of a whole class very completely, I think, when she said, "You have to be one of us to feel this question at all as it ought to be felt."

There, I think, I got something tangible. These emotions are a cult.

My globe-trotting impudence will seem, no doubt, to mount to its zenith when I declare that hardly any Americans at all seem to be in possession of the elementary facts in relation to this question. These broad facts are not taught, as of course they ought to be taught, in school; and what each man knows is picked up by the accidents of his own untrained observation, by conversation always tinctured by personal prejudice, by hastily read newspapers and magazine articles and the like. The quality of this discussion is very variable, but on the whole pretty low. While I was in New York opinion was greatly swayed by an article in, if I remember rightly, the *Century Magazine*, by a gentleman who had deduced from a few weeks' observation in the slums of Khartoum the entire incapacity of the negro to establish a civilization of his own. He never had, therefore he never could; a discouraging ratiocination. We English, a century or so ago, said all these things of the native Irish. If there is any trend of opinion at all in this matter at present, it lies in the direction of a generous decision on the part of the North and West to leave the black more and more to the judgment and mercy of the white people with whom he is locally associated. This judgment and mercy points, on the whole, to an accentuation of the colored man's natural inferiority, to the cessation of any other educational attempts than those that increase his industrial usefulness (it is already illegal in Louisiana to educate him above a contemptible level), to his industrial exploitation through usury and legal chicanery, and to a systematic strengthening of the social barriers between colored people of whatever shade and the whites.

Meanwhile, in this state of general confusion, in the absence of any determining rules or assumptions, all sorts of things are happening—according to the accidents of local feeling. In Massachusetts you have people with, I am afraid, an increasing sense of sacrifice to principle, lunching and dining with people of color. They do it less than they did, I was told. Massachusetts stands, I believe, at the top of the scale of tolerant humanity. One seems to reach the bottom at Springfield, Missouri, which is a county seat with a college, an academy, a high school, and a zoological garden. There the exemplary method reaches the nadir. Last April three unfortunate negroes were burned to death, apparently because they were negroes, and as a general corrective of impertinence. They seem to have been innocent of any particular offence. It was a sort of racial sacrament. The edified Sunday-school children hurried from their gospel-teaching to search for souvenirs among the ashes, and competed with great spirit for a fragment of charred skull.

It is true that in this latter case Governor Folk acted with vigor and justice, and that the better element of Springfield society was evidently shocked when it was found that quite innocent negroes had been used in these instructive pyrotechnics; but the fact remains that a large and numerically important section of the American public does think that fierce and cruel reprisals are a necessary part of the system of relationships between white and colored man.

"Things are better in Jamaica and Barbados," said I, in a moment of patriotic weakness, to Mr. Booker T. Washington.

"Eh!" said he, and thought in that long silent way he has. . . . "They're worse in South Africa—much. Here we've got a sort of light. We know generally what we've got to stand. *There*—"

His words sent my memory back to some conversations I had quite recently with a man from a dry-goods store in Johannesburg. He gave me clearly enough the attitude of the common white out there; the dull prejudice; the readiness to take advantage of the "boy"; the utter disrespect for colored womankind; the savage, intolerant resentment, dashed dangerously with fear, which the native arouses in him. (Think of all that must have happened in wrongful practice and wrongful law and neglected educational possibilities before our Zulus in Natal were goaded to face massacre, spear against rifle!) The rare and culminating result of education and experience is to enable men to grasp facts, to balance justly among their fluctuating and innumerable aspects, and only a small minority in our world is educated to that pitch. Ignorant people can think only in types and abstractions, can achieve only emphatic absolute decisions, and when the commonplace American or the commonplace colonial Briton sets to work to "think over" the negro problem, he instantly banishes most of the material evidence from his mind—clears for action, as it were. He forgets the genial carriage of the ordinary colored man, his beaming face, his kindly eye, his rich, jolly voice, his touching and trusted friendliness, his amiable, unprejudiced readiness to serve and follow a white man who seems to know what he is doing. He forgets—perhaps he has never seen— the dear humanity of these people, their slightly exaggerated vanity, their innocent and delightful love of color and song, their immense capacity for affection, the warm romantic touch in their imaginations. He ignores the real fineness of the indolence that despises servile toil, of the carelessness that disdains the watchful aggressive economies, day by day, now a wretched little gain here and now a wretched little gain there, that make the dirty fortune of the Russian Jews who prey upon color in the Carolinas. No; in the place of all these tolerable everyday experiences he lets his imagination go to work upon a monster, the "real nigger."

"Ah! You don't know the *real* nigger," said one American to me when I praised the colored people I had seen. "You should see the buck nigger down South, Congo brand. Then you'd understand, sir."

His voice, his face had a gleam of passionate animosity.

One could see he had been brooding himself out of all relations to reality in this matter. He was a man beyond reason or pity. He was obsessed. Hatred of that imaginary diabolical "buck nigger" blackened his soul. It was no good to talk to him of the "buck American, Packingtown brand," or the "buck Englishman, suburban race-meeting type," and to ask him if these intensely disagreeable persons justified outrages on Senator Lodge, let us say, or Mrs. Longworth. No reply would have come from him. "You don't understand the question," he would have answered. "You don't know how we Southerners feel."

Well, one can make a tolerable guess.

II

I CERTAINLY did not begin to realize one most important aspect of this question until I reached America. I thought of those eight millions as of men, black as ink. But when I met Mr. Booker T. Washington, for example, I met a man certainly as white in appearance as our Admiral Fisher, who is, as a matter of fact, quite white. A very large proportion of these colored people, indeed, is more than half white. One hears a good deal about the high social origins of the Southern planters, very many derive indisputably from the first families of England. It is the same blood flows in these mixed colored people's veins. Just think of the sublime absurdity, therefore, of the ban. There are gentlemen of education and refinement, qualified lawyers and doctors, whose ancestors assisted in the Norman Conquest, and they dare not enter a car marked "white" and intrude upon the dignity of the rising loan-monger from Esthonia. For them the "Jim Crow" car. . . .

One tries to put that aspect to the American in vain. "These people," you say, "are nearer your blood, nearer

your temper, than any of those bright-eyed, ringleted immigrants on the East Side. Are you ashamed of your poor
relations? Even if you don't like the half, or the quarter of
negro blood, you might deal civilly with the three-quarters
white. It doesn't say much for your faith in your own racial
prepotency, anyhow."

The answer to that is usually in terms of mania.

"Let me tell you a little story just to illustrate," said one
deponent to me in an impressive undertone—"just to illustrate, you know. . . . A few years ago a young fellow
came to Boston from New Orleans. Looked all right. Dark
—but he explained that by an Italian grandmother. Touch
of French in him, too. Popular. Well, he made advances to a
Boston girl—good family. Gave a fairly straight account of
himself. Married."

He paused. "Course of time—offspring. Little son."

His eye made me feel what was coming.

"Was it by any chance very, very black?" I whispered.

"Yes, *sir*. Black! Black as your hat. Absolutely negroid.
Projecting jaw, thick lips, frizzy hair, flat nose—everything. . . .

"But consider the mother's feelings, sir, consider that!
A pure-minded, pure white woman!"

What can one say to a story of this sort, when the taint
in the blood surges up so powerfully as to blacken the
child at birth beyond even the habit of the pure-blooded
negro? What can you do with a public opinion made of this
class of ingredient? And this story of the lamentable results
of intermarriage was used, not as an argument against intermarriage, but as an argument against the extension of quite
rudimentary civilities to the men of color. "If you eat with
them, you've got to marry them," he said, an entirely
fabulous post-prandial responsibility.

It is to the tainted whites my sympathies go out. The
black or mainly black people seem to be fairly content with

their inferiority; one sees them all about the States as waiters, cabdrivers, railway porters, car attendants, laborers of various sorts, a pleasant, smiling, acquiescent folk. But consider the case of a man with a broader brain than such small uses need, conscious, perhaps, of exceptional gifts, capable of wide interests and sustained attempts, who is perhaps as English as you or I, with just a touch of color in his eyes, in his lips, in his fingernails, and in his imagination. Think of the accumulating sense of injustice he must bear with him through life, the perpetual slight and insult he must undergo from all that is vulgar and brutal among the whites! Something of that one may read in the sorrowful pages of Du Bois's *The Souls of Black Folk*. They would have made Alexandre Dumas travel in the Jim Crow car if he had come to Virginia. But I can imagine some sort of protest on the part of that admirable but extravagant man. . . . They even talk of "Jim Crow elevators" now in Southern hotels.

III

BUT WHATEVER ASPECT I recall of this great taboo that shows no signs of lifting, of this great problem of the future that America in her haste, her indiscriminating prejudice, her lack of any sustained study and teaching of the broad issues she must decide, complicates and intensifies, and makes threatening, there presently comes back to mind the browned face of Mr. Booker T. Washington, as he talked to me over our lunch in Boston.

He has a face rather Irish in type, and the soft slow negro voice. He met my regard with the brown sorrowful eyes of his race. He wanted very much that I should hear him make a speech, because then his words came better; he talked, he implied, with a certain difficulty. But I preferred to have his talking, and get not the orator—every one tells me he is an altogether great orator in this country where oratory is still esteemed—but the man.

He answered my questions meditatively. I wanted to know with an active pertinacity. What struck me most was the way in which his sense of the overpowering forces of race prejudice weighs upon him. It is a thing he accepts; in our time and conditions it is not to be fought about. He makes one feel with an exaggerated intensity (though I could not even draw him to admit) its monstrous injustice. He makes no accusations. He is for taking it as a part of the present fate of his "people," and for doing all that can be done for them within the limit it sets.

Therein he differs from Du Bois, the other great spokesman color has found in our time. Du Bois is more of the artist, less of the statesman; he conceals his passionate resentment all too thinly. He batters himself into rhetoric against these walls. He will not repudiate the clear right of the black man to every educational facility, to equal citizenship, and equal respect. But Mr. Washington has statecraft. He looks before and after, and plans and keeps his counsel with the scope and range of a statesman. I use "statesman" in its highest sense; his is a mind that can grasp the situation and destinies of a people. . . .

I argued strongly against the view he seems to hold that black and white might live without mingling and without injustice, side by side. That I do not believe. Racial differences seem to me always to exasperate intercourse unless people have been elaborately trained to ignore them. Uneducated men are as bad as cattle in persecuting all that is different among themselves. The most miserable and disorderly countries of the world are the countries where two races, two inadequate cultures, keep a jarring, continuous separation. "You must repudiate separation," I said. "No peoples have ever yet endured the tension of intermingled distinctness."

"May we not become a peculiar people—like the Jews?" he suggested. "Isn't that possible?"

But there I could not agree with him. I thought of the dreadful history of the Jews and Armenians. And the negro cannot do what the Jews and Armenians have done. The colored people of America are of a different quality from the Jew altogether, more genial, more careless, more sympathetic, franker, less intellectual, less acquisitive, less wary and restrained—in a word, more Occidental. They have no common religion and culture, no conceit of race to hold them together. The Jews make a ghetto for themselves wherever they go; no law but their own solidarity has given America the East Side. The colored people are ready to disperse and interbreed, are not a community at all in the Jewish sense, but outcasts from a community. They are the victims of a prejudice that has to be destroyed. These things I urged, but it was, I think, empty speech to my hearer. I could talk lightly of destroying that prejudice, but he knew better. It is the central fact of his life, a law of his being. He has shaped all his projects and policy upon that. Exclusion is inevitable. So he dreams of a colored race of decent and inaggressive men silently giving the lie to all the legend of their degradation. They will have their own doctors, their own lawyers, their own capitalists, their own banks—because the whites desire it so. But will the uneducated whites endure even so submissive a vindication as that? Will they suffer the horrid spectacle of free and self-satisfied negroes in decent clothing on any terms without resentment?

He explained how at the Tuskegee Institute they make useful men, skilled engineers, skilled agriculturalists, men to live down the charge of practical incompetence, of ignorant and slovenly farming and house management.

"I wish you would tell me," I said, abruptly, "just what you think of the attitude of white America towards you. Do you think it is generous?"

He regarded me for a moment. "No end of people help us," he said.

"Yes," I said; "but the ordinary man. Is he fair?"

"Some things are not fair," he said, leaving the general question alone. "It isn't fair to refuse a colored man a berth on a sleeping car. I?—I happen to be a privileged person, they make an exception for me; but the ordinary educated colored man isn't admitted to a sleeping car at all. If he has to go a long journey, he has to sit up all night. His white competitor sleeps. Then in some places, in the hotels and restaurants—it's all right here in Boston—but southwardly he can't get proper refreshments. All that's a handicap. . . .

"The remedy lies in education," he said; "ours—*and theirs*.

"The real thing," he told me, "isn't to be done by talking and agitation. It's a matter of lives. The only answer to it all is for colored men to be patient, to make themselves competent, to do good work, to live well, to give no occasion against us. We feel that. In a way it's an inspiration. . . .

"There is a man here in Boston, a negro, who owns and runs some big stores, employs all sorts of people, deals justly. That man has done more good for our people than all the eloquence or argument in the world. . . . That is what we have to do—it is all we *can* do." . . .

Whatever America has to show in heroic living today, I doubt if she can show anything finer than the quality of the resolve, the steadfast effort hundreds of black and colored men are making today to live blamelessly, honorably, and patiently, getting for themselves what scraps of refinement, learning, and beauty they may, keeping their hold on a civilization they are grudged and denied. They do it not for themselves only, but for all their race. Each educated colored man is an ambassador to civilization. They know they have a handicap, that they are not exceptionally brilliant nor clever people. Yet every such man stands, one likes to think, aware of his representative and vicarious character, fighting against foul imaginations, misrepresentations, injustice, insult, and the naïve unspeakable meannesses of base antagonists. Every one of them who keeps decent and honorable does a little to beat that opposition down.

But the patience the negro needs! He may not even look contempt. He must admit superiority in those whose daily conduct to him is the clearest evidence of moral inferiority. We sympathetic whites, indeed, may claim honor for him; if he is wise he will be silent under our advocacy. He must go to and fro self-controlled, bereft of all the equalities that the great flag of America proclaims—that flag for whose united empire his people fought and died, giving place and precedence to the strangers who pour in to share its beneficence, strangers ignorant even of its tongue. That he must do—and wait. The Welsh, the Irish, the Poles, the white South, the indefatigable Jews may cherish grievances and rail aloud. He must keep still. They may be hysterical, revengeful, threatening, and perverse; their wrongs excuse them. For him there is no excuse. And of all the races upon earth, which has suffered such wrongs as this negro blood that is still imputed to him as a sin? These people who disdain him, who have no sense of reparation towards him, have sinned against him beyond all measure. . . .

No, I can't help idealizing the dark submissive figure of the negro in this spectacle of America. He, too, seems to me to sit waiting—and waiting with a marvellous and simple-minded patience—for finer understandings and a nobler time.

V. I. Lenin

American imperialism—the freshest, strongest and latest in joining the world-wide slaughter of nations for the division of capitalist profits—at this very moment has turned an exceptionally tragic page in the bloody history of bloody imperialism.

Vladimir Ilyich Ulyanov-Lenin (1870–1924) never came to America, but he knew a great deal about the development of this, the most successful capitalist venture in history. The authentic founder of twentieth-century communism and still its most influential theoretician, Lenin knew more about the United States than either Marx or Engels. He studied census reports for a massive work on capitalism and agriculture; he pored over statistics comparing the plight of Russian serfs and American Negroes; and he established the biting framework for antiimperialist rhetoric. The tone of his analysis and his provocative style—filled with epithet and denigration, pointedly caustic, often redundant, and invariably heroic—still shapes the character of Soviet anti-American writings today.

America, through Lenin's stringently Marxist eyes, was the

C. Leiteizen, ed., *Lenin on the United States: Selected Writings* (Moscow, Progress Publishers, 1969), pp. 123, 137–39, 343–48.

country of a triumphant bourgeoisie which was realizing all the predictions of "scientific socialism"—increasing monopoly, exhaustion of internal markets for capital exploitation, imperialist expansion in quest of raw materials and foreign markets. Political parties were simply agents of the most powerful capitalists, tools of Wall Street, lackeys of private property.

Lenin blamed American capitalism for the wretched life of Negroes, their high level of illiteracy and poor economic conditions. This racist oppression, he said, "is a disgrace to a civilized, advanced country like the North American republic. . . . Shame on America for the plight of the Negroes! Capitalism cannot give either complete emancipation or even complete equality." Negroes were "an oppressed people" held in semifeudal barbarism by an avaricious capitalism.

The following selections cover three areas of Lenin's involvement with American issues. The first is a report on the presidential elections of 1912 written while in exile from czarist Russia; the second is a bitter description of Frederick Taylor's experiments in "scientific management"; and the third includes excerpts from Lenin's famous "Letter to American Workers," written shortly after the Bolshevik revolution, during the period of armed intervention by the Allied powers (including the United States) against the Soviet Union on behalf of counterrevolutionary forces.

———◆———

CAPITALIST POLITICS

[*1912*]

[WOODROW] WILSON, a "Democrat," has been elected President of the United States of America. He has polled over six million votes. [Theodore] Roosevelt (the new National Progressive Party) over four million, [William Howard]

Taft (Republican Party) over three million, and the socialist Eugene Debs 800,000 votes.

The world significance of the U.S. elections lies not so much in the great increase in the number of socialist votes as in the far-reaching *crisis* of the *bourgeois* parties, in the amazing force with which their decay has been revealed. Lastly, the significance of the elections lies in the unusually clear and striking revelation of *bourgeois reformism* as a means of combating socialism.

In *all* bourgeois countries, the parties which stand for capitalism, i.e., the bourgeois parties, came into being a long time ago, and the greater the extent of political liberty, the more solid they are.

Freedom in the U.S.A. is most complete. And for a whole *half-century*—since the Civil War over slavery in 1860–65—*two* bourgeois parties have been distinguished there by remarkable solidity and strength. The party of the former slave-owners is the so-called Democratic Party. The capitalist party, which favored the emancipation of the Negroes, has developed into the Republican Party.

Since the emancipation of the Negroes, the distinction between the two parties has been diminishing. The fight between these two parties has been mainly over the height of customs duties. Their fight *has not had* any *serious* importance for the mass of the people. The people have been deceived and diverted from their vital interests by means of spectacular and meaningless *duels* between the two bourgeois parties.

This so-called bipartisan system prevailing in America and Britain has been one of the most powerful means of preventing the rise of an independent working-class, i.e., genuinely socialist, party.

And now the bipartisan system has suffered a fiasco in America, the country boasting the most advanced capitalism! What caused this fiasco?

The strength of the working-class movement, the growth of socialism.

The old bourgeois parties (the Democratic and the Republican parties) have been facing towards the past, the period of the emancipation of the Negroes. The new bourgeois party, the National Progressive Party, is facing towards the *future*. Its programme turns entirely on the question whether capitalism is to be or not to be, on the issues, to be specific, of protection for the workers and of "trusts," as the capitalist associations are called in the U.S.A.

The old parties are products of an epoch whose task was to develop capitalism as speedily as possible. The struggle between the parties was over the question *how* best to expedite and facilitate this development.

The new party is a product of the present epoch, which raises the issue of the very existence of capitalism. In the U.S.A., the freest and most advanced country, this issue is coming to the fore more clearly and broadly than anywhere else.

The entire programme and entire agitation of Roosevelt and the Progressives turn on how to *save capitalism* by means of *bourgeois reforms*.

The bourgeois reformism which in old Europe manifests itself in the chatter of liberal professors has all at once come forward in the free American republic as a party four millions strong. This is American style.

We shall save capitalism by reforms, says that party. We shall grant the most progressive factory legislation. We shall establish state control over *all* the trusts (in the U.S.A. that means over *all* industries!). We shall establish state control over them to eliminate poverty and enable everybody to earn a "decent" wage. We shall establish "social and industrial justice." We revere *all* reforms—*the only "reform"* we don't want is *expropriation of the capitalists*!

The national wealth of the U.S.A. is now reckoned to

be 120 billion (thousand million) dollars, i.e, about 240 billion rubles. Approximately *one-third* of it, or about 80 billion rubles, belongs to *two* trusts, those of Rockefeller and Morgan, or is subordinated to these trusts! Not more than 40,000 families making up these two trusts are the masters of 80 million wage-slaves.

Obviously, so long as these modern slave-owners are there, all "reforms" will be nothing but a deception. Roosevelt has been *deliberately* hired by the astute multi-millionaires to preach this deception. The "state control" they promise will become—if the capitalists keep their capital—a means of combating and crushing strikes.

But the American proletarian has already awakened and has taken up his post. He greets Roosevelt's success with cheerful irony, as if to say: You lured four million people with your promises of reform, dear impostor Roosevelt. Very well! Tomorrow those four million will see that your promises were a fraud, and don't forget that they are following you *only* because they feel that it is *impossible* to go on living in the old way.

THE TAYLOR SYSTEM—MAN'S ENSLAVEMENT BY THE MACHINE

[*1914*]

CAPITALISM cannot be at a standstill for a single moment. It must forever be moving forward. Competition, which is keenest in a period of crisis like the present, calls for the invention of an increasing number of new devices to reduce the cost of production. But the domination of capital converts all these devices into instruments for the further exploitation of the workers.

The Taylor system is one of these devices.

Advocates of this system recently used the following techniques in America:

An electric lamp was attached to a worker's arm, the worker's movements were photographed and the movements of the lamp studied. Certain movements were found to be "superfluous" and the worker was made to avoid them, i.e., to work more intensively, without losing a second for rest.

The layout of new factory buildings is planned in such a way that not a moment will be lost in delivering materials to the factory, in conveying them from one shop to another, and in dispatching the finished products. Films are systematically employed for studying the work of the best operatives and increasing their intensity, i.e., "speeding up" the workers.

For example, a mechanic's operations were filmed in the course of a whole day. After studying the mechanic's movements the efficiency experts provided him with a bench high enough to enable him to avoid losing time in bending down. He was given a boy to assist him. This boy had to hand up each part of the machine in a definite and most efficient way. Within a few days the mechanic performed the work of assembling the given type of machine in *one-fourth* of the time it had taken before!

What an enormous gain in labor productivity! . . . But the worker's pay is not increased fourfold, but only half as much again, at the very most, and *only for a short period* at that. As soon as the workers get used to the new system their pay is cut to the former level. The capitalist obtains an enormous profit, but the workers toil four times as hard as before and wear down their nerves and muscles four times as fast as before.

A newly engaged worker is taken to the factory cinema where he is shown a "model" performance of his job; the worker is made to "catch up" with this performance. A week later he is taken to the cinema again and shown pictures of his own performance, which is then compared with the "model."

All these vast improvements are introduced *to the detriment* of the workers, for they lead to their still greater oppression and exploitation. Moreover, this rational and efficient distribution of labor is confined *to each factory*.

The question naturally arises: What about the distribution of labor in society as a whole? What a vast amount of labor is wasted at present owing to the disorganised and chaotic character of capitalist production as a whole! How much time is wasted as the raw materials pass to the factory through the hands of hundreds of buyers and middlemen, while the requirements of the market are unknown! Not only time, but the actual products are wasted and damaged. And what about the waste of time and labor in delivering the finished goods to the consumers through a host of small middlemen who, too, cannot know the requirements of their customers and perform not only a host of superfluous movements, but also make a host of superfluous purchases, journeys, and so on and so forth!

Capital organizes and rationalizes labor within the factory for the purpose of increasing the exploitation of the workers and increasing profit. In social production as a whole, however, chaos continues to reign and grow, leading to crises when the accumulated wealth cannot find purchasers, and millions of workers starve and die because they are unable to find employment.

The Taylor system—without its initiators knowing or wishing it—is preparing the time when the proletariat will take over all social production and appoint its own workers' committees for the purpose of properly distributing and rationalizing all social labor. Large-scale production, machinery, railways, telephones—all provide thousands of opportunities to cut by three-fourths the working time of the organized workers and make them four times better off than they are today.

And these workers' committees, assisted by the workers'

unions, will be able to apply these principles of rational distribution of social labor when the latter is freed from its enslavement by capital.

LETTER TO AMERICAN WORKERS

[*1918*]

COMRADES! A Russian Bolshevik who took part in the 1905 revolution, and who lived in your country for many years afterwards, has offered to convey my letter to you. I have accepted his proposal all the more gladly because just at the present time the American revolutionary workers have to play an exceptionally important role as uncompromising enemies of American imperialism—the freshest, strongest and latest in joining in the world-wide slaughter of nations for the division of capitalist profits. At this very moment, the American multimillionaires, these modern slaveowners, have turned an exceptionally tragic page in the bloody history of bloody imperialism by giving their approval—whether direct or indirect, open or hypocritically concealed, makes no difference—to the armed expedition launched by the brutal Anglo-Japanese imperialists for the purpose of throttling the first socialist republic.

The history of modern, civilized America opened with one of those great, really liberating, really revolutionary wars of which there have been so few compared to the vast number of wars of conquest which, like the present imperialist war, were caused by squabbles among kings, landowners or capitalists over the division of usurped lands or ill-gotten gains. That was the war the American people waged against the British robbers who oppressed America and held her in colonial slavery, in the same way as these "civilized" bloodsuckers are still oppressing and holding in colonial slavery hundreds of millions of people in India, Egypt, and all parts of the world.

About 150 years have passed since then. Bourgeois
civilization has borne all its luxurious fruits. America has
taken first place among the free and educated nations in
level of development of the productive forces of collective
human endeavor, in the utilization of machinery and of all
the wonders of modern engineering. At the same time,
America has become one of the foremost countries in regard
to the depth of the abyss which lies between the handful
of arrogant multimillionaires who wallow in filth and
luxury, and the millions of working people who constantly
live on the verge of pauperism. The American people, who
set the world an example in waging a revolutionary war
against feudal slavery, now find themselves in the latest,
capitalist stage of wage-slavery to a handful of multimillionaires, and find themselves playing the role of hired
thugs who, for the benefit of wealthy scoundrels, throttled
the Philippines in 1898 on the pretext of "liberating" them,
and are throttling the Russian Socialist Republic in 1918
on the pretext of "protecting" it from the Germans.

The American multimillionaires were, perhaps, richest
of all, and geographically the most secure. They have pro-
fited more than all the rest. They have converted all, even
the richest, countries into their tributaries. They have
grabbed hundreds of billions of dollars. And every dollar
is sullied with filth: the filth of the secret treaties between
Britain and her "allies," between Germany and her vassals,
treaties for the division of the spoils, treaties of mutual "aid"
for oppressing the workers and persecuting the inter-
nationalist socialists. Every dollar is sullied with the filth
of "profitable" war contracts, which in every country made
the rich richer and the poor poorer. And every dollar is
stained with blood—from that ocean of blood that has been
shed by the ten million killed and twenty million maimed
in the great, noble, liberating and holy war to decide
whether the British or the German robbers are to get most

of the spoils, whether the British or the German thugs are to be *foremost* in throttling the weak nations all over the world.

While the German robbers broke all records in war atrocities, the British have broken all records not only in the number of colonies they have grabbed, but also in the subtlety of their disgusting hypocrisy. This very day, the Anglo-French and American bourgeois newspapers are spreading, in millions and millions of copies, lies and slander about Russia, and are hypocritically justifying their predatory expedition against her on the plea that they want to "protect" Russia from the Germans!

It does not require many words to refute this despicable and hideous lie; it is sufficient to point to one well-known fact. In October 1917, after the Russian workers had overthrown their imperialist government, the Soviet government, the government of the revolutionary workers and peasants, openly proposed a just peace, a peace without annexations or indemnities, a peace that fully guaranteed equal rights to all nations—and it proposed such a peace to *all* the belligerent countries.

It was the Anglo-French and the American bourgeoisie who refused to accept our proposal; it was they who even refused to talk to us about a general peace! It was *they* who betrayed the interests of all nations; it was they who prolonged the imperialist slaughter!

It was they who, banking on the possibility of dragging Russia back into the imperialist war, refused to take part in the peace negotiations and thereby gave a free hand to the no less predatory German capitalists who imposed the annexationist and harsh Brest peace upon Russia!

The American people have a revolutionary tradition which has been adopted by the best representatives of the American proletariat, who have repeatedly expressed their complete solidarity with us Bolsheviks. That tradition is

the war of liberation against the British in the eighteenth
century and the Civil War in the nineteenth century. In
some respects, if we only take into consideration the
"destruction" of some branches of industry and of the
national economy, America in 1870 was *behind* 1860. But
what a pedant, what an idiot would anyone be to deny on
these grounds the immense, world-historic, progressive and
revolutionary significance of the American Civil War of
1860–65!

The representatives of the bourgeoisie understand that
for the sake of overthrowing Negro slavery, of overthrowing the rule of the slaveowners, it was worth letting the
country go through long years of civil war, through the
abysmal ruin, destruction and terror that accompany every
war. But now, when we are confronted with the vastly
greater task of overthrowing capitalist *wage*-slavery, of
overthrowing the rule of the bourgeoisie—now, the representatives and defenders of the bourgeoisie, and also the
reformist socialists who have been frightened by the bourgeoisie and are shunning the revolution, cannot and do not
want to understand that civil war is necessary and legitimate.

The American workers will not follow the bourgeoisie.
They will be with us, for civil war against the bourgeoisie.
The whole history of the world and of the American labor
movement strengthens my conviction that this is so. I also
recall the words of one of the most beloved leaders of the
American proletariat, Eugene Debs, who wrote in the *Appeal to Reason*, I believe towards the end of 1915, in the
article "What Shall I Fight For" (I quoted this article at
the beginning of 1916 at a public meeting of workers in
Berne, Switzerland)—that he, Debs, would rather be shot
than vote credits for the present criminal and reactionary
war; that he, Debs, knows of only one holy and, from the
proletarian standpoint, legitimate war, namely, the war

against the capitalists, the war to liberate mankind from wage-slavery.

I am not surprised that Wilson, the head of the American multimillionaires and servant of the capitalist sharks, has thrown Debs into prison. Let the bourgeoisie be brutal to the true internationalists, to the true representatives of the revolutionary proletariat! The more fierce and brutal they are, the nearer the day of the victorious proletarian revolution.

We are blamed for the destruction caused by our revolution. . . Who are the accusers? The hangers-on of the bourgeoisie, of that very bourgeoisie who, during the four years of the imperialist war, have destroyed almost the whole of European culture and have reduced Europe to barbarism, brutality and starvation. These bourgeoisie now demand we should not make a revolution on these ruins, amidst this wreckage of culture, amidst the wreckage and ruins created by the war, nor with the people who have been brutalised by the war. How humane and righteous the bourgeoisie are! . . .

America is strong; she is everybody's creditor and everything depends on her; she is being more and more detested; she is robbing all and sundry and doing so in a unique fashion. She has no colonies. Britain emerged from the war with vast colonies. So did France. Britain offered America a mandate—that is the language they use nowadays—for one of the colonies she had seized, but America did not accept it. U.S. businessmen evidently reason in some other way. They have seen that, in the devastation it produces and the temper it arouses among the workers, war has very definite consequences, and they have come to the conclusion that there is nothing to be gained by accepting a mandate. Naturally, however, they will not permit this colony to be used by any other state. All bourgeois literature testifies to a rising hatred of America.

Sigmund Freud

Hate America? I don't hate America, I regret it! I regret that Columbus ever discovered it!

In 1908, Dr. G. Stanley Hall, the president of the small New England Clark University, invited a somewhat notorious Viennese doctor to give a course of lectures on his new ideas in the tentative field of psychology. In Vienna, Dr. Sigmund Freud accepted the invitation. He arrived in America on August 27, 1909. Freud gave five lectures on the general field of psychoanalysis after an English colleague persuaded him against speaking on "dream theory," as Americans might find that subject "not practical enough." After the lecture series, Freud received an honorary doctorate, remarking, "This is the first official recognition of our endeavors." While Freudian psychology was still in disrepute throughout scientific Europe, his theories of dynamic psychoanalysis were being applied to disturbed patients at New York's Ward's Island hospital.

Max Eastman, "Differing With Sigmund Freud," in *Great Companions*. Copyright © 1942, 1959 by Max Eastman. (New York, Farrar, Straus and Giroux, pp. 124-130.) Reprinted by permission of the publisher.

The founder of psychoanalysis was grateful to America, although unhappy with it as a civilization. His biographer, Dr. Ernest Jones, who was with him at Clark, tells us that "Freud himself attributed his dislike of America to a lasting intestinal trouble brought on . . . by American cooking. . . . He even went so far as to tell me that his handwriting had deteriorated since the visit to America." But Jones explained Freud's anti-Americanism as a result of his difficulty with the language. Once he heard one American ask another to repeat a phrase he seemed to have missed. Freud, Jones says, turned to his one-time associate, Dr. Jung, and remarked acidly: "These people cannot even understand each other." There were other things wrong with America. For example, Freud complained of the absence of convenient toilets: "They escort you along miles of corridors and ultimately you are taken to the very basement where a marble palace awaits you, only just in time." Bad food, poor communications, inaccessible bathrooms and a general lack of European deference led him to proclaim: "America is a mistake; a gigantic mistake, it is true, but none the less a mistake." Near the end of his life, in 1939, Freud's attitude softened. "America," he wrote to a friend seeking refuge from the Nazis, "seems to me an Anti-Paradise, but it has so much room and so many possibilities. Einstein told a friend recently that at first America looked to him like a caricature of a country, but now feels himself quite at home there."

The following memoir-interview of Freud was conducted by an American writer, Max Eastman, who moved from opposition to World War I and enthusiasm for the Bolsheviks (he was Trotsky's major translator) to become in his last years, a strident conservative and militant anti-communist.

———◆———

I WAS LIVING IN EUROPE in the mid-twenties and had published in London a book on Marxism which contained a chapter entitled "Marx and Freud." To my delight and excitement, Freud wrote me a letter about my book, calling it, generously, *"wirklich bedeutsam, wahrscheinlich auch richtig,"* * and then adding—as though not to be too generous—"I enjoyed it far more than former works of yours."

In thanking him, I said: "I'm sure you won't mind my quoting from your letter in advertising the American edition," and he wrote back, very stiff and caustic:

"I will thank you for *not* mentioning any of the remarks in my letter in public. I seem thus far to have failed to accustom myself to the American life forms."

I replied that I had not mentioned his remarks in public, but only asked permission to do so. And I think I intimated, as mildly as possible, that the American life forms are such as to make the difference between these two things usually quite readily perceptible. It may well be, however, that I merely wish I had said this, for my dominant feeling was one of mortification rather than resentment. Freud was not only in many things my teacher, but by proxy at least, my Father Confessor. More than one of his American apostles had given me psychoanalytic advice in time of trouble. I was not in a position, except so far as honest pride demanded it, to sass him back.

It all sharpened in me a long-cherished desire to set eyes on the great man. I knew I had a certain claim to his attention, for as a result of one of my sessions with his American apostle, Dr. Smith Ely Jelliffe, I had studied Freud's works very thoroughly and published, in *Everybody's Magazine* in 1915, the first popular exposition of his theories and methods of healing. Thus, happening to be in Vienna in 1926, I sent a note around and asked if I might call.

Berggasse 19 was a big roomy house full of books and pictures, the whole mezzanine floor padded with those thick rich rugs in which your feet sink like a camel's in the

* "Really important, probably also right."

sand. I was not surprised to see hanging beside Rembrandt's
Anatomy Lesson, without which no doctor's office would
be recognizable, a picture of *The Nightmare*—a horrid
monster with a semi-evil laugh or leer, squatting upon a
sleeping maiden's naked breast. Freud's early specialty had
been anatomy, and he had in him the hard scientific curiosity
suggested by Rembrandt's picture. But then he had too, in
my belief, a streak of something closely akin to medieval
superstition. He liked to talk about "*the* Unconscious," per-
sonifying the mere absence of a quality—and that, the
quality of awareness!—and making it into a scheming
demon for which anatomy certainly finds no place. Freud's
discovery that impulses suppressed out of our thoughts can
continue to control those thoughts, both waking and sleeping, and also our actions and bodily conditions, was certainly
a major event in the history of science. But what a lot of
purely literary mythology he built around it! Mental healing always did and always will run off into magic.

With such thoughts I sat there whetting my curiosity
until the door opened and he came in.

Well—he was smaller than I thought, and slender-
limbed, and more feminine. I have mentioned my surprise
at the feminineness of all the great men I have met. Genius
is a nervous phenomenon and, except for the steam-roller
variety that has come to the front in the totalitarian states, it
involves delicacy. An operation had altered Freud's features
a trifle when I met him, so that his nose seemed flatter than
I expected and bent slightly to one side. It made him, when
he threw his head clear back and laughed softly, as he
frequently did, seem quaint and gnomelike. His voice was a
little thin too, as though he were purposely holding back
half his breath in order to be mischievous.

"What did you want?" he said in English as we shook
hands.

"Not a thing," I said. "I just wanted to look you over."

"You want to quote my commendation of your book.

But why should I support you? Can't you stand up on your own legs?"

"I'm trying to," I said. "And that isn't what brought me here at all. Still, I do wonder why, if you think I got it right about you and Marx, you want to make a secret of it."

He made no answer and was not troubled by the silence this caused. It was a hard silence, a sort of weapon in his hand, and I made it worse by saying:

"There *is* one thing I always wanted to ask you. I don't see why you talk about unconsciousness as though it were a thing. The only *thing* there, when we are unconscious, is our brain and body. Wouldn't it clarify matters if you stopped using the noun and stuck to the adjective—instead of saying '*the* Unconscious,' say 'unconscious brain states'?"

"Well, haven't you read our literature?" he said tartly. "The Unconscious is not a thing, but a concept. It is a concept that we find indispensable in the clinic."

"It is a dangerous concept," I said, "because people inevitably think of it as a thing."

"Well, then, let them correct their thinking!"

It wasn't very pleasant, and I tried to say with a smile: "You're perfectly sure you're not resurrecting the soul?"

"No, there's no soul," he said. "There's only a concept which those of us engaged in practical work find indispensable.

"Perhaps you're a behaviorist," he went on. "According to your John B. Watson, even consciousness doesn't exist. But that's just silly. That's nonsense. Consciousness exists quite obviously and everywhere—except in America."

He enjoyed that crack at America so much that he began to laugh and be genial. In fact, he began to lecture me in a fatherly way about the relations between the psychic and the physical. He talked fluently, and I am a good listener, and we were soon very friendly.

"You mustn't confuse the psychic with the conscious," he said. "My old psychology teacher here in Vienna, Theodore Lipps, used to warn us against that. Psychic entities are not necessarily conscious."

My answer, of course, was: "Then the unconscious is not merely a concept after all, but a thing, an 'entity,' just as I thought!"

However, I did not make this answer until I got home and was putting down our conversation in a notebook. I was too far on the underside of my inferiority complex to catch a great man up like that. Perhaps it is just as well, for the contradiction, left standing, is very neat and pretty. It shows Freud in the very act of being both a scientist and a demonologist. Freud would not let his discoveries be a contribution to psychology. They had to be psychology— "Freud's psychology." And there had to be quite a little of the infallibility of the Pope in his pronunciamentos.

He had now become so genial, however, that he even said a good word for America—namely, that she had produced John Dewey.

"John Dewey is one of the few men in the world," he said, "for whom I have a high regard."

I said that I had taught and studied under Dewey at Columbia, and thought very highly of him too, though the World War had divided us. "The war was a watershed in America."

That remark interested him, and he kept returning to it afterward. Indeed, he had a way of calling the conversation back to where it had been going, not letting it get lost, that reminded me of Plato's Socrates.

For instance, I said that the war was a watershed in America, dividing radicals from liberals, but not in Europe because in Europe everybody was in it whether he wanted to be or not.

"Officially," he put in with a sly inflection. And then

he exclaimed: "You should not have gone into the war at all. Your Woodrow Wilson was the silliest fool of the century, if not of all centuries."

He paused for an answer, which got stuck accidentally in my throat.

"And he was also probably one of the biggest criminals —unconsciously, I am quite sure."

I said that Woodrow Wilson's literary style was a perfect instrument of self-deception, and that delighted him. He asked me if I had read *The Story of a Style*, a psychoanalytic character reading of Wilson on the basis of the relative predominance of certain types of words in his speeches. I said I had, and we agreed in praising the ingenuity of its author, William Bavard Hale. We were a long way from my remark about the watershed, but Freud called me back to it.

"I would like you to say some more about that watershed business," he said.

"Well, take Dewey, for instance. He went over on the war side, and wrote a book against Germany, and it seemed for a time to change his whole way of thinking. Most of our intellectual leaders who did that stopped thinking altogether."

"Why?" Freud asked.

"You know why people stop thinking," I said. "It's because their thoughts would lead them where they don't want to go."

That amused him again, and the whole of his gentleness came back, including the delighted little crinkles at the corners of his eyes. He put his head way back finally and laughed like a child. Sometimes a child at play reminds you of an odd little old man; there was something of that odd little old man in Freud's ways. He waggled his head and hands about all the time, looking up at the ceiling and closing his eyes, or making funny little pouts and wry faces, when he was trying to think of a word or an idea. I never ceased feeling that underneath it all was an obdurate hard cranky streak, but I also never ceased feeling its great charm.

He was curious about the support I gave to the Russian Bolsheviks.

"You believe in liberty," he said, "and there you get just the opposite."

I gave him our glib explanation: the class dictatorship is transitional—a method of moving toward a more real and universal liberty.

He made gestures like a man fighting with cobwebs or doing the Australian crawl.

"That is all up in the air," he said. "People who are going to produce liberty some time in the future are just the same for me as people who are going to have it ready for you in the celestial paradise. I live in this real world right here. This is the only world I am interested in."

I told him the very thing I admired about Lenin was his way of taking the real world exactly as it is, and yet trying to do something with it.

"The Bolsheviks," I said, "have a hypothesis and they're trying it out."

That appealed to the scientist in him, and he became both serious and mild.

"It *is* an intensely interesting experiment," he said. "Really, it's all *terra incognita* to me. I don't know anything about it."

"What are you politically?" I asked.

"Politically I am just nothing."

He settled down in his chair and squinted at me.

"What are you going to do when you get back to that America of yours?" he asked.

"What makes you hate America so?" I queried.

"Hate America?" he said. "I don't hate America, I regret it!"

He threw back his head again and laughed hilariously. "I regret that Columbus ever discovered it!"

I laughed with him, and rather egged him on, no doubt, for I am not touchy about our national faults.

"America," he went on, "is a bad experiment conducted by Providence. At least, I think it must have been Providence. I at least should hate to be held responsible for it."

More laughter, and then I asked: "In what way bad?"

"Oh, the prudery, the hypocrisy, the national lack of independence! There is no independent thinking in America, is there?"

I said there was a new and lively spirit among people.

"Mostly among Jews, isn't it?"

"The Jews are not so free from prudery and hypocrisy," I replied.

He seemed to change the subject.

"You didn't answer my question; what are you going to do when you get home? Have you any definite plans?"

"None except that I am going to write."

"I'll tell you what I want you to do. I want you to go home and write a book on America, and I'll tell you what to call it. *Missgeburt*—What is that word in English?"

"Abortion?"

"No, not abortion."

"Monster?"

"Well, that will do. You write a book about the monstrous thing that America turned out to be. . . ." He paused. "The word is 'miscarriage.' *The Miscarriage of American Civilization*—that shall be the title of your book. You will find out the causes and tell the truth about the whole awful catastrophe."

He was standing up now.

"That book will make you immortal. You may not be able to live in America any more, but you could go and live very happily somewhere else!"

I had risen too, and he extended his hand.

"Now I want to see that next book of yours without fail. So please remember to send it to me, and I'll read it with happy memories of this conversation. . . ."

A very gracious dismissal! How suave and charming—on the face of it.

As I went down the steps, my thoughts recurred to his similarly gracious letter about my book: "Really important; probably also correct. . . . I enjoyed it far more than former works of yours!"

Are those—I thought—the European life forms? Is Freud a little vain and cranky with too much peering into other people's complexes? Is it perhaps our rather hard-headed skepticism about some of the more mythological of his reported discoveries in "the Unconscious" that caused this extreme feeling? His American friend and translator, Dr. A. A. Brill, told me that this feeling dated back to his visit to this country in 1909 and the meager recognition he received from scientific circles then. It seemed a strange thing for an admiring disciple of Freud to say so casually and calmly. For was it not to deliver mankind from just that kind of displaced emotion that this hero of self-knowledge was born into the world?

THAT VISIT IN VIENNA was but an incident in a one-way companionship which had begun with a deep plunge into Freud's books in 1914 and has never ended. When my account of it first appeared, I received a letter from Freud's sister, Anna Bernays, saying—very politely—that although I had met her brother, it was evident I did not know him. On the other hand, two distinguished psychoanalysts, one a former close colleague of the master, congratulated me on the justness of the impression I had gathered so quickly. The contrast intrigued me, and when another close colleague, Dr. Ernest Jones, began to publish his intimate biography, I seized eagerly the opportunity to know Freud a little better. I wanted especially to continue our argument about the concept of the Unconscious.

So far as concerns Freud's charm and the "obdurate hard cranky streak" I felt underlying it, Dr. Jones bore me out, I thought, completely. Freud's confession, quoted by Dr. Jones on page 8 of the first volume, sounded "cranky" enough in all conscience: "An intimate friend and a hated enemy have always been indispensable to my emotional life; I have always been able to create them anew, and not infrequently . . . friend and enemy have coincided in the same person. . . ." As for Freud's passion against America, that proved only more obdurate on better acquaintance, and more morbidly bitter, than I had realized in our conversation. To the end of his days—according to Dr. Jones— or at least until it moved down and became recognized as mucous colitis—he used to describe his intestinal disorder as "my American indigestion." His nephew, Edward L. Bernays, who is also the nephew of Freud's wife, gave me an explanation of this anti-American fixation which differs somewhat from that of Dr. Brill. He said that William James attended those pioneer lectures at Clark University in 1909, and being intrigued both by Freud and his ideas, invited him up to his summer camp in the Adirondacks. To entertain the distinguished guest, they all went out in the woods and cooked a beefsteak dinner, picnic fashion, over an open fire. That dinner was the awful beginning of Freud's indigestion, according to Bernays, and of his anti-Americanism.

"Why they're still savages over there," he grumbled, "they cook their food on heated stones out in the woods!"

Georges Duhamel

*By what frightful miracle does this land,
which stretches from the tropics to the icebergs, find itself so degraded and made ugly?*

The French novelist Georges Duhamel (born 1884) published
the most eloquent and devastating book on America in the
twentieth century. "He is the kind of man," one reviewer said
in 1931 when *America The Menace: Scenes from the Life of
the Future* appeared, "to whom one refuses to listen even when
he is right." Duhamel complained that he could make no distinction between America and Americans. Between us, he
wrote, "There rises I know not what monstrous phantom, a collection of laws, institutions, prejudices, and even myths. . . . I
see a system rather than a people." Harold J. Laski, who wrote

Georges Duhamel, *America The Menace: Scenes from the Life of
the Future* (Boston, Houghton, Mifflin and Company, 1931), pp.
78–82, 85–86, 88–92, 190–91, 194–95, 205–206, 214. Translated by
Charles Miner Thompson. Reprinted by permission of the publisher.

two brilliant studies of American life and culture, reviewed Duhamel, finding his tone extravagant, his style ironic, and his book, therefore, "of little value to the serious observer."

Duhamel visited the United States during the early days of the Great Depression. He saw the country in a state of remarkable economic despair, and when he looked at the desecration which a failed prosperity had wrought to landscape and city, he wondered if the effort had been worthwhile. Like H. G. Wells and others, Duhamel was saddened by the realization that this dirty, crowded, bustling and unaesthetic "culture" was the future of the world.

———————◆———————

LANDSCAPES
or
THE IMPOTENCE OF THE PAINTER

CHICAGO stretches along the shore of Lake Michigan for approximately twenty-eight miles—or rather, did stretch that distance, for, while I am writing my sentence, it has lengthened another mile. Chicago!—the tumor, the cancer among cities—about which all statistics are out of date when they reach you, and in regard to which every calculation must be done over again, since the figures always change before you finish it!

This urban monster is, nevertheless, but half a city. It radiates from a point on the shore of the lake; its heart is on the border of empty space. It is like half an apple. You are astonished to find so much noise and activity on the edge of nothing. For the lake, which is as big as a sea, is not the sea. It has not the breath, or the tumult, or the life, or the soul of the sea. With its marshy smell, which you meet everywhere, even in the bathroom and in the ice water from the special tap, with its gloomy horizon, and its great, livid, shimmering surface, reflecting a dull sky with slow smoky clouds in it, the color of pewter, it lies there like an enormous piece of absence, like a warning of death, like a symbol of non-existence. Chicago comes howling to a standstill on the edge of eternity. Certain fishing villages are said to lie "in the peril of the waves"; I greet with a solemn hymn Chicago, the proud, lying in peril of nothingness.

Of what use is it in these days to be "the youngest metropolis in the world?" Hardly risen from the marshes, Chicago already seems old, already too narrow, stifled by its very strength. Though it has only been in existence for a few decades, it already suffers as much as a city that has endured for centuries. It did not foresee the automobile, which stuffs and suffocates it. It has scarcely the years of a grown man, and yet the wave of time has already submerged and condemned it. Some years ago, the city reclaimed from the lake a large strip of land on which now run roads that serve as race-courses for automobiles, roads for which America has borrowed the name of boulevard. Cars are turned loose there like toys that have gone mad. They seem free at last to rush against one another, to defy one another. There are no pedestrians and no horses. That space they have conquered for themselves—for their very own.

"Here," muttered Mr. Merriman, "wheel to wheel, bumper to bumper in a solid block, every one does at least thirty-five miles an hour."

"Is it against the law to go slower?"

"Oh," murmured Mr. Merriman, "imagine a blood corpuscle that let itself go slower than the rest, and loiter along at its own convenience."

The automobiles formed, indeed, a horizontal cataract—a compact, well-directed flood, the drops of which must not touch one another.

Night fell. A thousand cruel lamps lighted and clashed

like so many daggers. I did not see the lake, but I divined its presence on my right—an abyss of silence, an infinity of cotton-wool in which the noise of the demoniac city was lost.

"Wait," said Mr. Merriman, "wait. We are still only on the edge of things. You have not yet seen the real face of the city. There is more to Chicago than all this."

I half closed my eyes, for I wanted to pull myself together and to muster my strength. The high range of buildings with a skyline that makes you think of a man with some teeth out, I refused to look at, and glimpsed only from the corner of my eye. By an ingenious system of approaches, the automobile returned little by little to more congested regions where the blood of the city became thicker and flowed less rapidly, where the trains of the Elevated roared like iron storms over an unclean and stupid crowd—men, beasts, and machines—and suddenly, without my being able to understand how we got there, we rolled into a large subterranean passage full of light and noise.

A short walk brought us to some stone steps on the bank of the Chicago River.

I said to myself, "I salute thee, ancient river. On thy lone and marshy banks, Cavalier de La Salle camped when, driven by his wandering spirit, he sought the great inland valley. Is it indeed thou, O ancient Indian river, thou whom the white man hath chained, thou whose course he hath altered, thou flowing no longer into Lake Michigan at the will of thine own lazy waters, but changed to a sewer, running, ashamed and enslaved, to the Mississippi that, with other foulness, carries thee on to the shark-haunted Gulf of Mexico?"

Wide, deep, and fetid, the river was at this point a harbor. The two superimposed roads crossed it on a two-story bridge, on which two rivers of men, vehicles, and noise flowed above the river of dirty water. . . .

Allow me for a moment to disgress from this scrappy narrative. Let Chicago stand back for a moment, behind its tainted fogs. As I write these lines, I am in my own home, in my own country, in my garden in Île-de-France, caressed for yet a little time by the smile of a civilization that is ancient, wise, and noble. And yet even here I am harried by crazy visions. There comes to me sometimes again a hideous desire once more to be at the window of the monstrous hotel where a man can change his room every night for seven years without sleeping twice in the same one, to be high up there for yet another moment as on the balcony of death, and to gaze with my whole strength, trying to comprehend this wretched, demented world, this world that has no witness, this hell that lacks a Dante.

O painters, my friends and brothers, you can never make anything of Chicago! You will never paint this world, for it is beyond human grasp. Chicago is no more paintable than the desert. It is prodigious and untamed; it is not a living thing. It has nothing in common with that familiar spirit who had no dearer wish than to find again the features of a face.

Everything that for centuries the artists of old Europe have painted has been in scale with man. True greatness is not a matter of absolute dimension: it is the effect of happy proportion.

America is devoted to its ephemeral works. It erects, not monuments, but merely buildings. Should it fall into ruins tomorrow, we should seek in its ashes in vain for the bronze statuette that is enough to immortalize a little Greek village. Ruins of Chicago!—prodigious heap of iron-work, concrete, and old plaster, the sole beauty of which will be gay plants and moss—I evoke you with horror and weariness of spirit. . . .

Sole interpreter of the genius of America, architecture seems debased in its designs, in its methods, and in its achievements. It does not know the soundest ambition of all: the ambition to defy time.

In that ridiculous moral atmosphere in which swarms, not a great nation, but a confusion of races, how can one possibly find that sublime serenity which art must have if it is to quicken and flower? I do not view the theories of Taine without suspicion. A post-hoc explanation, by a geographical determinism that a wise man would never make a basis for prophecy, is too easy. Yet all the same it is curious to observe that the moral climate of North America imitates in its sharp changes the variable humor of the great valley that extends from Labrador to the Gulf of Mexico. When the wind blows from the south, it is like the breath from a stove. If the wind shifts, it becomes on the same day like a killing blast of winter. Almost all America works in a draught, now burning, now icy. You are forced to conclude that man has adapted himself to it and likes it; at any rate, in the manner in which the Americans heat their houses and their railway trains, they follow the same programme: that is, sudden bursts of heat interspersed with shivering intervals. It is the climate of the "boom" and the "crash." We are far indeed here from Touraine with its smiling horizons, from the moderate Seine and from pure and sonorous Provence.

The American people have raised their inhuman cities on a soil that never invites moderation. Lakes, valleys, rivers, forests, plains—all are huge; nothing seems made to incline man to thoughts of harmony. Everything is too big; everything discourages Apollo and Minerva.

I have gazed on the Father of Waters, the legendary Mississippi. I found it hard to see. The greatest river in the world is very often invisible. It is strangled among the docks of New Orleans; as it will not endure the bridge from which you might at least look at it, it remains hidden, as secret as the Cloaca Maxima. Mile after mile in the plains of Louisiana, where the oil tanks glisten among the fields of sugarcane, I have pursued it. The great river is necessarily invisible: it traverses the dull plain between immense levees, like a shameful prisoner.

I have seen Southern forests that sadly dip their gray, mossy branches into the somnolent waters of the bayous. I have seen millions of birds desert the burning savannahs and under a wave of smoke, I have seen the boiling of the yellow marsh water. I have seen the Texan prairies parched by the summer sun. I have seen the Negroes picking cotton in Alabama. I have seen the Appalachian Mountains, where you can find a peaceful retreat. By what frightful miracle does this land, which stretches from the tropics to the icebergs, this country, which may be without grace, but yet is not without nobility, find itself so degraded and made ugly? The people who inhabit it seem more anxious to plunder it than to love it and beautify it. These fields are not ugly, but despised, slaughtered, and squalid, for they are left in prey to "renters" who seek nothing except an ignoble profit. Near the amorphous villages burn mountains of rubbish. The great cities like Chicago and Pittsburgh, in spite of their wealth, live on certain days bowed down under a lid of greasy, pestilential smoke. Seek—and find, as you find in Connecticut, for example—some charming landscapes in which there are water, pasture land, and cliffs, and they will be disfigured with boardings that display advertisements that fairly scream. Discover in the mountains a green valley traversed by a lively brook, and it will inevitably be encumbered with a steel bridge like a cage, soiled with a funereal whitewash. I understand clearly that a new country cannot provide itself with the little ancient stone bridges that are the pride and treasure of our provinces. But think! Natural riches that are asserted to be inexhaustible, the effort of millions of brave men, administrative ability that we are required to respect, and three centuries of conquest without a halt or retreat, have been able to produce nothing but a churlish civilization, whose hostile ugliness defies description.

North America, which has not inspired painters—which has not raised up any sculptors, which has prompted the song of no musicians, unless it be that of the monotonous Negro, and whose barbarously industrial architecture seems to care not at all for the judgment of future times, has yet produced poets and writers. Almost all of them—oh mockery!—have turned from their native soil, in bitterness of spirit. I am not speaking of the numberless scribblers whose obscure labors go to feed the thousands of magazines and of daily newspapers as thick as dictionaries. I speak of the clear-eyed men who are striving today to evoke and to judge the mad society in which they grew up, the men whose work expresses now despair, now anguish, now a furious disdain, and now a vengeful irony.

But to paint Chicago? How can one do it with mere words or colors? Music alone, it seems to me, could accomplish the task. And rather than any imitative rhythm, soon lost in this tumult, it should be bitter funereal chords, a heavy prelude to chaos.

MEDITATION ON
THE CATHEDRAL OF COMMERCE

MY CRITIC WILL RISE, red with anger, and with his proofs in his hand will point out to me that I have not understood.

Yet I have given my life to gaining knowledge of man, to the love, to the defense, and to the praise of man. Have I made all the long pilgrimage of life only to meet this rebuff; that is, this failure to understand, this renunciation of my hopes? Have I written all my long chant of confidence in man only to end in refusing my adhesion? Last bitterness of all: I have failed to love.

Behind the first critic, I divine another. He smiles, and shakes his head. "America," he says, with a wink, "is like a woman, like life, like the world. Everything that you can say of America is true, and the most violently contradictory thoughts and words have all some truth in them."

America? I am not talking of America. By means of this America I am questioning the future; I am trying to determine the path that, willy-nilly, we must follow. . . .

In the United States, that far western land which has already made us aware of the promises of the future, what strikes the European traveler is the progressive approximation of human life to what we know of the way of life of insects—the same effacement of the individual, the same progressive reduction and unification of social types, the same organization of the group into special castes, the same submission of every one to those obscure exigencies which Maeterlinck names the genius of the hive or of the ant-hill.

The essential difference between insect and human civilizations is that, whether for agriculture or breeding— which they practice with skill—for their surgery, their industry, or their architecture, insects seem never to have recourse to apparatus capable of prolonging, or supplementing, or multiplying the strength of the organs. They have invented neither tools nor arms. They have obtained everything from certain anatomical modifications. They have demanded laboratories, tools, and arsenals from their own physical structure. The troublesome question of occupations and social castes is solved by differentiations of structure. All their chemistry, which is not simple, and which is at once alimentary and therapeutic, industrial and military, remains an affair of glands and secretions. We have seen the feet, the mandibles, the antennae, and the sting all transformed to meet the needs of a civilization that is none the less masterly because it often inspires us with an unconquerable terror.

It seems to me that if mechanical progress should some day find itself impeded, either by the play of economic laws or by any other inveterate obstacle, future society would certainly find inspiration in the insects.

At the point to which American genius has attained, it will almost surely be obliged to seek an outlet in that direction. . . .

There are many who take no part in the game. There are those who hope for nothing more than to eat each day something edible, and to sleep each night under a roof. If you care to see some examples, take a seat in the subway or in the Elevated between midnight and one o'clock in the morning.

In front of you there are ten old fellows of indeterminate age and with no appearance of life. They would pass well enough for ghosts. Where are they going? From what morose hell have they come? Their features are sunken and drawn, as if they had been subjected to torture. With closed eyes, they doze, thrown one against the other by the swaying of the car. Almost all of them are chewing gum as they sleep: any one would think that this movement of chewing was that involuntary trembling of the jaw which during severe famines you can see in the dying. Sometimes one of them spurts a long white streak of saliva on the floor, in contempt of comminatory notices. Sometimes one of the miserable creatures opens his eyes, and rests upon you a look full of despair, of hate, or of boredom.

They are not the legendary workmen who, as all the world knows, receive a hundred dollars a week, and who consecrate to the "movies" all the time that they do not pass among the delights of the standard factory. They are those who people the hideous quarters of Brooklyn, or those miserable suburbs that stretch as far as the eye can reach along the plain of Chicago.

In brilliant New York I have seen as many beggars as

I saw in Moscow. I have seen wandering along the frenzied streets the strange old scarecrows who, on some evening of especial boredom and disgust, spend their last pennies for an old soap box, mount it at the corner of a square, utter a few vague words of sedition, and who then, if they are not yet citizens of the promised land, and, as such, reserved for different treatment, are locked up, conducted under sufficient guard to the port and generously supplied with a third-class ticket to take them back across the ocean.

Of what account are the avenues that look like deep streams of wealth flowing between illuminated banks! Of what account are the mountainous buildings that evening crowns with flame! Of what account are the docks overflowing with merchandise, the railway stations stuffed with trains like ranged artillery, the factories, the banks, and the palaces! Of what account is all that!

"Here," an American magistrate admitted to me, "here, when a man is poor, he is poor indeed." The civilization of ants extends over the continents from the cold of the North to the cold of the South. Perhaps here and there there is some palace revolt. But the civilization of the ants has lasted for centuries on centuries. There are no revolutions among the insects.

No revolution in the American ant-heap can be imagined —unless indeed some day without anyone's knowing why, without anyone's foreseeing it, without any one's succeeding in explaining it after the event, the incredible machine goes off the track, collapses, and falls in cinders. For in the case of man, you never know.

America may fall, but American civilization will never perish; it is already mistress of the world.

Are we also to be conquered, we people of ordinary lands?

I have seen the strangest "Americanisms" in Germany, that country where the young men on returning from their first trans-Atlantic trip speak of New York as "not bad, but not American enough." In the wake of the architects I visited the new city of Frankfort, a city of blocks that in their monotony were like white chalk cliffs inhabited by disciplined little animals.

There are on our continent, in France as well as elsewhere, large regions that the spirit of old Europe has deserted. The American spirit colonizes little by little such a province, such a city, such a house, and such a soul.

How can the universe avoid being dazzled? Behold, people of Europe, behold the new empire! It has had two centuries of success, a constant rise; few wars, all of happy issue; it has kept its many problems at a safe distance; it feels the pride of being a numerous people, rich, feared, admired, a pride that begins to stir in the humblest passer-by, lost in the corridors of the ant-heap, a pride that is capable tomorrow of delivering a hundred million souls to the enterprises of their intoxicated leaders.

Emilio Cecchi

Branching out in the most tangled way, ultimate political power often passes finally into the hands of the last gangster.

Leslie Fiedler has remarked in his *An End to Innocence* that Italians rediscovered America in the 1930's through the force of a literary critic's travel report: Emilio Cecchi's *America Amara* ("Bitter America"). This book, Fiedler tells us, "transformed America from a geographical and social entity to a fact of the Italian imagination." Cecchi hated the people but loved their literature, especially that of Poe, Faulkner and Melville. American writers served as "witnesses against their own civilization," a barbarous and perhaps contagious civilization, Cecchi feared. He lived at peace with Mussolini's fascism since he had a self-confessed sympathy for "cops on horses." But both pro- and anti-fascists used Cecchi's mirror of America for their own purposes.

Emilio Cecchi, *America Amara* (Firenze, G. C. Sansoni, 1946), "Impressions of his American visits of 1930–31 and 1937–38," pp. 207–21, 278–87. Translated by Robert Connolly.

Cecchi's *America*, written after two visits in 1931 and 1938, is a drama of soup kitchens and bloody gangsters, frenetic wives dominating materialist husbands, lynchings and murders—all acted out on a stage of vulgarity. "Cecchi has scrupulously collected a museum of horrors," a fellow-countryman wrote, "where he has isolated diseases and decadence, and recognized a world in which it is impossible to trust."

The following excerpts are drawn from Cecchi's discussion of lynchings, the generally crime-ridden state of America during the Depression, as well as a patronizing glance at the black bourgeoisie.

———————◆———————

5000 LYNCHINGS

FROM 1882 UNTIL TODAY [1938], over 5110 persons have been lynched in the United States. Lynching is usually reserved for Negroes. But it has also happened to whites, both men and women. Of the thirty-nine lynchings which took place during the period 1935–36, four of the victims were white. One of these four lynchings (Tampa, Florida, December 9, 1935) was carried out by a gang of masked people. The victim had not even committed a definable crime. He was merely, and vaguely, charged with "extremism." In the case of Negroes, the most frequent crime or charge is that of the abduction or rape of a white woman. In many cases, the charge is true; in others, it turns out to be false, but by then it is too late. Usually the victim is taken from prison, under the nose of the sheriff or the police, thrown into an automobile and taken to some lonely spot where the slaughter is carried out. Afterwards, the reports of the sheriffs and governors invariably conclude: "murder by unknown persons."

I have no love for sensational journalism and literature.

But one must tell things as they are, at the risk of offending timorous souls. On April 13, 1937, in Duck Hall, Mississippi, two Negroes, Roosevelt Townes and "Boot Jack" Mac-Daniels, both recently accused of having killed a shopkeeper, G. S. Windham, in December, were abducted in broad daylight, while the sheriff and two agents were escorting them back from the courtroom. They were taken to a spot ten miles away where three or four hundred men, women and children were waiting for them. "They were chained to a tree and holes were burned in them with blowtorch soldering irons; and after hours of this torture, they were shot repeatedly with revolvers. Finally, oil-soaked stubble was piled around them and they were burned; the fire was lit while they were still alive and screaming." (Reports from the local press and from *Can the States Stop Lynching?*, published by the NAACP.) Outcome of the legal investigation—no clues regarding the guilty, no arrests.

Even more terrible and incredible was the lynching of twenty-three-year-old Claude Neal, in Greenwood, Florida, on October 26, 1934. The youth's family had lived for years near the farm of a certain Cannidy. Young Neal and Lola Cannidy grew up together in the fields. Few among the Negroes didn't realize that, for some time, the two had been lovers. One morning that October, the girl went out of the house with the pretext of going to water the pigs. She was seen speaking to Claude, but no one paid any attention. The following day, her body was found a short distance from the farm. It was covered with twigs and branches, completely dressed. Around the neck were signs of strangulation; on the ground a watch, a ring and a hammer.

Claude was arrested immediately: "When she told me she didn't want me to speak to her any more, or she would get the whites after me, I went crazy and killed her." It was a common crime of passion, heightened by the racial difference and the threat that "she would get the whites after me." That alone would have been enough to lynch him. It is certainly not my intention to whitewash this blackest of crimes. Even though it is clear, for example, that the crime of Othello is infinitely more unjustified and in- human. But listen to the response of the crowd.

"They took him to a woods, about four miles from Greenwood; they castrated him, and made him eat that flesh. They cut his belly and chest to shreds; and they burned him from head to toe with red-hot irons. Every so often they hung him by a rope and left him there until he was on the point of strangling; then they would let him down and begin torturing him again. They cut off three fingers from one hand, two from another, and several toes. Finally they decided to finish him off. They tied the corpse in back of an automobile and dragged it to the front door of the Cannidy house. A woman came out of the house and plunged a butcher knife into the dead man's chest. Some kicked the corpse, while others squashed it by running over it with their cars. Children poked it with sticks. The fingers and toes were put into alcohol and preserved like precious relics. One, as a very special favor, split a finger in half and gave it to a friend. The Dothan, Alabama, radio station invited the crowd to witness the lynching." And the news- papers of Richmond, Savannah, Tampa, Miami, etc., carried the news of the imminent lynching. (Accounts of the press, and *The Lynching of Claude Neal*, edited by the NAACP, February, 1937.) The results of the legal investigation? No indication of those responsible, no arrests.

Not all lynchings are of such diabolical dimensions. And it would be foolish to assume that a lynching can be per- formed with kid gloves. But one can easily imagine the terror that such slaughter can spread in isolated regions, such as those of the South, where there is a very high per- centage of Negroes and a limited police force; and where a hard-bitten populace of property owners, tenants and farm workers, obsessed by the suspicion of intermingling and of the sexual threat of the Negroes and by equally serious economic reasons, will stop at nothing to keep the Negro in submission—even committing horrors such as those described above.

Thus, into the South has been transplanted that Puritanical hysteria which one writer ascribed to those pioneers of New England who barricaded themselves against the Indians during the middle of the seventeenth century: "To the generations raised in this moral climate, the Indians must have seemed children of the Devil. The Puritan traditions of evil and guilt received daily confirmation. The community swarmed with 'witches.' An anxious, neurotic people, in that land full of betrayal, fought invisible enemies, and ghostlike figures seemed to fly through the air." And to quote [Andre] Siegfried: "The cordial and well-mannered gentleman with whom you are speaking may well be a murderer who, at night, in the woods, led the pack of a hundred against one. . . . Texas, Georgia and South Carolina at first glance seem to be states of the twentieth century, but in reality must be included among those lands where pogroms are still commonplace." The uneasiness and ill-feeling stemming from racial diversity are aggravated by economic grievances. Negroes will work for little money with great discipline. And not only in menial positions. Despite the obstacles placed before them, they are developing skills, a fact already observed by Siegfried in 1925, and which has become increasingly evident. And at the Ford factory I saw Negroes tirelessly sweeping the plant to keep it spotless at all times. But I also saw others who had become skilled workers.

THE NEGRO PETIT BOURGEOIS

ALL THIS is not being written to disparage the Negro! He was born that way, and nothing can be done about it. Superimposed over his wild, bestial nature is a "petit bourgeois" mentality, the most "petit" imaginable. He thinks only of momentary needs, becomes an infant when confronted with a pair of fancy shoes, a record player, or a radio. He moans and cries at the Passion of Our Father, yet would sell his soul for a nickel. He wavers between the vaudeville show and the Apocalypse. Among city Negroes, socialist agitators can find elements who will organize riots and fights. When recruiting "scabs," agents for factory owners go first to the ranks of the Negroes. But, whether it be for revolution or counterrevolution, the Negro will never fight with enthusiasm: he lacks the strength of his own convictions. He has a congenital distrust of every historical process. He is as strong in his need and desire for money—and his refusal to sweat to earn it—as he is weak in his capacity to save and utilize it constructively. He is improvident, a big spender, a show-off—a child.

As an example of how this almost unbelievable childishness is reflected even in the most serious matters, I cite the feature article in the Christmas issue of the *Afro-American,* one of the most widely read newspapers in Harlem, Washington, Baltimore, and all of the principal Negro sections of the East. In it were dispatches from its correspondents in Rome, Jerusalem, Bethlehem, and Samaria, which described and interpreted the birth of Christ as though it took place today, grotesquely drawing from it political inferences useful to the democrats in their diatribes against the totalitarian states.

These are some of the more tangible reasons why such a fetid odor emanates from the Negro chicken coop in America. The whole of America is unstable and constantly changing. But Negro communities, whether on the fringes or in the very hearts of cities, as in Washington, represent the most turbulent, swarming concentration of that particular kind of deeply embedded savagery in which the American life still has its roots. One can see everywhere—in waiting rooms and in certain train compartments, in hotels and clubs, etc.—the segregation of Negroes. But this does not nor will it ever succeed in preventing an imperceptible and continuing osmosis of material, and, above all, moral values.

G-MEN

WITH THE ABOLITION OF PROHIBITION (1934), there was a sigh of relief in America and elsewhere: "This is the end of gangsters." Those who said that should have kept their mouths shut. Before Prohibition there were dozens of kidnappings, and many trains and banks were robbed. The correlation between gangsters and Prohibition was, to a large degree, incidental. In fact it was artificially inflated by the anti-Prohibitionists. However, there was at least this advantage: because of conflicting interests, gangs of bootleggers sometimes found it necessary to kill each other. With their sharpshooter's precision, they did, on their own, the cleanup job that the police should have done.

There was still another reason why the relationship between gangsters and Prohibition acquired such an exaggerated importance. And that was the fault of the movies. It is easy to see how the world of the bootleggers could lend itself to the most exciting and imaginative film thrillers, in the best cinematographic tradition, with settings of Rembrandt-like cellars, of bleak and lonely houses in the country. How could one effectively portray on the screen the drug traffic, or the white slave trade? One is hardly picturesque, the other too indecent. Not to mention what would have happened if some courageous director had gotten the idea of showing the gangs in their political and electoral functions—that complex and unknown sphere which constitutes the basis of their strength and their *raison d'etre*. The Americans, covering their eyes with both hands, would have been scandalized. The traffic in alcohol, by comparison, was a trivial thing, easily admitted. And so the movies did their work, until finally people believed that gangsters practically hadn't existed before Prohibition, and above all, that they would disappear along with Prohibition.

This was not the case, however, as anyone knows who has even an inkling of the history of American politics and its connections with racketeering and organized crime.

How can such obnoxious elements continue to exist in a modern state? Let me refer to the recent and authoritative testimony of J. Edgar Hoover, director of the American Division of Investigation [FBI], whose name, inasmuch as he is the chief of police in America, appears constantly in the newspapers. In his preface to the book of a specialist, Courtney Ryley Cooper's *Ten Thousand Public Enemies*, Hoover is asked to name the insurmountable difficulties of the police and of justice against this appalling American lawlessness. And he responds: "There are a number of contributing factors. The laziness and indifference of those who think that it is not their problem. The snobbery of another part of the public who see the gangster in a kind of heroic light. There are lawyers who not only defend the criminal if he is captured, but advise him at all times, and who devise with him schemes for evading capture." There are the tentacles of the underground which reach out into many walks of life, plus the penalty for squealers. The accomplice who is arrested and doesn't talk merely risks a trial and a mild sentence. For the one who talks, death is certain.

And there is another reason. In the actual words of Hoover: "There is the morass of ineffective laws, many of which were made by men whose fortunes were directly tied to those of the criminals." And, most important of all: "There is the political labyrinth, from the small-time crooked politician, whose electoral influence can often mean life or death, to the powerful 'boss' who rules an entire city by criminal means."

It is a terrible thing that the chief of police of one of the strongest states in the world has had to write these words, and that no one has thought of discharging him. What it boils down to is that, from the rhetoric of technical progress, the skyscraper, ice cream, there has sprung up a widespread idea of America which flatters and greatly falsifies its true moral and political physiognomy. The truth is that while this is an extremely vigorous civilization, with great potential, it is still primitive—all weaknesses and contradictions.

In this civilization, as various writers have observed, the civil and political power often resembles that of the barbarian emperors, who, in exchange for the concession of certain privileges, were elected and supported by feudal lords and barons, and were therefore constantly subject to threats. Branching out in the most tangled way, ultimate political power often passes finally into the hands of the last gangster. And the head of his nation's police force, who directs the hunt for this gangster, laments that it is so difficult, or so impossible, to catch him.

Adolph Hitler

*When one reads a book like this about them,
one sees that they have the brains of a hen!*

Adolph Hitler believed that American racial tension was so
grave that the government must fall apart. "It's a decayed country," Hitler told his aides, "and they have their racial problem
and the problem of social inequalities. Everything about the
behavior of American society reveals that it's half Judaised
and the other half negrified. How can one expect a state like
that to hold together?" During the Second World War Hitler's
deputy Martin Bormann gave him a copy in translation of the
English writer Eric Linklater's spoof on Prohibition, *Juan in
America*. Written in jest, the book confirmed everything he

Joseph Goebbels, *The Story of the Statue of Liberty* (Berlin and
Lisbon, 1942). Translated from the Portuguese by George Jacob.
Pictures reproduced by permission of the director of the Franklin
Delano Roosevelt Library, Hyde Park, New York.

always felt about that country; Hitler remarked, "And when one reads a book like this about them, one sees that they have the brains of a hen!" He instructed Joseph Goebbels, his propaganda minister, to use the failures of America—and especially the racial paradox—in all propaganda ventures. Late in 1942, Goebbels' ministry published a cartoon pamphlet showing President Franklin D. Roosevelt leading the Statue of Liberty off her pedestal to see the "glories" of American civilization: lynchings, miscegenation, "Negroid rhythms," the contrast between rich and poor—all the "glories" of America. The Statue, distraught by the tour, commits suicide by jumping into the ocean, where she finds the Constitution already sinking.

On December 28, 1942, Nelson Rockefeller, the Coordinator of Inter-American Affairs, sent Roosevelt this Nazi booklet, which was being distributed in Portugal and Brazil. Rockefeller told Roosevelt that he thought the Goebbels booklet "might be amusing for you." The booklet is rather clumsy as a propaganda effort and is, of course, openly and crudely anti-American. But it provides continuity in the themes of nearly two hundred years of anti-American thought. Roosevelt thanked Rockefeller for the cartoons. "I am delighted to see just what Goebbels thinks I look like and am doing. I should hate to disabuse his mind and it would, therefore, probably be best for him to jump into the Baltic before I catch him."

THE TALE OF THE STATUE OF LIBERTY

. . . and one day it happened that the Statue of Liberty
called Mr. Roosevelt and said to him: "I would finally like
to see something of America. Please show me everything
that you have achieved, behind my back, in the last 50
years." Roosevelt helped her descend from the pedestal
and accompanied her on a tour.

First, they arrived at Wall Street. "Here, dear Goddess of
Liberty, you can see how our ideals are well guarded.
There, on the top of the steps, are the latest, true idealists
of our century protecting against selfish interests in the
community."

"Here, on Broadway," Roosevelt explained, "the happy
inhabitants of our democracy satisfy their hunger for culture. We are the guardians of Western Culture."

"Here, in the newspaper district, you see one of your principal objectives realized: Freedom of the Press. Anyone can write freely what he thinks or sees."

"Here, in the heart of New York, your ideal of Freedom of Speech has become a fact. With our flag in his hands, anyone can say anything, as long as it is not against me."

"The postman is delivering new tax rates. All the residents are happy. They finally realize that I am a good statesman. Because, truthfully, everything that is good is also expensive."

"Here, dear Goddess, you can see one of my principal triumphs: All these men live free from misery and worries. They don't have to work any longer and can dedicate themselves to their private desires."

"In this beautiful community, you see Negro and white joined together for a traditional, popular celebration. Here we do not recognize racial differences!"

Finally, Roosevelt led the Statue of Liberty to his office. "From here," he said, "I direct the war against imperialism and against the appetite of conquerors."

"And what do those arrows signify?" asked the Goddess.

"These are my plans for the moment," Roosevelt said.

Roosevelt accompanied the Statue back to her pedestal. "Tell me, Mr. Roosevelt," the Statue asked, "Wasn't everything you just explained to me intended as ironic or in jest?"

Roosevelt answered: "Of course not! How could such an idea occur to you? I said everything in all seriousness!"

"In that case," the Statue of Liberty exclaimed, "*you* climb on the pedestal!" And then she threw herself into the ocean.

Kingsley Martin

The effect of the [McCarthyite] witch hunt is to produce a general level of conformity, a new orthodoxy from which a man dissents at his economic peril.

The Allied victory in the Second World War led to the emergence of two aggressive Superpowers, Soviet Russia and the United States, both heavily armed with devastating nuclear weapons, both competing for military supremacy. The worst features of the American response to Russia found expression in the notorious demagoguery of Senator Joseph R. McCarthy, a crafty seditionist who came to symbolize the more hysterical aspects of our anti-Communist crusade.

McCarthy charged that spies and "dupes", following orders from Moscow and Peking, plotted the overthrow of the repub-

"The American Witch-Hunt," *The New Statesman and Nation*, July 5, 1952, Volume XLI, Number 1044. Reprinted by permission of the publisher.

lic and its surrender into the waiting arms of Stalinist Russia. Defeat would come, McCarthy warned, not from military failures so much as through internal subversion. Treason lurked deep within the councils of government. How else could one explain the "loss" of China to Mao's forces in 1949; the Soviet occupation and domination of East Europe; the Russian achievement of nuclear parity with the United States within so short a time. "Twenty years of treason" was the cause, Mc-Carthy shouted, a "treason" presided over by liberal Democrats and "gutless" Republicans. Fortunately, McCarthy uncovered this "conspiracy so immense . . . this infamy so black." "I hold in my hand," McCarthy proclaimed from time to time, "51" or "87" or "200" names of high officials working to subvert national policy, steal secrets and poison the minds of patriotic citizens. Few of his charges were ever documented; none proved in court. "McCarthyism", a word meaning irresponsible, defamatory charges, blatantly hurled, was added to the language.

McCarthyism thrived in the nineteen fifties. Loyalty oaths were demanded from school children and generals alike. Accusations were made against prominent people in arts and letters for past beliefs and associations. Black lists were posted denying work to the "accused" or suspect. It was an age of domestic suspicion amidst an age of international terror.

Kingsley Martin, the left-wing editor of the British weekly, *New Statesman*, was a frequent critic of America throughout the period. He was especially distressed by what he considered the brutalization of American sensibilities hardened by the Cold War enthusiasm of the people. He protested against the "indoctrination of G.I.'s . . . being taught to regard all Asians as 'gooks,' and to make no distinction in Korea between soldiers and civilians." He challenged the total war policies of General Douglas MacArthur. He was appalled by talk of using Britain as an "American aircraft carrier" for a nuclear assault against Russia. However, Martin denied being narrowly anti-American. World hostility, he remarked, could be summarized by the tauntingly ironic phrase of Arnold Toynbee: "No Annihilation without Representation."

The following essay appeared in 1952 while both the Korean War and McCarthyism raged. The war ended in a bitter truce in 1953. A year later McCarthy was censured by the Senate for "rude and improper" treatment of his colleagues. He died in 1957 a rejected and pathetic alcoholic.

———◆———

MR. ROOSEVELT'S FAMOUS REMARK that America had nothing to fear except fear itself is often quoted in the United States today. Nothing more astonishes the European visitor than evidence of fear—the directions to public underground shelters in New York, the periodic air-raid practices; the awkward hush that may fall over a dinner table if someone ventures a "subversive" remark; the unhappy position of a professor who is suspected of once having been associated with someone who had signed a document that was also signed by a Communist. This, let us be clear, is in the background, not on the surface of social life. On the surface everything is normal except that the prosperity is fantastic, that, in short, America is the first country in history to produce guns and butter simultaneously and in immense quantities.

One result of this prosperity is to sever the alliance which normally exists in a Western democracy between manual and intellectual workers. Democratic progress has usually been the fruit of this alliance. Workers have struggled against intolerable conditions and eventually obtained the right to form unions; in the struggle they have accepted the alliance and often the leadership of middle-class liberals and socialists who are themselves concerned primarily with the right to speak and write and agitate as their conscience and interests dictate. Today this alliance is broken because the working classes are for the moment substantially satisfied. There are badly paid groups; there are white-collar workers who complain that salaries have not kept pace with inflated prices; there is a disgraceful housing shortage. Even so, some C.I.O. unions have manfully passed resolutions protesting against grave infringements of basic American rights, including academic liberty. But by and large the powerful unions are conservative and not much concerned with preserving the Bill of Rights. Never before has so large a proportion of the population had a chance of going to college, nor has anyone ever before imagined a day when so many working-class families would have their own cars, refrigerators, washing machines and television sets.

What signs are there then that liberty is in danger? The average citizen knows that Senator McCarthy is shooting wide and that he has failed to unearth one Communist in the State Department, where he declared he could name two hundred. They notice that a paper like the *New York Times* will sometimes point to excesses in the witch hunt, but they say, shrugging their shoulders: "After all, we are at war with Communists, aren't we? We can't run any risks of leaving them in positions of importance, and if a few innocent people suffer with the guilty, that can't be helped. No use saying that McCarthy's charges are ridiculous: if there were doubts about Hiss, there were none about Fuchs or any of the other Communist spy trials."

In England it is hard to remember that the United States believes itself at war, even if a strange and unfightable war, with China. In this atmosphere few realize how remote the present witch hunt is from any real effort to discover spies. The F.B.I. is specially equipped for dealing with espionage; certainly it knows better than to imagine that any spy would have joined any of the Attorney General's list of subversive organizations; the spy would not be trapped by a questionnaire; he would be a communicant as well as an ex-Communist; he would be more plausible and pious than McCarthy, more patriotic than MacArthur and more ready to testify than Budenz. He would work very closely (and very safely) with the F.B.I., learning much to his advantage from the association and helping to defame liberals who are the natural enemies of Communism, as of all totalitarian creeds.

The success of the ex-F.B.I. men who compiled *Red Channels* and who were responsible for the periodical *Counterattack* is well known. One or two notorious cases have informed the public which wished to be informed how the process worked. Details of how film stars, actors and writers have been deprived of their livelihoods by this smear technique can be found in a careful piece of research sponsored by the American Civil Liberties Union. Frequently the newspapers carry accounts of hearings before the McCarran Committee, of Communists who are excused from answering questions only by in effect incriminating themselves by pleading the First Amendment, which protects them from self-incrimination. Occasionally a sensation is caused by a star like Lillian Hellman who had the courageous idea of offering to answer all questions relating to herself but refusing to answer any which might incriminate others. Owen Lattimore, who has now won an apology from the State Department, has been criticised by some who call themselves liberal on the ground that to have fought back has deprived the academic world of the dubious distinction of always remaining polite even when filth is thrown in its face. But these are the headline examples which tell as little about what is really happening, as the original dismissal of the ten Hollywood actors and writers. The real pressure is a continuous day-by-day affair which has the effect of rewarding mediocrity, cowardice, and sycophancy and silencing independence and creative talent.

Let me give one example which happened to come my way. An American citizen who worked closely with the Administration during the war was recently asked to deliver a four weeks' course of lectures for a thousand dollars to an institute of higher learning. He accepted, pleased with the honor and the fee. He received a fourteen-page questionnaire which, he was informed, must be completed in every detail before he could be allowed to give the lectures. There were about 800 questions. They included medical inquiries—I noted them down myself—about whether he had "ever had terrifying nightmares" or was addicted to bedwetting! He was asked whether he had ever "received literature" from any of the Attorney General's subversive organizations (it would indeed have been suspicious if he had not). Every possible detail of his public and private life, that of his father and mother, that of his wife and her father and mother had to be given. To complete this part of the questionnaire alone, as he said in his letter of refusal, would have taken a month's research. The last question read:

> Are there any unfavourable incidents in your life not mentioned above which may be discovered in subsequent investigation, whether you were directly involved or not, which might require investigation? If so, describe. If not, answer "No."

He was informed that the correctness of his answers would be investigated. I should point out here that purges now go by perjury, and that to omit some "unfavorable" incident might well be accounted perjury. Supposing, for example, that he failed to give some details of his work in the New Deal? Would not that land him with a charge of

perjury if President Truman's Administration should give
way to one which regarded it as criminal (as many Republicans now apparently do) to have given aid to the Soviet
Union in the last war? My friend, being a man of independence and integrity, refused to complete this preposterous
questionnaire and lost the job and the honorarium attached
to it.

I have heard it argued that these things are not important
since American democracy has never been tolerant and
such hysterical periods have occurred in the past. The atmosphere in the Twenties, when Professor Chafee wrote
his great book on free speech, was similar. I am not, however, consoled by this consideration, since the psychological
background for witch-hunting will remain as long as the
Cold War continues. In the meantime, liberties which may
be hard to win back are apparently being lost. Since Communists threaten the overthrow of the State, few people
worried when ten leading Communists were jailed on
the charge, not of any overt acts, but on the plea that their
"conspiracy" to advocate Communist doctrine was itself an
incitement to violence. American purges are not to be
confused with those of the Soviet Union, since no one in
America has been shot for heresy. But the principle which
has shocked the Western world about Soviet trials appears
to be also at work in the U.S. People are defamed or lose
their jobs because they once held views or gave advice
which some authority retrospectively considers mistaken.
The withdrawal of passports on purely political grounds is
again a step in imitation of the Soviet Union. Distinguished
scientists find themselves unable to attend scientific confer-
ences which, as one New York paper pointed out, may in
future have to be held underground, where Communists
will be able to work with greater safety!

Most important of all, the effect of the witch hunt is
to produce a general level of conformity, a new orthodoxy

from which a man dissents at his economic peril. From the point of view of big business this has the advantage that if there is a slump, there will be no effective advocacy of another New Deal. Leaders of the Republican Party still do not understand that Mr. Roosevelt and Maynard Keynes saved capitalism, and that no one will have so much cause to rejoice at the destruction of liberalism as the Communist Party.

David Holbrook

Few Americans know what it is like to be bombed, blown up, invaded or to have one's country wasted. Mentally they are back in the "Spirit of '76": a fatal anachronism. No wonder they are so preoccupied with the dinosaur: Tyrannosaurus rex *could be their symbol.*

In 1967 an international group of prominent writers and artists were invited to respond to the following questionaire:

1. "Are you for, or against, the intervention of the United States in Vietnam?"

And:

2. "How, in your opinion, should the conflict . . . be resolved?"

Most replies were strongly against the American presence in Indo-China, the brutal nature of the fighting and the apparent

Cecil Woolf and John Bagguley, eds., *Authors Take Sides on Vietnam.* Copyright © 1967 by Simon and Schuster. (New York, Simon and Schuster), pp. 40–41. Reprinted by permission of the publisher.

illogic of the United States' role in the Cold War. Several writers went beyond mere criticism of foreign policy, suggesting that Vietnam was the true expression of American national defects, the culmination of a mindless civilization using criminal means to achieve corrupt ends.

David Holbrook (b. 1923) is a prominent English poet and novelist.

———————

FOR OR AGAINST. Against! I have recently been in America and the jingoism there appalled and terrified me. It manifested a naïve, fatal ignorance of present-day realities only possible 3,000 miles from Europe. In no European country could you parade "The Mothers of World War II" in a lorry: and nowhere else could newspaper leaders appear of the kind you read in the *Chicago Tribune* on "The American Mettle."

The great industrial and financial powers in America, urging their politicians from the background, play on this naïve jingoism, in promoting their wars here and there intended to "contain communism." For them the wars help to test strength, equipment and tactics; to draw attention away from the consequences of corruption, neglect and bad government at home; to consolidate the nation, so that it feels it has a common identity (even pleasant and otherwise humane people say savage things against "Communists" in America). War maintains a false boost to a rickety economy, as is so often recognized in financial comment there. The wars also provide a symbolic externalization of the fear and hate which lurk beneath the cosmetic surface of American life. They go with that divided conscience by which America lives—the neat opulence of suburbia only being possible because of the wastes of slums and poverty at home, and the wastes of corruption and destruction caused by American arrogance abroad.

Before I went to America I felt there must be an energy of democratic sincerity and integrity of principle there, in which there was hope. I came home dismayed, for it seemed to me that there was simply insufficient discrimination there to prevent America pouring out hate and evil into the world—even to the extent of being prepared to sacrifice the world's very survival, to preserve the American way of maintaining a sense of identity—which is mostly achieved at the expense of others.

Social responsibility, humane care and service, a disinterested concern for culture, learning and education—these count for little in America, where good government is distrusted, and graft prevents even such urgently needed developments as housing schemes. Despite its claims, in its relationships with the world America is not motivated by an essential concern for human rights and equality, in terms of the needs and potentialities of beings and life, but by power. So, they will buy out nations where they can, corrupt where they can, burn and torture where they can, and poison or deliberately spread disease where they can. They are utterly not to be trusted, and are unlikely to be restrained from destroying the world unless a majority of large nations can, by material and forceful sanctions, force them to behave, internationally.

One tries to hope for a change to come from within America; but here the most disturbing feature is that contempt for opinion, ideas and thought at large manifested by a society in which pragmatic utilitarianism and *laissez-faire* are triumphant. Education in America has been badly neglected and startlingly lacks those traditions and kinds of content which foster inquiring and challenging minds: The craven intellectual sellout at the time of McCarthy was symptomatic.

How should the conflict be resolved? Britain could take a leading part here, if our leadership were not so nervously concerned not to offend the American government and risk disturbing the holy precinct of American financial investment in England. Of course, for a substantial body of nations to meet together to reject and condemn America would cause a world economic crisis, as America tried (as she tries now with France) to corrupt, wreck, or undermine them—as a penalty for not fawning to Uncle Sam and bowing to American policies.

But Britain could have led such a group of nations; and what a relief it would be to grapple with such a consequent crisis! What a clean feeling one would have in Europe if a group of nations coldly dissociated themselves from Uncle Sam in his Far Eastern antics! But nothing so clear comes from the Labour Government, who have chosen to forfeit the world's future in consequence. I was deeply shocked to read, when in Rome in 1965, of Harold Wilson's endorsement of American policy in Vietnam. What dismay and contempt one found around one, at England's sycophancy!

Mr. Brown's new points* are concerned more to preserve Mr. Brown and to keep the Labour Party in power than to meet the situation—for who is going to negotiate under a threat of the resumption of bombing if negotiation fails?

America, believing so much in "mettle" and gallantry, is not going to withdraw. Every proposal from the West is based on the assumption that Hanoi will be broken. The proposals sound like armistice proposals, with a tinge of

* [The British Foreign Secretary's proposals, first put forward at the Labour Party Conference at Brighton on October 6, 1966, and repeated before the United Nations General Assembly on October 11, consisted of three main points: A conference between all the interested parties, a cessation of the bombing of the North, and an end to the introduction of US and North Vietnamese troops into South Vietnam. EDS.]

conditional surrender about them. Just as they wasted thousands of lives on Omaha Beach in Normandy because they refused to have waterproofed engineer tanks, the Americans will sacrifice thousands of lives in Vietnam rather than lose face, or risk any suspicion of hesitation that might be interpreted as "cowardice." To them peace doesn't yet seem tolerable. War is an expression of the American *raison d'être*—because American society lacks a peaceful sense of identity so badly. So, the more American "boys" are killed, the more jingoistic the local feeling in their newspapers, the more excitement in *Life*, the more impossible it will be to withdraw—or to act sanely in diplomacy. Few Americans know what it is like to be bombed, blown up, invaded or to have one's country wasted. Mentally they are back in the "Spirit of '76": a fatal anachronism. No wonder they are so preoccupied with the dinosaur: *Tyrannosaurus rex* could be their symbol.

Only the most forcible group of nations, called together by such a power as Britain or France, could so alarm the Americans by the threat of sanctions and material resistance (I mean economic resistance—which is where it will hurt them), could force the Americans to look at the Vietnam situation realistically. And here "realistic" means that they must stop bombing and withdraw the preponderance of their forces *before* negotiation can be acceptable. Every other kind of move will be taken for bluff or treachery—and very likely will be.

The other hope is that the situation at home becomes so delicate that America will not be able to afford the Vietnam war. The consequences of her *laissez-faire* attitude to planning are variously disastrous. Besides the derelict state of her education, such things as her production rates and her infant mortality rates are nothing to be proud of: they are behind those of many European nations. The racial problem is (with every reason to be) explosive. Indeed, this weakness of America at home makes Labour's treachery even more craven: America is very sensitive, and a little of the only treatment she respects—tough handling—might well provoke an internal regeneration by a healthy shock to American arrogance and complacency—which is our only hope.

Michel Legris

American pornographers, by pushing specialization to an extreme degree, have succeeded in catering to the infinite variety of tastes and desires, if not perversions, of their clients.

Since the end of the Second World War, television and movies have informed the world of American defects. The underside of American life is made public on an international scale. Foreigners no longer write of America in sensationalist tones for purposes of exposure. In the past ten years the image we have projected to the world is that of a nation which has assassinated a President; killed his brother; murdered a black saint; devastated a remote country for obscure reasons; shot its idealistic children; polluted landscapes and cities with mindless energy; debased culture; corrupted officials; indulged a traditional and strident hypocrisy; wasted billions on foolish projects while impoverishing a remarkably high percentage of

Michel Legris, "The American Way of Lust," *Le Monde*, July 8, 1970 (*Weekly Selection*, London). Reprinted by permission of *Le Monde*.

its own people; consumed a glutton's share of world resources —all the while proclaiming its virtues, its noble mission of freedom, and its surging destiny as the last, best hope on earth. The world sees an America at once brutal and violent, racist and hypocritical, pathetic, sick and, above all, threatening— to itself, civilization and perhaps, the planet. If our Golden Image of Perfection were ever a living thing, then we have become our own executioners.

The last two essays are drawn from recent (1970) accounts of two disturbing aspects of American life: the revolution in sexual freedom and the frequently displayed brutality of the police against demonstrators for peace and civil rights.

Michel Legris' "The American Way of Lust" tells the story of the new, though still tentative, American sexual freedom.

———————— ◆ ————————

WHEN FUTURE HISTORIANS study the morals of our times, will they see two distinct styles, Danish and American, in the pornographic "movement" which came into being in the 1970's?

It is tempting to lump together in one sweeping condemnation the pornographic films and illustrated publications produced in Denmark and their American counterparts, but the products of the two countries have at least until now shown marked differences in style.

Where the Copenhagen variety is rawer and frankly clinical, American pornography has to submit to certain restraints which tend to produce material offering more psychological satisfactions.

The fact that in sexual matters there is no censorship at all in Denmark—a stage yet to be reached in the United States—no doubt has something to do with it, although it may also be the result of varying mentalities, of two kinds of perverted imaginations. Perhaps, in this domain, there is an "American way of love."

In less than three years many of the stores around Times Square, New York, which used to offer films, photos, and gadgets to the often too-trusting buyer, have been turned into "pornoshops," "sex shops" or establishments of a similar nature. And they are multiplying rapidly, jostling one another, competing shoulder to shoulder, as it were.

Such an impressive volume of business would indicate that the market is vast. From the time offices close in the afternoon to two o'clock in the morning, crowds of men can be seen stopping to examine and leaf through, quite unselfconsciously, the "works" displayed in racks and on counters.

In Paris the purveyors of pornography are, so to speak, still in the apostolic stage. The customer can freely enter their stores; they can do everything to encourage him to browse, inspect and appreciate with no obligation to buy anything. If an occasional publication is offered under cellophane wraps, it is generally only a precautionary measure intended to avert the wrath of the police.

In the United States, however, business is business. It is somewhat old-fashioned to let customers see too closely what they may or may not buy. The important thing is to keep the merchandise moving. To discourage the curious who merely remain curious, some store owners place a good part of their stock of books and periodicals under cellophane covers. Whoever wants to find out more must buy— at prices that range from three to fifteen dollars. No more free thrills, no more casual snatching of stealthy pleasures. Other stores charge an entry fee—usually fifty cents— which is deducted from the price of any article eventually bought by the customer.

American pornographers seem to have discovered another way to widen and titillate their circle of clients. By pushing specialization to an extreme degree, they have succeeded in catering to the infinite variety of tastes and desires, if not perversions, of their clients.

Their subjects range well beyond the three categories —the heterosexual, male and female homosexual relations— which continue to be exploited by the Danes, who, however broad their minds, have such narrow vision that they reduce the sexual act to its physiological expression; the height of imagination as far as they are concerned is an orgy involving half a dozen men and women.

Examined in this light, all the recent illustrated pornographic literature published in the United States deserves to be carefully studied by sociologists and psychologists. Perhaps they will discern in the use of Negro "models" an intent which goes beyond the mere exploitation of their bodies. It seems designed to cater to certain fantasies, racist, or anti-racist, associated with an issue which looms so large in the country's politics.

HAUNTING FEAR OF ISOLATION

IN A SIMILAR FASHION, any of the favorite subjects dealt with in pornographic magazines seem to be expressions of the fear of being isolated which haunts so many Americans. Illustrations of group sex practices, first imported from the Scandanavian countries, are perhaps one manifestation of this fear.

The very large number of dramatis personae used here, compared to the modest Danish casts, are not just a reflection of the superior financial resources of the American "producers." Nor are they merely trying to perpetuate the Hollywood tradition of glossy extravaganzas, of which Cecil B. De Mille's productions remain the classical examples. It is no longer small groups of persons, but masses of human beings who grapple together, clutching at one another in an incredibly confused heap, as if each of them were trying, through sex and nakedness, to become one with the mass, to merge with it, seeking in the one gesture both oblivion and total awareness.

Friendship and camaraderie, the usual ways of avoiding solitude, inspire many pornographic scenarios, which also exploit the legends that surround sport. The intimacy prevailing in dressing rooms and shower cabins serves as a backdrop for body contacts which quite naturally have the blanket excuse of being accidental.

Violence, that other constant of American life, evidently provides an abundance of material for the purveyors of pornographic literature, whose "productions" give pride of place—noblesse oblige!—to masochism and sadism.

An addiction to scenes in which whips play a prominent part betrays a very Anglo-Saxon preoccupation with corporal punishment. So, for instance, a fat paperback flaunts the title *Encyclopaedia of Birching*, and the Marquis de Sade's writings are shamelessly plundered for suitable illustrations.

But what seems to hold the greatest fascination for customers is "realistic" cruelty, which is not limited to the glorification of the overpowering virility of leather-garbed police officers, but sometimes shows open disregard for particular sensibilities. A paperback now being sold in the United States portrays on its front cover beautiful nude women cowering at the feet of strapping young men wearing storm trooper uniforms complete with swastikas on the brassards. The caption underneath reads: "Young Jewish girls in a Nazi camp."

The greater attention which is so obviously paid to details in the scenario, setting, atmosphere, and the explanations—for texts are printed along with photographs—in American magazines, as compared with Danish publications, is probably intended to make up for the fact that the American illustrations do not go "all the way."

American law forbids it. The code even defines the

point at which an illustration may be considered obscene. So in page after page the reader is treated to a ridiculous procession of naked males embracing equally naked females, involved in the most studied acrobatic exercises, while avoiding any direct contact and preserving the frozen expressions of marble statuary.

Perhaps some American customers feel frustrated by the restriction, for already a few bookstores have begun to offer under-the-counter novelties—photographic copies of magazines produced in Copenhagen.

There are not too many of these magazines around, but one wonders whether it is the law as it stands today which is really holding back publishers. It would be helpful to discover to what extent male readers of these magazines identify more readily with a hero when he is apparently afflicted by that cursed weakness of hard-driving men in a highly civilized society—impotency.

The fact that a few restraints are still being imposed permits pornography to cling to its last fig leaf—hypocrisy. The nude photographs displayed under glass in stores are adorned with "pasties," which serve as much to attract attention as to hide details.

Entrances to pornoshops carry the notice required by law: "You must be over 21." But underneath there is the tantalizing proscription: "Men only." Excluding minors does not prevent them being offered up to the delectation of the customers. Once inside, the client can take his pick of albums that display the beauties of children ranging in age from eight to fourteen. The albums are never advertised for what they really are; the nudes are referred to as "sun children" as though the principal purpose was to glorify the benefits of fresh air and naturism.

They are not the only publications to use nudism as a cover for pornography. Others exploit the educational use of sport in their displays of "American athletes." Another category subtly flatters national pride by offering lusty, godlike "young American males" for adoration by male readers.

The purpose of some of these publications being manifestly uplifting, it is not surprising to find the "models" thinking of making a career of their activities. Unlike in Denmark, the models in American pornographic magazines do not always remain anonymous, and some publications even carry lists of credits with the names of the "artists." Which, again, is typically American.

Needless to say, the Times Square stores do not confine themselves to the illustrated magazine trade. They all have plentiful stocks of films which are sold at an astonishingly low price, varying from eight to ten dollars per reel. More than that, the films are also distributed on a nationwide basis through a vast vending machine circuit.

In busy streets, at crowded corners, doors open onto strange dark halls furnished with half a dozen, a dozen or a score of tiny cubicles, each no larger than a coin-in-the-slot photo cabin. Once seated inside, the customer draws a curtain, slips a quarter into a slot and a screen before him lights up for a few minutes. A complete film consists of several episodes, usually six, and entails a total expenditure of $1.50. In spite of, or perhaps because of, the relatively greater liberty that the films enjoy compared to illustrated magazines, these establishments are subjected to stricter rules. Only one person at a time in a cabin . . .

SUPERMAN GETS INTO THE ACT

ONE WONDERS whether it is possible to go any further than behind a shabby curtain. And the answer is: Yes. West . . .

The appearance of pornographic funny magazines may be considered as the beginning of an attempt to question pornography itself, or they may be, on the contrary, one more proof of its corrupting power.

The magazines take the form of comic strips, where the playboy has replaced the cowboy, and Superman, in addition to righting wrongs and displaying his conqueror's prowess, excels in more earthly feats, even if they are accomplished with extra-terrestrial partners.

In any case, the profusion of illustrated "pornographics" has been a contributory factor in damaging the trade in pornographic literature proper. Since 1967, when a series of United States Supreme Court decisions legalized the distribution of such books in a country which until 1959 had banned the publication of *Lady Chatterley's Lover*, the trade in pornographic books has made a fortune for several publishers.

Today many of these same men find their businesses threatened. The reason is simple: it lies in the greater impact of the picture over the written word, of the image over that which is imagined. Some publishers have hastily turned to producing illustrated magazines and films.

Can the gradual disappearance of poorly written material (in 1967 they were selling around 60,000 copies per title, but today the figure has dropped to a bare 6,000) be considered a boon to the "good" pornographic authors? That, at any rate, is the view of a former Paris publisher, Maurice Girodias, who left France because of government curbs on the output of his Olympia Press and settled in New York three years ago, where his new venture, Olympia Press, publishes a dozen titles a month, each priced at $1.95 and running into between thirty thousand and forty thousand copies.

Despite the success he claims for his publishing venture, M. Girodias plans to diversify his activities. He has just finished work on a full-length feature film, *Barbara*, and, in association with a partner, he intends to have translations of his authors published in Holland, Italy, Germany and France.

One of his projects this summer is to have his books

translated into Russian. He sees the works being snapped
up by Soviet sailors in Western ports, and through them
Olympia Press writers would be able to get into the Soviet
Union's blackmarket book trade. The object of all this
is not just to corner the potential Soviet market; as a poker-
faced M. Girodias puts it, "There's a revolution to be
carried out."

It is easy, after all, to understand why New York
pornography can now only hope to dream of conquering
the East. Pornography in the West, the Far West, has so
outstripped the products of New York that it has nothing
more to learn from the East.

Like New York, Chicago, and other large cities, San
Francisco and Los Angeles also have their pornographic
bookstores where the same magazines are sold, at slightly
higher prices. But pornographers here have an added source
of revenue in the sale of erotic plastic objects which make
up "between thirty and forty per cent of the receipts," as
one dealer in such prosthetics estimated. In Los Angeles the
trade is largely concentrated on Santa Monica Avenue,
and the customers are mostly men.

Private projection studios in the back rooms of certain
stores are as common here as elsewhere, but these are not
the principal outlets for the industry, which has given rise
to highly specialized cinemas. For a relatively steep fee—
between five and ten dollars—the public is treated to a
series of short films which run continuously.

Two or three big Hollywood cinemas now show fea-
ture-length films produced in the studios of the larger com-
panies, a few of which have begun, very timidly, it is true,
to exploit the pornographic field.

FROM PICTURES TO LIVE FLESH

BUT A PICTURE is after all only a picture. The California
pornographers understood that they could do better simply

by offering models . . . in living flesh. The cocktail lounge-type establishments in New York and relatively prudish Washington which try to lure the passer-by with a promise of "topless" or "bottomless" service are in reality just playing with words.

The young women whose job it is to stand jiggling all day long on a platform usually wear two stars and a tiny triangle. In San Francisco the stars have fallen. Between street numbers 8000 and 9000 Sunset Boulevard, Los Angeles, a forest of neon signs proclaim "Total Nudity."

Two or three nightclubs in Los Angeles are doing a better trade than their competitors. Here the customer has to pay an entry fee of two dollars and is given a seat at a long counter, but it is not for drinking. An unbroken procession of young girls and women walk down the counter, each going through the same tired old bump-and-grind routine of the striptease dancer until she stands there quite naked.

When a spectator waves a bill, she minces up to him and bends forward to take the money. It is the act of bending, performed more or less slowly, depending on the size of the proffered bill, which constitutes the supreme moment for the spectator. His neighbors crane over his shoulders to take a closer look, and some do not hesitate to use their cigarette lighters to discover what the shadows hide.

What is astonishing in all this is the incredible calm of the spectators. There is no rush, not the slightest attempt to indulge in a misplaced gesture, no obscene comments (they are banned) directed at the dancers. On the contrary, absolute silence prevails in the room.

The appearance of this kind of establishment gives some idea of the extent of Asian influence on America's West Coast. It is an influence which is even more perceptible in the countless "massage salons" flourishing in Los Angeles and San Francisco; they compare favorably with those

whose charms have profoundly impressed travelers to the
Far East. But it is an influence which has been warped in
its passage to the United States and it has undergone a
further mutilation in its desire to adapt itself to American
laws and American tastes.

It is warped because California's "massage salons" are
a copy of the establishments which mushroom in Hong
Kong and Bangkok, where local color has been sacrificed
in order to meet the growing demand created by tourists
and, much more important, American troops. In Bangkok
alone their number has risen to six hundred within a few
years: six hundred establishments in each of whose ultra-
modern show windows a dozen young Thai girls, wearing
a number on their white blouses, pass their time reading
magazines or knitting while they wait for the visitor seeking a spinal massage. The very high degree of Americanization which these places have undergone is evident in their
standardization, not to mention their streamlined efficiency.

It is a warped influence, for the gentleness and delicacy
of the Asian girls is cruelly missing in their white counterparts in Los Angeles and San Francisco, who are apparently concerned solely with efficiency and who know no
other rule than that of hypocrisy. The means employed by
massage parlors to sell their services are suggestive. Advertisements, which even appear in telephone directories,
promise a satisfying massage at Lolita's, or offer to lead
clients to the "utmost limits of relaxation," or sing the
praises of some establishment where "six well-trained Scan-
dinavian girls are waiting to serve you." Businessmen are
given every assurance that they can relax without neglect-
ing their principal interests: "We provide private massage
rooms with telephone and Wall Street Journal."

Having spent fifteen dollars or so, the massage parlor
client—especially if he is new to the establishment—risks
experiencing some rude disappointments with no possibility

of complaining, for the trickery is cleverly practiced and stops short of outright illegality.

The client is first made to strip completely naked, which is understandable since these places are provided with saunas, and he is expected to take a shower before he receives the attentions of the masseuse. The young girl assigned to look after him drapes his body with a sheet first, and the ensuing treatment is technically unimpeachable, soothing and genuinely relaxing. After all, that was what the advertisement promised.

But—and this is the catch—the softness of her touch and the manipulations of her fingers may sometimes induce a certain tension in the client who, thus led to the threshold of total relaxation, runs a good risk of being left just there. Should he make the slightest gesture, or improper suggestion, he will be met with a scandalized refusal.

"We do nothing illegal here," snorted a virtuously indignant operator of a massage parlor. And she was probably telling the truth, for in reality these establishments merely provide the ingredients for concocting pleasure, not pleasure itself. They resemble, in some ways, those stores catering to "do-it-yourself" enthusiasts where one can buy all the parts needed to make an article, but not the article itself.

These young women and girls who so expertly practice massage would be surprised, perhaps even hurt, were they to be told they are the near-virgins of prostitution. They do however offer to practice their skills in the homes of clients, and some of them even hint they would not mind being invited out after work, which usually ends around two in the morning. In such a case, the bargain is sealed with a wad of notes slipped into the palm of the compliant masseuse. The rest is predictable.

To stay within the law, to keep up appearances, to exploit to the maximum all that is suggestive in sham and pretense—this seems to be the final stage of Anglo-Saxon Puritanism. After all, what is the law in question? A religious law? If so, it is one that has become extremely flexible.

The law permits citizens to heap derision on law-enforcement officers. At the Runway Nightclub on Cienaga Boulevard, where women are not just naked but expose even the most intimate parts of their anatomy to spectators, the doorman is dressed up like a policeman, complete with nightstick, helmet and badge. That there is in fact a law which forbids the wearing of police uniforms by unauthorized persons compounds this contempt for the law.

FEW WANT TO BE POLICEMEN

ANOTHER NIGHTCLUB similar to the Runway carries a notice indicating that it must restrict admission to one hundred thirty-nine persons. Hygiene, personal air space, safety—these are the latest embodiments of virtue.

Sometimes even justice seems to take pleasure in putting itself in ludicrous positions. A recent Los Angeles court decision over *Oh Calcutta!* was, for instance, greeted with gibes and hoots of derision. Since the musical was the object of an obscenity charge, the judge ruled that in order to ascertain at first hand the grounds for the complaint the entire show should be filmed.

Meanwhile, however, the show closed in Los Angeles, because it had been playing to very poor houses. Indignant that the cameramen who had been assigned to the job were left with raw film on their hands, the judge slapped a contempt-of-court charge on the theater director.

The changes in laws from state to state, even sometimes from county to county within a single state, only add to the contradictions and the confusion. What is permitted in Hollywood is illegal in Beverly Hills.

Little by little the authorities have relaxed the strict bans they had imposed on the use of live models in pornographic representations. Everyone is carefully watching the decisions handed down by the Supreme Court which invoke the First Amendment to the Constitution to set more and more liberal precedents.

The Supreme Court has for some time been grappling with another problem—postmen who have begun to object to handling pornographic mail (its volume has been increasing recently) on grounds of conscience. Even this hurdle is likely to be overcome before too long. Publishers of salacious magazines have only to wait—impatiently perhaps, but quite hopefully—for the day when the Supreme Court will authorize the erect male member to figure in pornographic tableaux. "It will only be a matter of months," they say.

In addition to the general permissiveness and the woolliness of legal definitions, there is also the great difficulty experienced by California cities in recruiting police officers. Few people want to join a service that is so disparaged today. San Francisco, with its population of seven hundred fifty thousand in the city proper, of whom ninety thousand are homosexuals with two hundred fifty bars for their own use, has hardly one thousand seven hundred men on its police force. A police official recently expressed concern about the incredible difficulty of infusing enthusiasm for the profession. In certain wealthy and fashionable areas of Los Angeles, the residents have set up their own security forces.

Are these materially privileged people now beginning to discover the dead end to which the worship of Mammon leads? When all is said and done, wherever the ultimate moral criterion may lie, it is most visible in pornography, where a sort of absolution appears to be granted in advance to those who make a fortune out of it.

"All that is not forbidden is allowed" appears to be the rule implicitly followed by these businessmen, all avid readers of the Bible, who might have interpreted Saint Paul according to their lights: "All things are lawful unto me, but all things are not expedient."

Their idea of what is lawful and expedient is probably the same which, consciously or otherwise, is being questioned by some young people, whose charges on one particular point are, however, based on shaky premises. If, as they say, it is possible to speak of a commercial civilization in connection with pornography, one should logically abandon the idea of a consumer civilization. For pornography merely supplies a substitute for sexual satisfaction; it is the substitute that pornography is engaged in promoting.

Edward Thorpe

*"When you see one of those sonsa-bitches
make the peace sign you're gonna be drilled
so's you can place your baton right between
his goddammed fingers."*

Edward Thorpe's *Blueprint for Brutality* is a report by a young
English novelist of a "riot"-control training session held by the
New Mexico State police. The sanction of government is now
joined to the violence of the mythic West, and now the "posse"
is armed with credentials. Now the "lynchers" wear badges of
legitimacy.

I WAS IN NEW MEXICO doing research for a novel, and the
State Police had been very helpful. I got a call from Billy,
a friendly highway patrolman: would I care to go along

Edward Thorpe, "Blueprint for Brutality," (Manchester) *Guardian
Weekly*, November 14, 1970.

and watch their riot training? It wasn't in the line of my research but I was interested to go.

Billy picked me up at a hamburger bar on the outskirts of town, and we tore down the highway in his souped-up patrol car to the new, fortresslike State Police Headquarters. He was proud to show me around the comfortable, carpeted administration block, the canteen, the cells, the bleak interrogation room complete with two-way mirror. From a file he produced a pile of photographs, mostly Polaroid pictures, taken the night before when there had been a big hash bust. They showed a roomful of smiling hippies, with several close-ups of a naked girl with a mound of marijuana on her chest, like a third breast. At the bottom of the pile were some black-and-white photographs of people walking in the main shopping streets and sitting in the town square. "What are these?" I asked. "Have they come from a family album?" "No," said Billy, "they're jus' our reg'lar undercover photos." I remembered then that when we had first been introduced, quite by chance, he already knew where I was staying and how long I had been in the town.

I felt I was passing some sort of test when Billy handed me a folder containing pictures of the decomposing body of a murdered Navajo; he watched me closely as I stared at the gruesome evidence but I kept, I think, a poker face. "You must have had a problem of identification," I said. "Yeah, we never did find the killer."

We went along to the lecture room and I was introduced to Billy's colleagues, big muscular men in tight black uniforms, highly polished black gunbelts and boots, and black peaked caps. They all wore dark glasses which they never took off, and most of them sported large, elaborate turquoise and silver rings and bracelets made by the Pueblo Indians on the local reservations. We sat around a table and listened to the instructor. It seemed there had been a little trouble on the local campus a week or so before and the cops had been criticized for being indecisive and uncoordinated, hence the need for riot training. "You can take it from me, men," the instructor said, "there's more trouble comin' an' when it does we're gonna be good an' ready. When you see one of those sonsa-bitches make the peace sign you're gonna be drilled so's you can place your baton right between his goddammed fingers."

On the blackboard he showed us how the police would be deployed on the campus: two lines of men to face the students, with back-up groups behind and others waiting with strategically placed patrol cars and paddy wagons to take charge of prisoners. There would also be an ambulance group for casualties. The forward lines of men would advance shoulder to shoulder, with helmets on and batons at the ready in the approved position.

There are many approved positions for the baton, so many, in fact, that even with the illustrated manuals we had in front of us the men found it all rather bewildering. To make it easier the instructor demonstrated in slow motion: "Pull the baton from the ring in your belt, holding it just in front of the rubber grommet, so; present it at your opponent's chest, so—that will distract him; then swing it in a tight arc above your head and bring it down against the side of his neck; from this position you can come forward again, jabbing him in the balls; as he goes down you can hit him on the knee or head."

We spent an hour or so watching his smooth, practiced baton-work. There were lots of questions about the practical difficulties of advancing together, of making the same blows in unison as the manual advised, of hearing the orders clearly with helmets on, of what to do if one of the cops was himself struck down. There were comments on the seemingly overcomplicated riot drill and complaints about how their helmets were scratched and knocked about and insufficently smart to make an impression on the recalcitrant students. On the other hand, someone said, dented helmets might help to intimidate the rioters. "Kinda looks like we're used to brawlin'." When all the questions and suggestions had been dealt with, we piled into five or six patrol cars and went off to the National Guard gymnasium for practice.

It was a swelteringly hot afternoon, so the men took off their caps and shirts and gunbelts. Some of them took off their bracelets, too. There were five basic Striking Exercises in the manual, so the instructor decided to concentrate on the first two. Trouble, he said, was not far off, and it was better to be proficient in two exercises than make a mess of all five.

They started slowly, almost elegantly, repeating each stroke several times before attempting to run them together in the complete cycle of movements. When they did it was a shambles.

Some men were caught off balance when the instructor pushed them; some went faster than others so that the line became wavy as they surged forward, and some completed the exercise while others were only halfway through. One man got a nasty crack on the elbow when the man next to him wielded his baton rather wide. He danced about holding his arm and yelling while the others laughed. The instructor waited patiently for the noise to subside, then in order to try and keep them together he made them call out the strokes by numbers, flourishing their batons and doing the accompanying footwork as if they were a line of Radio City Rockettes rehearsing grotesque routines.

After an hour they were managing to keep together pretty well; at the end of the afternoon they were performing the two Striking Exercises in perfect unison. For the last twenty minutes, when the men were sweating and irritable and exhausted, the instructor worked a little on their psyches, exhorting them to "give those motherfuckers hell," ordering them to curse and scream and shout and make spine-chilling ritual noises like Samurai in Japanese films.

I sat nervously at the end of the gymnasium watching the flailing phalanx advance across the floor, shoulder to shoulder, beating imaginary opponents across the head and neck and knees, thrusting their batons into stomach, ribs and groin, mouths agape as they bellowed hate, eyes still invisible behind the blank sockets of their sunglasses. But I imagine they will take those off when they actually reach the campus.

SOURCES

The foreign literature on the United States is vast. I examined nearly one thousand articles and books, much of the material boring and repetitive. Rather than clutter the text excessively with detailed citations and bibliographical listings, I've attempted to combine both functions in the following chapter notes.

For purposes of abbreviation I've used the following citations:

DNB: *Dictionary of National Biography* (London, Smith, Elder and Company, 1888)

COMMAGER: Henry Steele Commager, *America in Perspective* (New York, Random House, 1947)

NEVINS: *America Through British Eyes* (New York, Oxford University Press, 1948)

INTRODUCTION

The remark by Freud is from Ernest Jones, *Sigmund Freud* (New York, Basic Books, 1955), Vol. II, p. 60. For a suggestive discussion of Freud's anti-Americanism, see Paul Roazen, *Freud: Political and Social Thought* (New York, Alfred A. Knopf, 1968), pp. 97–101. "Like Marx in his distaste for Russia," Roazen concludes, "Freud detested the country which chose him as its prophet."

Classic foreign writings on America include: M. G. St. John de Crevecouer, *Letters from an American Farmer* (London, Printed for T. Davies, 1782); Alexis de Tocqueville, *Democracy in America* (London, Saunders and Otley, 1835); James Bryce, *The American Commonwealth* (London, Macmillan and Company, 1888); Andre Siegfried, *America Comes of Age* (New York, Harcourt, Brace and Company, 1927); and D. W.

Brogan, *The American Character* (New York, Alfred A. Knopf, 1944).

For various interpretations and collections of foreign writings in addition to COMMAGER and NEVINS, see: H. T. Tuckerman, *America and Her Commentators* (New York, Charles Scribner's Sons, 1864); J. G. Brooks, *As Others See Us* (New York, Macmillan Company, 1908); Oscar Handlin, ed., *This Was America* (Cambridge, Mass., Harvard University Press, 1949); Alan F. Westin, Julian H. Franklin, Howard R. Swearer, and Paul E. Sigmund, eds., *Views of America* (New York, Harcourt, Brace and World, 1966); G. D. Lillibridge, ed., *The American Image: Past and Present* (Boston, D. C. Heath and Company, 1968). Marcus Cunliffe's brilliant essay "Europe and America," *Encounter* (London), December, 1961, led to the chapter on Duhamel. *The Harvard Guide to American History* (Cambridge, Belknap Press, 1961), Second Edition, has detailed listings on travel literature which should be supplemented by the bibliographies in NEVINS, COMMAGER, Handlin, Brooks and Lillibridge.

De Pauw

Henry Steele Commager and Elmo Giordanetti, eds., *Was America a Mistake: An Eighteenth Century Controversy* (New York, Harper and Row, 1967), includes biographical details as well as extracts from other philosophical works on mythical America. Durrand Echeverria, *Mirage in the West: A History of the French Image of American Society to 1815*, (Princeton, Princeton University Press, 1968, Revised Edition), is a brilliant analysis of the most influential European writers during this period. Howard Mumford Jones, *O Strange New World: American Culture, The Formative Years* (New York, Viking Press, 1964), provides background on the world image of America before and after discovery. All of the above studies are indebted to Gilbert Chinard, "Eighteenth Century Theories of America as a Human Habitat," *Proceedings of the American Philosophical Society*, Vol. XCI (1947), pp. 25–57.

Beaujour

Echeverria, *Mirage in the West*, is a perceptive account. See also the excellent chapter (VIII, "The Radical Republic") in Jones, *O Strange New World*. Seymour Martin Lipset, *The First New Nation* (New York, Basic Books, 1963), suggests that Beaujour anticipates later criticisms of America.

Smith

For Smith's life see the *DNB* and NEVINS. Commager and Giordanetti, eds., *Was America a Mistake*, show that the dismissal of American culture was anticipated in the eighteenth century by the *philosophes*. Herman Melville has an angry and chauvinistic "reply" to Smith in "Hawthorne and His Mosses" written in 1850. For a discussion of American writers' inferiority complex, see F. O. Matthiessen, *American Renaissance: Art and Expression in the Age of Emerson and Whitman* (New York, Oxford University Press, 1941), p. 372. Travel literature during this period is discussed in J. L. Mesick, *The English Traveller in America, 1785–1835* (New York, Columbia University Press, 1922), and Max Berger, *The British Traveller in America, 1836–1860* (New York, Columbia University Press, 1943).

Hamilton

For Hamilton's life, I used the *DNB*, NEVINS, and Mesick, *The British Traveller*. Lewis Feuer, *Marx and the Intellectuals: A Set of Post-Ideological Essays* (New York, Anchor Books, 1969), led me to Hamilton's influence on the early Marx. Maximilien Rubel's essay "Notes on Marx's Conception of Democracy" appeared in *New Politics* (New York), Volume I (1962), pp. 83–85. The working-class movement in Jacksonian America is studied in Walter Hugins, *Jacksonian Democracy and the Working Class: A Study of the New York Workingman's Movement, 1829–1837* (Stanford, Stanford University Press, 1960), and Edward Pessen, *Most Uncommon Jacksonians: The Radical Leaders of the Early Labor Movement* (Albany, State University of New York Press, 1967).

Frances Anne Kemble

Margaret Armstrong, *Fanny Kemble: A Passionate Victorian* (New York, Macmillan Company, 1938), is the standard biography which I used with interest. See also the newest, annotated edition of her plantation journal edited by John A. Scott (New York, Alfred A. Knopf, 1961). NEVINS and Max Berger, *The British Traveller in America*, are helpful.

Dickens

On Dickens in America, see Edgar Johnson, *Charles Dickens: His Tragedy and Triumph* (Boston, Little, Brown, 1965), the definitive biography. NEVINS and COMMAGER reprint sections of Dickens' *American Notes* with comments. The newly discovered letter was written on April 1, 1842, to his English friend William C. Macready while Dickens was on a steamboat from Pittsburgh to Cincinnati. Excerpts quoted in the headnote are used with the kind permission of Mr. Charles Ryskamp, director of the J. Pierpont Morgan Library (New York), owners of the original. The condition of free blacks during Dickens' visit is well sketched in Leon Litwack, *North of Slavery: The Negro in the Free States, 1790–1860* (Chicago, University of Chicago Press, 1961). See also a contemporary of Dickens, Harriet Martineau, *Society in America* (London, Saunders and Otley, 1837), which was read by Dickens before his trip here. Max Berger, *The British Traveller in America*, mentions a number of Dickens' fellow countrymen who defended slavery as an institution and sympathized with the burdens of slaveholders.

Martí

Biographical material is from M. Isidoro Mendez, ed., *José Martí: Obras Completas* (Havana, Editorial Lex, 1946), two volumes, and Federico De Onis' Introduction to Juan De Onis, ed., *The America of José Martí* (New York, Noonday Press, 1954). D. H. Lawrence's attack on Franklin is in his *Studies in Classic American Literature* (New York, T. Seitzer, 1923).

For more recent views by Latin Americans, see Alan Westin, *et al.*, *Views of America*, and Lillibridge, ed., *The American Image*. Translated excerpts from Martí's last letter appear in Hugh Thomas' *Cuba: The Pursuit of Freedom* (New York, Harper and Row, 1971), p. 310.

Marx

Lewis Feuer's essay "Marxian Tragedians," *Encounter* (London), Vol. XIX (November, 1962), led me to the Aveling-Marx book on America. The essay is reprinted in Feuer, *Marx and the Intellectuals*. For biographical details and a more extended account of their American tour, see Chushichi Tsuzuki, *The Life of Eleanor Marx, 1855–1898, A Socialist Tragedy* (New York, Oxford, Clarendon Press, 1967). Frederick Engels' involvement in the Aveling scandal and his (and Marx's) interest in America is covered in Alexander Trachtenberg, ed., *Letters to Americans, 1848–1895, by Karl Marx and Frederick Engels* (New York, International Publishers, 1953).

Hamsun

Biographical information is in Knut Hamsun, *The Cultural Life of Modern America* (Cambridge, Mass., Harvard University Press, 1969), edited and translated by Barbara Gordon Morgridge. Henry David, *The History of the Haymarket Affair* (New York, Russell and Russell, 1957), Second Edition, is the standard account.

Bourget

Personal details are in COMMAGER, Handlin, *This Was America*, and J. G. Brooks, *As Others See Us*. French accounts of violence in the West are used by Georges Sorel, *Reflections on Violence* (New York, Collier Books, 1961: original edition, 1906, Paris). See especially Sorel on lynchings, pp. 180–182. For the lively argument caused by Bourget's book, see Mark Twain, "What Paul Bourget Thinks of Us," in *How To Tell a Story and Other Essays* (New York, Harper and Brothers, 1900), pp. 140–180.

Ostrogorski

Biographical information is in Arthur Macmahon "Ostrogorski," *Encyclopedia of the Social Sciences* (New York, Macmillan Company, 1933), Vol. XI, pp. 503–504. Seymour Martin Lipset has edited an abridgement of *Democracy and the Organization of Political Parties* (New York, Anchor Books, 1964). For Max Weber's use of Ostrogorski's impressions, see his "Politics as a Vocation" in H. H. Gerth and C. Wright Mills, eds., *From Max Weber: Essays in Sociology* (New York, Oxford University Press, 1946), pp. 104–111. David Hecht: *Russian Radicals Look to America* (Cambridge, Harvard University Press, 1947) is useful for background.

Stead

Frederic Whyte, *Life of W. T. Stead* (London, Jonathan Cape, 1925), is the standard biography, which should be supplemented with Henry Pelling, *America and the British Left: From Bright to Bevan* (New York, New York University Press, 1957). Stead also wrote a prophetic book on *The Americanization of the World* (London, H. Markley, 1901). The "vice" quotation is from Robert Hutchinson, ed., *Mr. Dooley on Ivrything and Ivrybody by Peter Finley Dunne* (New York, Dover Publications, 1963). On other Chicago visitors, see B. L. Pierce, ed., *As Others See Chicago: Impressions of Visitors, 1673–1933* (Chicago, University of Chicago Press, 1933).

Griffin

On his life, see *DNB* and NEVINS. Matthew Arnold's writings are in *Civilization in the United States* (Boston, Little, Brown and Company, 1888), and J. G. Brooks, *As Others See Us*. The anecdote on frontier culture is from Oscar Wilde: *Writings* (London, Longmans, Green and Company, 1901), Vol. IX.

Munsterberg

On his life, see the *Dictionary of American Biography*, and Handlin, *This Was America*. Munsterberg was generally favorable to American life and a strong advocate of industrial efficiency. He met Freud during the Clark University lecture trip in 1909. For Munsterberg and the Fabians, see Pelling, *America and the British Left*, p. 95. COMMAGER reprints a number of impressions on American women, and see also the classic sketch by (Mrs.) Frances Trollope, *Domestic Manners of the Americans* (London, Whittaker, Treacher and Company, 1832).

Gorky

Hecht: *Russian Radicals Look to America*, and Bertram Wolfe: *Three Who Made a Revolution* (Boston, Beacon Press, 1955), are indispensable for Gorky's travels. Helen Muchnic: *Russian Writers: Notes and Essays* (New York, Random House, 1971), quotes Lenin on Gorky. For Stalin's persecution, see Robert Conquest, *The Great Terror* (New York, Macmillan Company, 1968). The Statue of Liberty as symbol and anti-American focal point continues to appeal to propagandists. See the chapter on Nazi propaganda (below) and the New York *Post*, December 7, 1970, for illustration of Moscow airport billboard depicting the statue with a crown of rockets, cowboys, KKK hangmen, etc., entitled: "Freedom, American Style." Gorky's encounter with Mark Twain is in Justin Kaplan, *Mr. Clemens and Mark Twain* (New York, Simon and Schuster, 1966), pp. 367–368.

Wells

Pelling, *America and the British Left*, is indispensable on Wells and other British radicals for this period. I used the *DNB* and the *Book Review Digest* (1906) for responses to Wells' first book on America. His other writings include: *Social Forces in England and America* (New York, Harper and Brothers, 1914), *The New America: The New World* (New York, Macmillan Company, 1935). Pelling shows that the Tory condescension toward America in the nineteenth century was gradually replaced by liberal and radical patronization in the twentieth century.

Lenin

Lenin's writings on America are well edited in *Lenin on the United States* (New York, International Publishers), the centenary publication of his work prepared in Moscow and published here in English. George F. Kennan, *Russia Leaves the War* (Princeton, Princeton University Press, 1956) is filled with impressions of Lenin by Americans, with reports of his views of this country during the early days of the Bolshevik revolution. On the continuing impact of Lenin's ideas and style relating to America, see O. Lawrence Burnette, Jr., and William Converse, eds., *A Soviet View of the American Past* (Chicago, Scott, Foresman, 1960), and Westin, *Views of America*.

Freud

See references cited above, Introduction. The interview with Eastman in the 1920's was especially embittered since Freud still retained a World War I bias against Woodrow Wilson and his apparent hypocrisy. At the time Freud was working with an American diplomat on a psychoanalytical biography of Wilson which did not appear until 1967. Jones, *Sigmund Freud*, *passim*, frequently refers to episodes of his uncritical anti-Americanism.

Duhamel

I am indebted to Cunliffe: "Europe and America" for this somewhat neglected French critic. See also *Book Review Digest*

(1931) for American reviews. Duhamel's hope for revolution in America is echoed in a recent French view of America: Jean-Francois Revel, *Ni Marx Ni Jesus* (Paris, R. Laffont, 1970). In addition to Siegfried: *America Comes of Age*, see J-P. Sartre, "The Respectful Prostitute," in *Three Plays* (New York, Alfred A. Knopf, 1949), and Simone de Beauvoir, *America Day by Day* (New York, Grove Press, 1953), for some of the more influential contemporary French views.

Cecchi

Leslie Fiedler's essay "Italian Pilgrimage: The Discovery of America," *Kenyon Review* (Summer, 1952), is reprinted in his *An End to Innocence* (Boston, Beacon Press, 1955). His observations on Cecchi were supplemented by me through conversations with the translator, Mr. Robert Connolly of Casa Italiana, Columbia University.

Hitler

The staff of the Franklin D. Roosevelt Library, Hyde Park, New York, worked with me in finding the Goebbels cartoon booklet. My original research was influenced by James Mac-Gregor Burns, *Roosevelt: The Soldier of Freedom, 1940–1945* (New York, Harcourt Brace Jovanovich, 1970). For Hitler's comments on Linklater, see *Hitler's Secret Conversations, 1941–1944* (New York, Farrar, Straus and Young, 1953), Introduction by H. R. Trevor-Roper, pp. 563–565. On Nazi propaganda during World War II, see Ernest K. Bramsted, *Goebbels and National Socialist Propaganda, 1929–1945* (East Lansing, Michigan, Michigan State University Press, 1965) and Z. A. B. Zeman: *Nazi Propaganda* (New York, Oxford University Press, 1964).

Martin, Holbrook, Legris and Thorpe

The weekly editions of *The Guardian* (Manchester) and *Le Monde* (English edition) are enormously interesting for gauging current views of America. *Atlas* magazine reprints excerpts from the world's press, in translation, and devotes considerable space to foreign impressions. *The Current Digest of the Soviet Press* reprints important materials on America, and recently the Academy of Science, Moscow, has started an Institute of American Affairs, a counterpart to our own Kremlinologists. *The Peking Review* invariably reprints the thoughts of Chairman Mao as they apply to contemporary Sino-American relations.

ACKNOWLEDGMENTS

Many people have assisted me in the research and assembling of materials for this book: John Cohen, Jean Pohoryles, and Nancy Inglis of Random House made several indispensable suggestions. Lenworth Gunther served as my research assistant throughout and did much of the reference checking. Sigrid Macrea, George Jacob, Robert Connolly, and Edward Seidentsicker translated a number of selections, many more than I was able to use. Istvan Deak, Nagayo Homma, and Professor Henry Steele Commager served as unofficial research associates by bringing to my attention sources which I had neglected to consult. The Director and staff of the Franklin D. Roosevelt Library, Hyde Park, helped uncover and prepare materials for publication. Georgianna Grant and David R. Turner did much to overcome the sheer physical burden of shaping this literary mosaic.

My interest in the American anti-image began with two articles by Marcus Cunliffe and Lewis Feuer which appeared originally in *Encounter* (London). Professor Cunliffe's work has been especially suggestive.

As is customary, let me stress that I alone am responsible for the final product.

GES

About the Author

GERALD EMANUEL STEARN edited the critical symposium, *McLuhan: Hot & Cool* (1967) and has contributed articles to *Encounter* and the *New York Times*. He studied at the University of Illinois and was a doctoral fellow of the Social Science Research Council at the London School of Economics and Political Science and Columbia University, where he taught American history from 1960 to 1964. He is the General Editor of the Great Lives Observed series.